GOD IN THE DOCK

GOD IN THE DOCK

ESSAYS ON THEOLOGY AND ETHICS

by

C. S. LEWIS

edited by

WALTER HOOPER

WILLIAM B. EERDMANS PUBLISHING COMPANY
GRAND RAPIDS, MICHIGAN

Printed in the United States of America

CONTENTS

PART II

PART III

PART IV

PREFACE

Dr Johnson, speaking of an eighteenth-century theologian, re-marked that he 'tended to unsettle every thing, and yet settle nothing'.[1] I wonder what the robust Doctor would make of our age: an age in which one sees in most bookshops and Sun-day papers the controversial — and, oftentimes, apostate — works of clergy who 'unsettle' every article of the Faith they are ordained and paid to uphold. It is, partly because of this, a pleasure for me to offer as an antidote this new book by C. S. Lewis.

I say 'new' because, though these essays and letters were written over a period of twenty-four years, almost all are published in book-form for the first time. Considering how rapidly theological fashions change, it might be expected that these pieces would already be old stuff. There are, how-ever, I expect, others like myself who are more concerned with whether a book is *true* than whether it was written last week. I believe that Lewis's refusal to compromise, neck or nothing, Heaven or Hell, does not for one moment detract from their relevance to the basic problems which still assail us.

Because of my desire to read everything that Lewis wrote, I undertook the long but happy task of 'excavating' his con-tributions to ephemeral publications. Now, at last, my years of searching libraries and reading faded newsprint are over. But, more important, I anticipate that the majority of them will have never been seen by most readers, and I hope they will derive as much satisfaction as I do from having them firmly stitched between two boards.

Since these new Lewisiana have been culled from such a wide variety of sources, they make, as might be expected, a very mixed bag. I do not apologize for this because so much

[1] James Boswell, *The Life of Samuel Johnson,* ed. George Birkbeck Hill (Oxford, 1887), vol. II, p. 124.

of their interest lies in the many different angles from which we are able to view the Christian religion. Lewis never received a penny for most of them. Some of the essays were written simply because he felt the topic badly needed ventilating and the healthy position defending; others at the request of a newspaper or a periodical; there are other pieces, such as the ones from *The Socratic Digest,* which he composed for the purpose of defending the Faith against the attacks of agnostics and atheists.

Because Lewis knew how to adapt his material to suit the audience he was writing for, the essays differ both in length and in emphasis. Nevertheless, all share a particular seriousness. Not 'gloominess', for they sparkle with wit and common sense; but 'seriousness' because of the high stakes which Lewis believed were involved in being a man — a possible son of God or a possible candidate for hell.

During his years as an agnostic, Lewis wanted to know the answers to such questions as why God allows pain, why Christianity — out of all other religions — was held to be the true one, why and if miracles actually happen. As a result, he quite naturally anticipated the questions other men ask. After his conversion in 1931, Lewis, who seldom refused an invitation to speak or write about the Faith, found himself moving in very different circles. He preached to and argued with fellow dons, industrial workers, members of the Royal Air Force, and university students. It was partly due to this varied experience that he came to see why the professional theologians could not make Christianity understandable to most people. As a result, he set himself the task of 'translating' the Gospel into language which men use and understand. He believed that if you found it difficult to answer questions from men of different trades it was probably because 'You haven't really thought it out; not to the end; not to "the absolute ruddy end".'[2]

There were many Christians in Oxford in the early 1940s who, like Lewis, felt that both the *pros* and the *cons* of the Christian religion should be discussed openly. This led to the foundation of the Socratic Club in 1941. Lewis was the obvious person for the presidency, a position he held until he

[2] P. 256.

went to Cambridge in 1954. Meetings were (and still are) held every Monday evening in Term. One Monday a Christian would read a paper, to be answered by an unbeliever, and the following Monday an agnostic or atheist would read a paper which was, in turn, answered by a Christian. Lewis had always relished 'rational opposition', and the Socratic Club served as the perfect arena for testing the strengths and weaknesses of his apologetics. One example of the kind of paper he read at the Socratic is 'Religion without Dogma?' which he wrote as a reply to Professor H. H. Price's paper on 'The Grounds of Modern Agnosticism'.

It was difficult for the most able unbeliever to contend with Lewis's formidable logic and immense learning in the Socratic Club. On the other hand, we find him, in his articles in *The Coventry Evening Telegraph* and popular magazines, adapting his language and logic to less educated people. Pieces such as 'Religion and Science' and 'The Trouble with "X". . .', with their lucidity and apt analogies, have unmasked many popular fallacies about the supposed opposition between religion and science, and have led many people to understand what Christianity is about.

Regardless of one's education, it is impossible to decide whether Christianity is true or false if you do not know what it is *about*. And, just as there were many who were totally ignorant of Christianity when Lewis began to write, so there are many today who do not know what the real issue is. It is foolish to pretend. The recent flood of autobiographical explanations why such and such a bishop or parson cannot accept the Christian Faith has, I expect, driven many people into deeper ignorance and also (perhaps) into the despairing belief that it could not be understood however hard one tried.

For Lewis, who believed that to be born meant either an eventual surrender to God or an everlasting divorce from Him, this was a serious matter. One day he and I were speculating as to what would happen if a group of friendly and inquisitive Martians suddenly appeared in the middle of Oxford and asked (those who did not flee) what Christianity is. We wondered how many people, apart from voicing their prejudices about the Church, could supply them with much in the way of accurate information. On the whole, we doubted whether the Martians would take back to their world much that is worth having. On the other hand, 'there is nothing', Lewis argued, 'in the nature of the younger generation which incapacitates them for receiving Christianity'. But, as he goes on to say, 'no generation can bequeath to its successors what it has not got.'[3]

What it has not got. The question as to *why* it has not got it is, obviously, too complex for me to answer. Nevertheless, having been a college chaplain for five years, I can see that much of the ignorance today is rightly attributed by Lewis to 'the liberal writers who are continually accommodating and whittling down the truth of the Gospel'.[4] And what Lewis would most emphatically *not* do is 'whittle down'.

He believed that, regardless of the temporary fashions which our ideas about God and morality pass through, there is nothing which can make the Everlasting Gospel out of date. ('All that is not eternal is eternally out of date.')[5] On the other hand, he believed that our methods of getting the truth across must often vary. Indeed, his own methods vary considerably: but he nowhere attempts to empty God out with the bath-water. For instance, we have from Lewis's pen straightforward apologetical works such as *Mere Christianity* and *The Problem of Pain,* theological satires such as *The Screwtape Letters* and *The Great Divorce,* and (for lack of a better word) his 'concealed' Christianity in the interplanetary novels and the Chronicles of Narnia.

Though Lewis's methods are not acceptable to liberal theologians (see, for example, his 'Rejoinder to Dr Pittenger'), he has probably got more orthodox Christianity into more heads than any religious writer since G. K. Chesterton. His graceful prose, his easy conversational style (almost all his books are written in the first person), his striking metaphors, and love of clarity are, no doubt, chiefly the result of his wide reading, his delight in writing, and his large share of mother wit. But they are more closely related than those who have read only his theological books might imagine to his abilities as a literary critic.

Beginning with his literary criticism and going on to his theological works, one will probably find that the process

[3] Pp. 115, 116.
[4] P. 260.
[5] C. S. Lewis, *The Four Loves* (London, 1960), ch. vi, p. 156.

10

works the other way round as well. However, the point I particularly want to emphasize is this. Lewis believed that the proper work of a literary critic is to write about the merits and faults of a book, rather than to speculate about the genesis of the book or the author's private life. Though he had a high regard for textual criticism (and lectured on it at one time), he never overlooked the obvious in favour of the hypothetical. Similarly, in his theological works Lewis (who never claimed to be more than a layman writing for other laymen) does not offer ingenious guesses about whether, say, such and such a passage in one of the Gospels was supplied by the early Church long after that Gospel was written, but what the Gospels as we have them do, in fact, say and mean.

The essays in this book which are more or less 'straight' theology fall into two groups. The first contains those in which the primary topic is miracles. Lewis maintained that the Faith stripped of its supernatural elements could not conceivably be called Christianity. Because the miraculous is too toned down or hushed up today, I feel that his essays on the miraculous are particularly ripe for publication. Though most of what he says about miracles and the self-refutation of Naturalists can be found in his full-length book on *Miracles* (London, 1947; revised, 1960), I believe that the short essays here could have one advantage over the book. They might appeal to readers who have not the leisure to read, or who might get bogged down in, longer works.

The second category is hinted at in the title of this book. 'The ancient man', Lewis wrote, 'approached God (or even the gods) as the accused person approaches his judge. For the modern man the roles are reversed. He is the judge: God is in the dock.'[6] It would be ridiculous to suppose we can easily put *man* back in the dock. Lewis discusses his own methods for attempting this in his essay on 'Christian Apologetics' (the only essay in this volume which has never been published in any form before). 'In my experience', he says in this essay, 'if one begins from the sin that has been one's chief problem during the last week, one is very often surprised at the way this shaft goes home.'[7] Those who have read *Screwtape* will recall numerous instances in which he pinpoints

[6] P. 244.
[7] P. 96.

11

those (seemingly) small sins which, if allowed to grow un-
checked, in the end dominate man. As for the essays that
follow, I should be surprised if those who read 'The Trouble
with "X". . .' do not have the sensation (which I do) of seeing their reflection in a mirror.

Lewis struck me as the most thoroughly *converted* man I
ever met. Christianity was never for him a separate department of life; not what he did with his solitude; 'not even', as
he says in one essay, 'what God does with His solitude'.[8] His
whole vision of life was such that the natural and the supernatural seemed inseparably combined. Because of this, I have
included in this collection his numerous semi-theological essays
on topics such as the proposed ordination of women and
vivisection. There are also a number of essays such as 'The
Humanitarian Theory of Punishment' which could more properly be called ethical. Lastly, because of my concern that
nothing be lost, I have added to the back of this book all
Lewis's letters on theology and ethics that have appeared in
newspapers and magazines.

The absence of moral values is so acutely felt today that
it would seem a pity not to make public whatever help is available to our confused and spiritually-starved world. There may
be contemporary writers who strike us as more humane, tender,
'original' and up to date than Lewis. But, like the Three Little
Pigs, we need, not straw, but firm brick houses. Those who are
concerned about the cheap religion and shoddy values so typical of our times will be aware of our immediate need for the
antidote which Lewis provides: his realism, his moral rectitude,
his ability to see beyond the partial perspectives which limit so
many existentialists.

It will be noticed that I have, in the footnotes, given the
sources of many of the quotations including the biblical ones.
This will, perhaps, seem pedantic to some readers. I may have
been at fault, but I hope that there will be some who might be
as grateful to have them as I was to find them. I have also
provided in the footnotes translations of the more difficult
Latin phrases. This book was prepared with American as well
as English readers in mind, and I have included in my footnotes relevant information which is not, I believe, as generally

[8] P. 128.

known in the United States as it is here. In order that my notes may be easily distinguished from the author's, I have used * for Lewis's and arabic numerals for mine. Those who compare the texts of the essays published here with their originals will discover, in a few instances, some minor changes. This is because I have Lewis's own published copies of some essays, and where he has made changes or corrections I have followed his emendations. I have also felt it my responsibility to correct obvious errors wherever I have found them.

Though these essays do not fall easily into neat sub-divisions, I have, nevertheless, felt that divisions of some sort would be helpful to the reader. I have, therefore, divided the essays into three parts, conscious while doing so that some of the essays would fit almost as well in one part as they would in another. Part I contains those essays which are clearly theological: Part II contains those which I term semi-theological, and Part III includes those in which the basic theme is ethics. Part IV is composed of Lewis's letters arranged in the chronological order in which they were published.

I am very grateful to the publishers who have allowed me to reprint these essays and letters. I hope they will not think me ungenerous and slovenly if, instead of listing them separately, I acknowledge their permission by citing the original sources of the essays in the list that follows. The sources of the letters are found in Part IV. It is to be understood that all the publishers are English except where I have stated otherwise.

PART I: (1) 'Evil and God' is reprinted from *The Spectator,* vol. CLXVI (7 February 1941), p. 141. (2) 'Miracles' was preached in St Jude on the Hill Church, London, on the 26th November 1942 and appeared in *St Jude's Gazette,* No. 73 (October 1942), pp. 4-7. A shorter and slightly altered version of this sermon was published in *The Guardian* (2 October 1942), p. 316. *The Guardian* was a weekly Anglican newspaper which was founded in 1846 and ceased publication in 1951. (3) 'Dogma and the Universe' was published in two parts in *The Guardian* (19 March 1943), p. 96 and (26 March 1943), pp. 104, 107. The second part originally bore the title 'Dogma and Science'. (4) 'Answers to Questions on Christianity' was first published as a pamphlet by the Electrical and Musical Industries Christian Fellowship, Hayes, Middlesex [1944]. (5) 'Myth Became Fact' first appeared in *World Dominion,* vol. XXII (September-October 1944), pp. 267-70. (6) 'Horrid Red Things' was originally published in the *Church of England Newspaper,* vol. LI (6 October 1944), pp. 1-2. (7) 'Religion and Science' is reprinted from *The Coventry Evening Telegraph* (3 January 1945), p. 4. (8) 'The Laws of Nature' is also from *The Coventry Evening Telegraph* (4 April 1945), p. 4. (9) 'The Grand Miracle' was preached in St Jude on the Hill Church, London, and afterwards published in *The Guardian* (27 April 1945), pp. 161, 165. (10) 'Christian Apologetics', which is published for the first time, was read to an assembly of Anglican priests and youth leaders at the 'Carmarthen Conference for Youth Leaders and Junior Clergy' at Carmarthen during Easter 1945. (11) 'Work and Prayer' first appeared in *The Coventry Evening Telegraph* (28 May 1945), p. 4. (12) 'Man or Rabbit?' was first published as a pamphlet by the Student Christian Movement in Schools. The pamphlet does not bear a date, but my guess is that it appeared sometime in 1946.

(13) 'On the Transmission of Christianity' is my title for Lewis's Preface to B. G. Sandhurst's *How Heathen is Britain?* (Collins Publishers, 1946), pp. 9-15. (14) 'Miserable Offenders' was preached at St Matthew's Church, Northampton, on the 7th April 1946 and afterwards published by St Matthew's Church in a booklet *Five Sermons by Laymen* (April-May 1946), pp. 1-6. (15) 'The Founding of the Oxford Socratic Club' is my title for Lewis's Preface to *The Socratic Digest,* No. 1 (1942-1943), pp. 3-5. This piece is obviously an intruder in this section, and would more properly fit into Part II. I have chosen, however, to give it the place it has because of its connection with the essay which follows. (16) 'Religion without Dogma?' was read to the Socratic Club on the 20th May 1946 and published as 'A Christian Reply to Professor Price' in *The Phoenix Quarterly,* vol. I, No. 1 (Autumn 1946), pp. 31-44. It was reprinted as 'Religion without Dogma?' in *The Socratic Digest,* No. 4 [1948], pp. 82-94. The 'Reply'

which I have appended to this essay is Lewis's answer to Miss G. E. M. Anscombe's article 'A Reply to Mr C. S. Lewis' Argument that "Naturalism" is Self-refuting', both of which appeared in issue No. 4 of *The Socratic Digest,* pp. 15-16 and pp. 7-15 respectively. (17) 'Some Thoughts' was written one evening in The White Horse Inn at Drogheda, Ireland, at the request of the Medical Missionaries of Mary who founded Our Lady of Lourdes Hospital at Drogheda, and was published in *The First Decade: Ten Years of Work of the Medical Missionaries of Mary* (Dublin, At the Sign of the Three Candles [1948]), pp. 91-94. (18) 'The Trouble with "X". . .' was first published in the *Bristol Diocesan Gazette,* vol. XXVII (August 1948), pp. 3-6. (19) 'What Are We to Make of Jesus Christ?' is reprinted from *Asking Them Questions,* Third Series, ed. Ronald Selby Wright (Oxford University Press, 1950), pp. 47-53. (20) 'The Pains of Animals: A Problem in Theology' first appeared in *The Month,* vol. CLXXXIX (February 1950), pp. 95-104. I am indebted to Miss M. F. Matthews for permission to include the late Dr C. E. M. Joad's part of this essay. (21) 'Is Theism Important? A Reply' is reprinted from *The Socratic Digest,* No. 5 (1952), pp. 48-51. (22) The 'Rejoinder to Dr Pittenger' first appeared in the columns of the American periodical *The Christian Century,* vol. LXXV (26 November 1958), pp. 1359-61. (23) 'Must Our Image of God Go?' is taken from *The Observer* (24 March 1963), p. 14.

PART II: The first three essays in this part are reprinted from the columns of *The Guardian.* (1) 'Dangers of National Repentance' is from the issue of 15 March 1940, p. 127. (2) 'Two Ways with the Self' is from that of 3 May 1940, p. 215, and (3) 'Meditation on the Third Commandment' from that of 10 January 1941, p. 18. (4) 'On the Reading of Old Books' is my title for Lewis's Preface to St Athanasius' *The Incarnation of the Word of God,* translated by A Religious of C.S.M.V., first published by Geoffrey Bles Ltd. in 1944 and by A. R. Mowbray and Co. Ltd. in 1953. (5) 'Two Lectures' is Lewis's title for an essay originally published as 'Who was Right — Dream Lecturer or Real Lecturer?' in *The Coventry Evening Telegraph* (21 February 1945), p. 4. (6) 'Meditation in a Toolshed' is reprinted from *The Coventry Evening Telegraph* (17 July 1945), p. 4. (7) 'Scraps'

15

originally appeared in the *St James' Magazine* (December 1945), pp. [4-5], which was published by St James' Church, Birkdale, Southport. (8) 'The Decline of Religion' is taken from an Oxford periodical, *The Cherwell,* vol. XXVI (29 November 1946), pp. 8-10. (9) 'Vivisection' was first published as a pamphlet by the New England Anti-Vivisection Society [1947]. (10) 'Modern Translations of the Bible' is a title I have chosen for Lewis's Preface to J. B. Phillips' *Letters to Young Churches: A Translation of the New Testament Epistles* (Geoffrey Bles Ltd., 1947), pp. vii-x.

(11) 'Priestesses in the Church?' was originally published as 'Notes on the Way' in *Time and Tide,* vol. XXIX (14 August 1948), pp. 830-31. (12) 'God in the Dock' is my title for 'Difficulties in Presenting the Christian Faith to Modern Unbelievers', *Lumen Vitae,* vol. III (September 1948), pp. 421-26. (13) 'Behind the Scenes' appeared first in *Time and Tide,* vol. XXXVII (1 December 1956), pp. 1450-51. (14) 'Revival or Decay?' is reprinted from *Punch,* vol. CCXXXV (9 July 1958), pp. 36-38. (15) 'Before We Can Communicate' was published in *Breakthrough,* No. 8 (October 1961), p. 2. (16) 'Cross-Examination' is the title I have chosen for an interview Mr Sherwood E. Wirt of the Billy Graham Association had with Lewis in Magdalene College, Cambridge, on the 7th May 1963. The interview was originally published in two parts under different titles. The first part was called 'I Was Decided Upon', *Decision,* vol. II (September 1963), p. 3, and the second 'Heaven, Earth and Outer Space', *Decision,* vol. II (October 1963), p. 4.

PART III: (1) A shortened form of 'Bulverism' appeared under the title 'Notes on the Way' in *Time and Tide,* vol. XXII (29 March 1941), p. 261. A longer version, which is the one found here, appeared in *The Socratic Digest,* No. 2 (June 1944), pp. 16-20. (2) 'First and Second Things' is Lewis's title for 'Notes on the Way' from *Time and Tide,* vol. XXIII (27 June 1942), pp. 519-20. (3) 'The Sermon and the Lunch' is reprinted from the *Church of England Newspaper,* No. 2692 (21 September 1945), pp. 1-2. (4) 'The Humanitarian Theory of Punishment' first appeared in *20th Century: An Australian Quarterly Review,* vol. III, No. 3 (1949), pp. 5-12. This same journal in vol. VI, No. 2 (1952), pp. 20-26 published Drs Norval Morris and Donald Buckle's

'Reply to C. S. Lewis'. Both pieces were later reprinted in *Res Judicatae,* vol. VI (June 1953), pp. 224-30 and pp. 231-37 respectively. Then followed Professor J. J. C. Smart's 'Comment: The Humanitarian Theory of Punishment' in *Res Judicatae,* vol. VI (February 1954), pp. 368-71, and Lewis's 'On Punishment: A Reply' — that is, a reply to all three men — in *Res Judicatae,* vol. VI (August 1954), pp. 519-23. (5) 'Xmas and Christmas: A Lost Chapter from Herodotus' first appeared in *Time and Tide,* vol. XXXV (4 December 1954), p. 1607. (6) 'What Christmas Means to Me' is reprinted from *Twentieth Century,* vol. CLXII (December 1957), pp. 517-18. (7) 'Delinquents in the Snow' appeared first in *Time and Tide,* vol. XXXVIII (7 December 1957), pp. 1521-22. (8) 'Willing Slaves of the Welfare State' is from *The Observer* (20 July 1958), p. 6. (9) 'We Have No "Right to Happiness"' is the last thing Lewis wrote for publication. It appeared shortly after his death in *The Saturday Evening Post,* vol. CCXXXVI (21-28 December 1963), pp. 10, 12.

Finally, as on many previous occasions, I would like to thank Major W. H. Lewis, Mr Owen Barfield, Mr Colin Hardie, Mr Roger Lancelyn Green, Professor John Lawlor and Miss Nan Dunbar for the assistance they have given me in making these Lewis 'excavations' available to others.

Jesus College, Oxford   WALTER HOOPER
May 1970

PART I

1

EVIL AND GOD

Dr Joad's article on 'God and Evil' last week[1] suggests the interesting conclusion that since neither 'mechanism' nor 'emergent evolution' will hold water, we must choose in the long run between some monotheistic philosophy, like the Christian, and some such dualism as that of the Zoroastrians. I agree with Dr Joad in rejecting mechanism and emergent evolution. Mechanism, like all materialist systems, breaks down at the problem of knowledge. If thought is the undesigned and irrelevant product of cerebral motions, what reason have we to trust it? As for emergent evolution, if anyone insists on using the word *God* to mean 'whatever the universe happens to be going to do next', of course we cannot prevent him. But nobody would in fact so use it unless he had a secret belief that what is coming next will be an improvement. Such a belief, besides being unwarranted, presents peculiar difficulties to an emergent evolutionist. If things can improve, this means that there must be some absolute standard of good above and outside the cosmic process to which that process can approximate. There is no sense in talking of 'becoming better' if better means simply 'what we are becoming' — it is like congratulating yourself on reaching your destination and defining destination as 'the place you have reached'. Mellontolatry, or the worship of the future, is a *fuddled* religion.

We are left then to choose between monotheism and dualism

[1] C. E. M. Joad, 'Evil and God', *The Spectator,* vol. CLXVI (31 January 1941), pp. 112-13.

— between a single, good, almighty source of being, and two
equal, uncreated, antagonistic Powers, one good and the other
bad. Dr Joad suggests that the latter view stands to gain
from the 'new urgency' of the fact of evil. But *what* new urgency? Evil may seem more urgent to us than it did to the
Victorian philosophers — favoured members of the happiest
class in the happiest country in the world at the world's happiest period. But it is no more urgent for us than for the
great majority of monotheists all down the ages. The classic
expositions of the doctrine that the world's miseries are compatible with its creation and guidance by a wholly good Being
come from Boethius waiting in prison to be beaten to death
and from St Augustine meditating on the sack of Rome. The
present state of the world is normal; it was the last century
that was the abnormality.

This drives us to ask why so many generations rejected
Dualism. Not, assuredly, because they were unfamiliar with
suffering; and not because its obvious *prima facie* plausibility
escaped them. It is more likely that they saw its two fatal
difficulties, the one metaphysical, and the other moral.

The metaphysical difficulty is this. The two Powers, the
good and the evil, do not explain each other. Neither Ormuzd
nor Ahriman can claim to be the Ultimate. More ultimate than
either of them is the inexplicable fact of their being there together. Neither of them chose this *tête-à-tête*. Each of them,
therefore, is *conditioned* — finds himself willy-nilly in a situation; and either that situation itself, or some unknown force
which produced that situation, is the real Ultimate. Dualism
has not yet reached the ground of being. You cannot accept
two conditioned and mutually independent beings as the self-
grounded, self-comprehending Absolute. On the level of pic-
ture-thinking this difficulty is symbolised by our inability to
think of Ormuzd and Ahriman without smuggling in the idea
of a common *space* in which they can be together and thus
confessing that we are not yet dealing with the source of the
universe but only with two members contained in it. Dualism
is a truncated metaphysic.

The moral difficulty is that Dualism gives evil a positive,
substantive, self-consistent nature, like that of good. If this
were true, if Ahriman existed in his own right no less than
Ormuzd, what could we mean by calling Ormuzd good except

22

that we happened to prefer *him*. In what sense can the one party be said to be right and the other wrong? If evil has the same kind of reality as good, the same autonomy and completeness, our allegiance to good becomes the arbitrarily chosen loyalty of a partisan. A sound theory of value demands something different. It demands that good should be original and evil a mere perversion; that good should be the tree and evil the ivy; that good should be able to see all round evil (as when sane men understand lunacy) while evil cannot retaliate in kind; that good should be able to exist on its own while evil requires the good on which it is parasitic in order to continue its parasitic existence.

The consequences of neglecting this are serious. It means believing that bad men like badness as such, in the same way in which good men like goodness. At first this denial of any common nature between us and our enemies seems gratifying. We call them fiends and feel that we need not forgive them. But, in reality, along with the power to forgive, we have lost the power to condemn. If a taste for cruelty and a taste for kindness were equally ultimate and basic, by what common standard could the one reprove the other? In reality, cruelty does not come from desiring evil as such, but from perverted sexuality, inordinate resentment, or lawless ambition and avarice. That is precisely why it can be judged and condemned from the standpoint of innocent sexuality, righteous anger, and ordinate acquisitiveness. The master can correct a boy's sums because they are blunders in arithmetic — in the same arithmetic which he does and does better. If they were not even attempts at arithmetic — if they were not in the arithmetical world at all — they could not be arithmetical mistakes.

Good and evil, then, are not on all fours. Badness is not even bad *in the same way* in which goodness is good. Ormuzd and Ahriman cannot be equals. In the long run, Ormuzd must be original and Ahriman derivative. The first hazy idea of *devil* must, if we begin to think, be analysed into the more precise ideas of 'fallen' and 'rebel' angel. But only in the long run. Christianity can go much further with the Dualist than Dr Joad's article seems to suggest. There was never any question of tracing *all* evil to man; in fact, the New Testament has a good deal more to say about dark superhuman powers than about the fall of Adam. As far as this world is concerned, a Christian can share most of the Zoroastrian outlook; we all live between the 'fell, incensed points'[2] of Michael and Satan. The difference between the Christian and the Dualist is that the Christian thinks one stage further and sees that if Michael is really in the right and Satan really in the wrong this must mean that they stand in two different relations to somebody or something far further back, to the ultimate ground of reality itself. All this, of course, has been watered down in modern times by the theologians who are afraid of 'mythology', but those who are prepared to reinstate Ormuzd and Ahriman are presumably not squeamish on that score.

Dualism can be a manly creed. In the Norse form ('The giants will beat the gods in the end, but I am on the side of the gods') it is nobler by many degrees than most philosophies of the moment. But it is only a half-way house. Thinking along these lines you can avoid Monotheism, and remain a Dualist, only by refusing to follow your thoughts home. To revive Dualism would be a real step backwards and a bad omen (though not the worst possible) for civilization.

[2] Shakespeare, *Hamlet,* V, ii, 60.

2

MIRACLES

I HAVE KNOWN ONLY ONE PERSON IN MY LIFE WHO CLAIMED to have seen a ghost. It was a woman; and the interesting thing is that she disbelieved in the immortality of the soul before seeing the ghost and still disbelieves after having seen it. She thinks it was a hallucination. In other words, seeing is not believing. This is the first thing to get clear in talking about miracles. Whatever experiences we may have, we shall not regard them as miraculous if we already hold a philosophy which excludes the supernatural. Any event which is claimed as a miracle is, in the last resort, an experience received from the senses; and the senses are not infallible. We can always say we have been the victims of an illusion; if we disbelieve in the supernatural this is what we always shall say. Hence, whether miracles have really ceased or not, they would certainly appear to cease in Western Europe as materialism became the popular creed. For let us make no mistake. If the end of the world appeared in all the literal trappings of the Apocalypse,[1] if the modern materialist saw with his own eyes the heavens rolled up[2] and the great white throne appearing,[3] if he had the sensation of being himself hurled into the Lake of Fire,[4] he would continue forever, in that lake itself, to regard his experience as an illusion and to find the explanation of it in psycho-analysis, or cerebral pathology. Experience by itself

[1] The book of Revelation.
[2] *Ibid.,* vi. 14.
[3] *Ibid.,* xx. 11.
[4] *Ibid.,* xix. 20; xx. 10; xx. 14-15; xxi. 8.

25

proves nothing. If a man doubts whether he is dreaming or waking, no experiment can solve his doubt, since every experiment may itself be part of the dream. Experience proves this, or that, or nothing, according to the preconceptions we bring to it.

This fact, that the interpretation of experiences depends on preconceptions, is often used as an argument against miracles. It is said that our ancestors, taking the supernatural for granted and greedy of wonders, read the miraculous into events that were really not miracles. And in a sense I grant it. That is to say, I think that just as our preconceptions would prevent us from apprehending miracles if they really occurred, so their preconceptions would lead them to imagine miracles even if they did not occur. In the same way, the doting man will think his wife faithful when she is not and the suspicious man will not think her faithful when she is: the question of her actual fidelity remains, meanwhile, to be settled, if at all, on other grounds. But there is one thing often said about our ancestors which we must *not* say. We must not say 'They believed in miracles because they did not know the Laws of Nature.' This is nonsense. When St Joseph discovered that his bride was pregnant, he was 'minded to put her away'.[5] He knew enough biology for that. Otherwise, of course he would not have regarded pregnancy as a proof of infidelity. When he accepted the Christian explanation, he regarded it as a miracle precisely because he knew enough of the Laws of Nature to know that this was a suspension of them. When the disciples saw Christ walking on the water they were frightened:[6] they would not have been frightened unless they had known the laws of Nature and known that this was an exception. If a man had no conception of a regular order in Nature, then of course he could not notice departures from that order: just as a dunce who does not understand the normal metre of a poem is also unconscious of the poet's variations from it. Nothing is wonderful except the abnormal and nothing is abnormal until we have grasped the norm. Complete ignorance of the laws of Nature would preclude the perception of the miraculous just as rigidly as complete disbelief in the supernatural precludes it, perhaps even more so. For while the materialist would have at

[5] Matthew i. 19.
[6] Matthew xiv. 26; Mark vi. 49; John vi. 19.

least to explain miracles away, the man wholly ignorant of Nature would simply not notice them.

The experience of a miracle in fact requires two conditions. First we must believe in a normal stability of nature, which means we must recognize that the data offered by our senses recur in regular patterns. Secondly, we must believe in some reality beyond Nature. When both beliefs are held, and not till then, we can approach with an open mind the various reports which claim that this super- or extra-natural reality has sometimes invaded and disturbed the sensuous content of space and time which makes our 'natural' world. The belief in such a supernatural reality itself can neither be proved nor disproved by experience. The arguments for its existence are metaphysical, and to me conclusive. They turn on the fact that even to think and act in the natural world we have to assume something beyond it and even assume that we partly belong to that something. In order to think we must claim for our own reasoning a validity which is not credible if our own thought is merely a function of our brain, and our brains a by-product of irrational physical processes. In order to act, above the level of mere impulse, we must claim a similar validity for our judgments of good and evil. In both cases we get the same disquieting result. The concept of nature itself is one we have reached only tacitly by claiming a sort of *super*-natural status for ourselves.

If we frankly accept this position and then turn to the evidence, we find, of course, that accounts of the supernatural meet us on every side. History is full of them — often in the same documents which we accept wherever they do not report miracles. Respectable missionaries report them not infrequently. The whole Church of Rome claims their continued occurrence. Intimate conversation elicits from almost every acquaintance at least one episode in his life which is what he would call 'queer' or 'rum'. No doubt most stories of miracles are unreliable; but then, as anyone can see by reading the papers, so are most stories of all events. Each story must be taken on its merits: what one must not do is to rule out the supernatural as the one impossible explanation. Thus you may disbelieve in the Mons Angels[7] because you cannot find a sufficient num-

[7] Lewis is referring to the story that angels appeared, protecting British troops in their retreat from Mons, France, on the 26th August 1914.

ber of sensible people who say they saw them. But if you found a sufficient number, it would, in my view, be unreasonable to explain this by collective hallucination. For we know enough of psychology to know that spontaneous unanimity in hallucination is very improbable, and we do not know enough of the supernatural to know that a manifestation of angels is equally improbable. The supernatural theory is the less improbable of the two. When the Old Testament says that Sennacherib's invasion was stopped by angels,[8] and Herodotus says it was stopped by a lot of mice who came and ate up all the bowstrings of his army,[9] an open-minded man will be on the side of the angels. Unless you start by begging the question, there is nothing intrinsically unlikely in the existence of angels or in the action ascribed to them. But mice just don't do these things.

A great deal of scepticism now current about the miracles of our Lord does not, however, come from disbelief of all reality beyond nature. It comes from two ideas which are respectable but I think mistaken. In the first place, modern people have an almost aesthetic dislike of miracles. Admitting that God can, they doubt if He would. To violate the laws He Himself has imposed on His creation seems to them arbitrary, clumsy, a theatrical device only fit to impress savages — a solecism against the grammar of the universe. In the second place, many people confuse the laws of nature with the laws of thought and imagine that their reversal or suspension would be a contradiction in terms — as if the resurrection of the dead were the same sort of thing as two and two making five.

I have only recently found the answer to the first objection. I found it first in George MacDonald and then later in St Athanasius. This is what St Athanasius says in his little book *On the Incarnation:* 'Our Lord took a body like to ours and lived as a man in order that those who had refused to recognize Him in His superintendence and captaincy of the whole universe might come to recognize from the works He did here

A recent summary of the event by Jill Kitson 'Did Angels appear to British troops at Mons?' is found in *History Makers*, No. 3 (1969), pp. 132-33.
  8 II Kings xix. 35.
  9 Herodotus, Bk. II, Sect. 141.

below in the body that what dwelled in this body was the Word of God.' This accords exactly with Christ's own account of His miracles: 'The Son can do nothing of Himself, but what He seeth the Father do.'[10] The doctrine, as I understand it, is something like this:

There is an activity of God displayed throughout creation, a wholesale activity let us say which men refuse to recognize. The miracles done by God incarnate, living as a man in Palestine, perform the very same things as this wholesale activity, but at a different speed and on a smaller scale. One of their chief purposes is that men, having seen a thing done by personal power on the small scale, may recognize, when they see the same thing done on the large scale, that the power behind it is also personal — is indeed the very same person who lived among us two thousand years ago. The miracles in fact are a retelling in small letters of the very same story which is written across the whole world in letters too large for some of us to see. Of that larger script part is already visible, part is still unsolved. In other words, some of the miracles do locally what God has already done universally: others do locally what He has not yet done, but will do. In that sense, and from our human point of view, some are reminders and others prophecies.

God creates the vine and teaches it to draw up water by its roots and, with the aid of the sun, to turn that water into a juice which will ferment and take on certain qualities. Thus every year, from Noah's time till ours, God turns water into wine. That, men fail to see. Either like the Pagans they refer the process to some finite spirit, Bacchus or Dionysus: or else, like the moderns, they attribute real and ultimate causality to the chemical and other material phenomena which are all that our senses can discover in it. But when Christ at Cana makes water into wine, the mask is off.[11] The miracle has only half its effect if it only convinces us that Christ is God: it will have its full effect if whenever we see a vineyard or drink a glass of wine we remember that here works He who sat at the wedding party in Cana. Every year God makes a little corn into much corn: the seed is sown and there is an increase, and men, according to the fashion of their age, say 'It is Ceres,

[10] John v. 19.
[11] John ii. 1-11.

29

it is Adonis, it is the Corn-King,' or else 'It is the laws of Nature.' The close-up, the translation, of this annual wonder is the feeding of the five thousand.[12] Bread is not made there of nothing. Bread is not made of stones, as the Devil once suggested to Our Lord in vain.[13] A little bread is made into much bread. The Son will do nothing but what He sees the Father do. There is, so to speak, a family *style*. The miracles of healing fall into the same pattern. This is sometimes obscured for us by the somewhat magical view we tend to take of ordinary medicine. The doctors themselves do not take this view. The magic is not in the medicine but in the patient's body. What the doctor does is to stimulate Nature's functions in the body, or to remove hindrances. In a sense, though we speak for convenience of healing a cut, every cut heals itself; no dressing will make skin grow over a cut on a corpse. That same mysterious energy which we call gravitational when it steers the planets and biochemical when it heals a body is the efficient cause of all recoveries, and if God exists, that energy, directly or indirectly, is His. All who are cured are cured by Him, the healer within. But once He did it visibly, a Man meeting a man. Where He does not work within in this mode, the organism dies. Hence Christ's one miracle of destruction is also in harmony with God's wholesale activity. His bodily hand held out in symbolic wrath blasted a single fig tree;[14] but no tree died that year in Palestine, or any year, or in any land, or even ever will, save because He has done something, or (more likely) ceased to do something, to it.

When He fed the thousands he multiplied fish as well as bread. Look in every bay and almost every river. This swarming, pulsating fecundity shows He is still at work. The ancients had a god called Genius — the god of animal and human fertility, the presiding spirit of gynaecology, embryology, or the marriage bed — the 'genial bed' as they called it after its god Genius.[15] As the miracles of wine and bread and healing showed who Bacchus really was, who Ceres, who Apollo, and

[12] Matthew xiv. 15-21; Mark vi. 34-44; Luke ix. 12-17; John vi. 1-11.
[13] Matthew iv. 3; Luke iv. 3.
[14] Matthew xxi. 19; Mark xi. 13-20.
[15] For further information on this subject see the chapter on 'Genius and Genius' in Lewis's *Studies in Medieval and Renaissance Literature,* ed. Walter Hooper (Cambridge, 1966), pp. 169-74.

that all were one, so this miraculous multiplication of fish reveals the real Genius. And with that we stand at the threshold of the miracle which for some reason most offends modern ears. I can understand the man who denies the miraculous altogether; but what is one to make of the people who admit some miracles but deny the Virgin Birth? Is it that for all their lip service to the laws of Nature there is only one law of Nature that they really believe? Or is it that they see in this miracle a slur upon sexual intercourse which is rapidly becoming the one thing venerated in a world without veneration? No miracle is in fact more significant. What happens in ordinary generation? What is a father's function in the act of begetting? A microscopic particle of matter from his body fertilizes the female: and with that microscopic particle passes, it may be, the colour of his hair and his great grandfather's hanging lip, and the human form in all its complexity of bones, liver, sinews, heart, and limbs, and pre-human form which the embryo will recapitulate in the womb. Behind every spermatozoon lies the whole history of the universe: locked within it is no small part of the world's future. That is God's normal way of making a man — a process that takes centuries, beginning with the creation of matter itself, and narrowing to one second and one particle at the moment of begetting. And once again men will mistake the sense impressions which this creative act throws off for the act itself or else refer it to some infinite being such as Genius. Once, therefore, God does it directly, instantaneously; without a spermatozoon, without the millenniums of organic history behind the spermatozoon. There was of course another reason. This time He was creating not simply a man, but the man who was to be Himself: the only true Man. The process which leads to the spermatozoon has carried down with it through the centuries much undesirable silt; the life which reaches us by that normal route is tainted. To avoid that taint, to give humanity a fresh start, He once short-circuited the process. There is a vulgar anti-God paper which some anonymous donor sends me every week. In it recently I saw the taunt that we Christians believe in a God who committed adultery with the wife of a Jewish carpenter. The answer to that is that if you describe the action of God in fertilizing Mary as 'adultery' then, in that sense, God would have committed adultery with every woman who ever had a baby. For what He did once

31

without a human father, He does always even when He uses a human father as His instrument. For the human father in ordinary generation is only a carrier, sometimes an unwilling carrier, always the last in a long line of carriers, of life that comes from the supreme life. Thus the filth that our poor, muddled, sincere, resentful enemies fling at the Holy One, either does not stick, or, sticking, turns into glory.

So much for the miracles which do small and quick what we have already seen in the large letters of God's universal activity. But before I go on to the second class — those which foreshadow parts of the universal activity we have not yet seen — I must guard against a misunderstanding. Do not imagine I am trying to make the miracle less miraculous. I am not arguing that they are more probable because they are less unlike natural events: I am trying to answer those who think them arbitrary, theatrical, unworthy of God, meaningless interruptions of universal order. They remain in my view wholly miraculous. To do instantly with dead and baked corn what ordinarily happens slowly with live seed is just as great a miracle as to make bread of stones. Just as great, but a different *kind* of miracle. That is the point. When I open Ovid,[16] or Grimm,[17] I find the sort of miracles which really would be arbitrary. Trees talk, houses turn into trees, magic rings raise tables richly spread with food in lonely places, ships become goddesses, and men are changed into snakes or birds or bears. It is fun to read about: the least suspicion that it had really happened would turn that fun into nightmare. You find no miracles of that kind in the Gospels. Such things, if they could be, would prove that some alien power was invading Nature; they would not in the least prove that it was the same power which had made Nature and rules her every day. But the true miracles express not simply a god, but God: that which is outside Nature, not as a foreigner, but as her sovereign. They announce not merely that a King has visited our town, but that it is *the* King, *our* King.

The second class of miracles, on this view, foretell what God has not yet done, but will do, universally. He raised one man (the man who was Himself) from the dead because He

[16] The reference is to Ovid's (43 B.C.-A.D. 18) *Metamorphoses.*
[17] The fairy tales of the brothers, Jacob Ludwig Carl (1785-1863) and Wilhelm Carl (1786-1859) Grimm.

will one day raise all men from the dead. Perhaps not only men, for there are hints in the New Testament that all creation will eventually be rescued from decay, restored to shape and subserve the splendour of re-made humanity.[18] The Transfiguration[19] and the walking on the water[20] are glimpses of the beauty and the effortless power over all matter which will belong to men when they are really waked by God. Now resurrection certainly involves 'reversal' of natural process in the sense that it involves a series of changes moving in the opposite direction to those we see. At death, matter which has been organic, falls back gradually into the inorganic, to be finally scattered and used perhaps in other organisms. Resurrection would be the reverse process. It would not of course mean the restoration to each personality of those very atoms, numerically the same, which had made its first or 'natural' body. There would not be enough to go round, for one thing; and for another, the unity of the body even in this life was consistent with a slow but perplexed change of its actual ingredients. But it certainly does mean matter of some kind rushing towards organism as now we see it rushing away. It means, in fact, playing backwards a film we have already seen played forwards. In that sense it is a reversal of Nature. But, of course, it is a further question whether reversal in this sense is necessarily contradiction. Do we know that the film cannot be played backwards?

Well, in one sense, it is precisely the teaching of modern physics that the film never works backwards. For modern physics, as you have heard before, the universe is 'running down'. Disorganization and chance is continually increasing. There will come a time, not infinitely remote, when it will be wholly run down or wholly disorganized, and science knows of no possible return from that state. There must have been a time, not infinitely remote, in the past when it was wound up, though science knows of no winding-up process. The point is that for our ancestors the universe was a picture: for modern physics it is a story. If the universe is a picture these things either appear in that picture or not; and if they don't, since

18 E.g. Romans viii. 22: 'We know that the whole creation groaneth and travaileth in pain together until now.'

19 Matthew xvii. 1-9; Mark ix. 2-10.

20 Matthew xiv. 26; Mark vi. 49; John vi. 19.

it is an infinite picture, one may suspect that they are contrary to the nature of things. But a story is a different matter; specially if it is an incomplete story. And the story told by modern physics might be told briefly in the words 'Humpty Dumpty was falling.' That is, it proclaims itself an incomplete story. There must have been a time before he fell, when he was sitting on the wall; there must be a time after he had reached the ground. It is quite true that science knows of no horses and men who can put him together again once he has reached the ground and broken. But then she also knows of no means by which he could originally have been put on the wall. You wouldn't expect her to. All science rests on observation: all our observations are taken *during* Humpty Dumpty's fall, because we were born after he lost his seat on the wall and shall be extinct long before he reaches the ground. But to assume from observations taken while the clock is running down that the unimaginable winding-up which must have preceded this process cannot occur when the process is over is the merest dogmatism. From the very nature of the case the laws of degradation and disorganization which we find in matter at present, cannot be the ultimate and eternal nature of things. If they were, there would have been nothing to degrade and disorganize. Humpty Dumpty can't fall off a wall that never existed.

Obviously, an event which lies outside the falling or disintegrating process which we know as Nature, is not imaginable. If anything is clear from the records of Our Lord's appearances after His resurrection, it is that the risen body was very different from the body that died and that it lives under conditions quite unlike those of natural life. It is frequently not recognized by those who see it:[21] and it is not related to space in the same way as our bodies. The sudden appearances and disappearances[22] suggest the ghost of popular tradition: yet He emphatically insists that He is not merely a spirit and takes steps to demonstrate that the risen body can still perform animal operations, such as eating.[23] What makes all this baffling to us is our assumption that to pass beyond what we call Nature — beyond the three dimensions and the five highly

[21] Luke xxiv. 13-31, 36-7; John xx. 14-16.
[22] Mark xvi. 14; Luke xxiv. 31, 36; John xx. 19, 26.
[23] Luke xxiv. 42-3; John xxi. 13.

specialized and limited senses — is immediately to be in a world of pure negative spirituality, a world where space of any sort and sense of any sort has no function. I know no grounds for believing this. To explain even an atom Schrödinger[24] wants seven dimensions: and give us new senses and we should find a new Nature. There may be Natures piled upon Natures, each supernatural to the one beneath it, before we come to the abyss of pure spirit; and to be in that abyss, at the right hand of the Father, may not mean being absent from any of these Natures — may mean a yet more dynamic presence on all levels. That is why I think it very rash to assume that the story of the Ascension is mere allegory. I know it sounds like the work of people who imagined an absolute up and down and a local heaven in the sky. But to say this is after all to say 'Assuming that the story is fake, we could thus explain how it arose.' Without that assumption we find ourselves 'moving about in worlds unrealised'[25] with no probability — or improbability — to guide us. For if the story is true then a being still in some mode, though not our mode, corporeal, withdrew at His own will from the Nature presented by our three dimensions and five senses, not necessarily into the non-sensuous and undimensioned but possibly into, or through, a world or worlds of super-sense and superspace. And He might choose to do it gradually. Who on earth knows what the spectators might see? If they say they saw a momentary movement along the vertical plane — then an indistinct mass — then nothing — who is to pronounce this improbable?

My time is nearly up and I must be very brief with the second class of people whom I promised to deal with: those who mistake the laws of Nature for laws of thought and, therefore, think that any departure from them is a self-contradiction, like a square circle or two and two making five. To think this is to imagine that the normal processes of Nature are transparent to the intellect, that we can say why she behaves as she does. For, of course, if we cannot see why a thing is so, then we cannot see any reason why it should not be otherwise. But in fact the actual course of Nature is wholly inexplicable.

[24] Arthur Schrödinger (1887-1961), the Austrian physicist.
[25] This is probably a misquotation of Wordsworth's 'Moving about in worlds not realised.' *Intimations of Immortality,* ix, 149.

I don't mean that science has not yet explained it, but may do so some day. I mean that the very nature of explanation makes it impossible that we should even explain why matter has the properties it has. For explanation, by its very nature, deals with a world of 'ifs and ands'. Every explanation takes the form 'Since A, therefore B' or 'If C, then D.' In order to explain any event you have to assume the universe as a going concern, a machine working in a particular way. Since this particular way of working is the basis of all explanation, it can never be itself explained. We can see no reason why it should not have worked a different way.

To say this is not only to remove the suspicion that miracle is self-contradictory, but also to realize how deeply right St Athanasius was when he found an essential likeness between the miracles of Our Lord and the general order of Nature. Both are a full stop for the explaining intellect. If the 'natural' means that which can be fitted into a class, that which obeys a norm, that which can be paralleled, that which can be explained by reference to other events, then Nature herself as a whole is *not* natural. If a miracle means that which must simply be accepted, the unanswerable actuality which gives no account of itself but simply *is,* then the universe is one great miracle. To direct us to that great miracle is one main object of the earthly acts of Christ: that are, as He himself said, Signs.[26] They serve to remind us that the explanations of particular events which we derive *from* the given, the unexplained, the almost wilful character of the actual universe, are not explanations of that character. These Signs do not take us away from reality; they recall us to it — recall us from our dream world of 'ifs and ands' to the stunning actuality of everything that is real. They are focal points at which more reality becomes visible than we ordinarily see at once. I have spoken of how He made miraculous bread and wine and of how, when the Virgin conceived, He had shown Himself the true Genius whom men had ignorantly worshipped long before. It goes deeper than that. Bread and wine were to have an even more sacred significance for Christians and the act of generations was to be the chosen symbol among all mystics for the union of the soul with God. These things are no accidents. With Him

[26] Matthew xii. 39; xvi. 4; xxiv. 24, 30; Mark xiii. 22; xvi. 17, 20; Luke xxi. 11, 25.

there are no accidents. When He created the vegetable world He knew already what dreams the annual death and resurrection of the corn would cause to stir in pious Pagan minds, He knew already that He Himself must so die and live again and in what sense, including and far transcending the old religion of the Corn King. He would say 'This is my Body.'[27] *Common* bread, miraculous bread, sacramental bread — these three are distinct, but not to be separated. Divine reality is like a fugue. All His acts are different, but they all rhyme or echo to one another. It is this that makes Christianity so difficult to talk about. Fix your mind on any one story or any one doctrine and it becomes at once a magnet to which truth and glory come rushing from all levels of being. Our featureless pantheistic unities and glib rationalist distinctions are alike defeated by the seamless, yet ever-varying texture of reality, the liveness, the elusiveness, the intertwined harmonies of the multidimensional fertility of God. But if this is the difficulty, it is also one of the firm grounds of our belief. To think that this was a fable, a product of our own brains as they are a product of matter, would be to believe that this vast symphonic splendour had come out of something much smaller and emptier than itself. It is not so. We are nearer to the truth in the vision seen by Julian of Norwich, when Christ appeared to her holding in His hand a little thing like a hazel nut and saying, 'This is all that is created.'[28] And it seemed to her so small and weak that she wondered how it could hold together at all.[29]

[27] Matthew xxvi. 26; Mark xiv. 22; Luke xxii. 19; I Corinthians xi. 24.
[28] *Sixteen Revelations of Divine Love,* ed. Roger Hudleston (London, 1927), ch. 5, p. 9.
[29] See Letter 3.

3

DOGMA AND THE UNIVERSE

I T IS A COMMON REPROACH AGAINST CHRISTIANITY THAT ITS
dogmas are unchanging, while human knowledge is in continual growth. Hence, to unbelievers, we seem to be always
engaged in the hopeless task of trying to force the new knowledge into moulds which it has outgrown. I think this feeling
alienates the outsider much more than any particular discrep-
ancies between this or that doctrine and this or that scientific
theory. We may, as we say, 'get over' dozens of isolated 'difficulties', but that does not alter his sense that the endeavour
as a whole is doomed to failure and perverse: indeed, the more
ingenious, the more perverse. For it seems to him clear that,
if our ancestors had known what we know about the universe,
Christianity would never have existed at all: and, however
we patch and mend, no system of thought which claims to be
immutable can, in the long run, adjust itself to our growing
knowledge.

That is the position I am going to try to answer. But before
I go on to what I regard as the fundamental answer, I would
like to clear up certain points about the actual relations between Christian doctrine and the scientific knowledge we already have. That is a different matter from the continual
growth of knowledge we imagine, whether rightly or wrongly,
in the future and which, as some think, is bound to defeat us
in the end.

In one respect, as many Christians have noticed, contemporary science has recently come into line with Christian doctrine, and parted company with the classical forms of ma-

38

terialism. If anything emerges clearly from modern physics, it is that nature is not everlasting. The universe had a beginning, and will have an end. But the great materialistic systems of the past all believed in the eternity, and thence in the self-existence of matter. As Professor Whittaker said in the Riddell Lectures of 1942, 'It was never possible to oppose seriously the dogma of the Creation except by maintaining that the world has existed from all eternity in more or less its present state.'[1] This fundamental ground for materialism has now been withdrawn. We should not lean too heavily on this, for scientific theories change. But at the moment it appears that the burden of proof rests, not on us, but on those who deny that nature has some cause beyond herself.

In popular thought, however, the origin of the universe has counted (I think) for less than its character — its immense size and its apparent indifference, if not hostility, to human life. And very often this impresses people all the more because it is supposed to be a modern discovery — an excellent example of those things which our ancestors did not know and which, if they had known them, would have prevented the very beginnings of Christianity. Here there is a simple historical falsehood. Ptolemy knew just as well as Eddington[2] that the earth was infinitesimal in comparison with the whole content of space.[3] There is no question here of knowledge having grown until the frame of archaic thought is no longer able to contain it. The real question is why the spatial insignificance of the earth, after being known for centuries, should suddenly in the last century have become an argument against Christianity. I do not know why this has happened; but I am sure it does not mark an increased clarity of thought, for the argument from size is, in my opinion, very feeble.

When the doctor at a post-mortem diagnoses poison, pointing to the state of the dead man's organs, his argument is rational because he has a clear idea of that opposite state in which the organs would have been found if no poison were

[1] Sir Edmund Taylor Whittaker, *The Beginning and End of the World*, Riddell Memorial Lectures, Fourteenth Series (Oxford, 1942), p. 40.
[2] Sir Arthur Stanley Eddington (1882-1944) who wrote *The Expanding Universe* (1933).
[3] Ptolemy lived at Alexandria in the 2nd century A.D. The reference is to his *Almagest*, bk. I, ch. v.

present. In the same way, if we use the vastness of space and the smallness of earth to disprove the existence of God, we ought to have a clear idea of the sort of universe we should expect if God did exist. But have we? Whatever space may be in itself — and, of course, some moderns think it finite — we certainly perceive it as three-dimensional, and to three-dimensional space we can conceive no boundaries. By the very forms of our perceptions, therefore, we must feel as if we lived somewhere in infinite space. If we discovered no objects in this infinite space except those which are of use to man (our own sun and moon), then this vast emptiness would certainly be used as a strong argument against the existence of God. If we discover other bodies, they must be habitable or uninhabitable: and the odd thing is that both these hypotheses are used as grounds for rejecting Christianity. If the universe is teeming with life, this, we are told, reduces to absurdity the Christian claim — or what is thought to be the Christian claim — that man is unique, and the Christian doctrine that to this one planet God came down and was incarnate for us men and our salvation. If, on the other hand, the earth is really unique, then that proves that life is only an accidental by-product in the universe, and so again disproves our religion. Really, we are hard to please. We treat God as the police treat a man when he is arrested; whatever He does will be used in evidence against Him. I do not think this is due to our wickedness. I suspect there is something in our very mode of thought which makes it inevitable that we should always be baffled by actual existence, *whatever* character actual existence may have. Perhaps a finite and contingent creature — a creature that might not have existed — will always find it hard to acquiesce in the brute fact that it is, here and now, attached to an actual order of things.

However that may be, it is certain that the whole argument from size rests on the assumption that differences of size ought to coincide with differences of value: for unless they do, there is, of course, no reason why the minute earth and the yet smaller human creatures upon it should not be the most important things in a universe that contains the spiral nebulae. Now, is this assumption rational or emotional? I feel, as well as anyone else, the absurdity of supposing that the galaxy could be of less moment in God's eyes than such an atom as a human being. But I notice that I feel no similar absurdity in supposing that a man of five-feet high may be more important than another man who is five-feet three and a half — nor that a man may matter more than a tree, or a brain more than a leg. In other words, the feeling of absurdity arises only if the differences of size are very great. But where a relation is perceived by reason it holds good universally. If size and value had any real connexion, small differences in size would accompany small differences in value as surely as large differences in size accompany large differences in value. But no sane man could suppose that this is so. I don't think the taller man *slightly* more valuable than the shorter one. I don't allow a slight superiority to trees over men, and then neglect it because it is too small to bother about. I perceive, as long as I am dealing with the small differences of size, that they have no connexion with value whatsoever. I therefore conclude that the importance attached to the great differences of size is an affair, not of reason but of emotion — of that peculiar emotion which superiorities in size produce only after a certain point of absolute size has been reached.

We are inveterate poets. Our imaginations awake. Instead of mere quantity, we now have a quality — the sublime. Unless this were so, the merely arithmetical greatness of the galaxy would be no more impressive than the figures in a telephone directory. It is thus, in a sense, from ourselves that the material universe derives its power to over-awe us. To a mind which did not share our emotions, and lacked our imaginative energies, the argument from size would be sheerly meaningless. Men look on the starry heavens with reverence: monkeys do not. The silence of the eternal spaces terrified Pascal,[4] but it was the greatness of Pascal that enabled them to do so. When we are frightened by the greatness of the universe, we are (almost literally) frightened by our own shadows: for these light years and billions of centuries are mere arithmetic until the shadow of man, the poet, the maker of myth, falls upon them. I do not say we are wrong to tremble at his shadow; it is a shadow of an image of God. But if ever the vastness of matter threatens to overcross our spirits, one must remember that it is matter spiritualized which does so. To puny man,

[4] Blaise Pascal, *Pensées,* No. 206.

41

the great nebula in Andromeda owes in a sense its greatness.

And this drives me to say yet again that we are hard to please. If the world in which we found ourselves were not vast and strange enough to give us Pascal's terror, what poor creatures we should be! Being what we are, rational but also animate, amphibians who start from the world of sense and proceed through myth and metaphor to the world of spirit, I do not see how we could have come to know the greatness of God without that hint furnished by the greatness of the material universe. Once again, what sort of universe do we demand? If it were small enough to be cosy, it would not be big enough to be sublime. If it is large enough for us to stretch our spiritual limbs in, it must be large enough to baffle us. Cramped or terrified, we must, in any conceivable world, be one or the other. I prefer terror. I should be suffocated in a universe that I could see to the end of. Have you never, when walking in a wood, turned back deliberately for fear you should come out at the other side and thus make it ever after in your imagination a mere beggarly strip of trees?

I hope you do not think I am suggesting that God made the spiral nebulae solely or chiefly in order to give me the experience of awe and bewilderment. I have not the faintest idea why He made them; on the whole, I think it would be rather surprising if I had. As far as I understand the matter, Christianity is not wedded to an anthropocentric view of the universe as a whole. The first chapters of Genesis, no doubt, give the story of creation in the form of a folk-tale — a fact recognized as early as the time of St Jerome — and if you take them alone you might get that impression. But it is not confirmed by the Bible as a whole. There are few places in literature where we are more sternly warned against making man the measure of all things than in the Book of Job: 'Canst thou draw out leviathan with an hook? Will he make a covenant with thee? wilt thou take him for a servant? Shall not one be cast down even at the sight of him?'[5] In St Paul, the powers of the skies seem usually to be hostile to man. It is, of course, the essence of Christianity that God loves man and for his sake became man and died. But that does not prove

[5] Job xli. 1, 4, 9.

that man is the sole end of nature. In the parable, it was the one lost sheep that the shepherd went in search of:[6] it was not the only sheep in the flock, and we are not told that it was the most valuable — save in so far as the most desperately in need has, while the need lasts, a peculiar value in the eyes of Love. The doctrine of the Incarnation would conflict with what we know of this vast universe only if we knew also that there were other rational species in it who had, like us, fallen, and who needed redemption in the same mode, and that they had not been vouchsafed it. But we know none of these things. It may be full of life that needs no redemption. It may be full of life that has been redeemed. It may be full of things quite other than life which satisfy the Divine Wisdom in fashions one cannot conceive. We are in no position to draw up maps of God's psychology, and prescribe limits to His interests. We would not do so even for a man whom we knew to be greater than ourselves. The doctrines that God is love and that He delights in men, are positive doctrines, not limiting doctrines. He is not less than this. What more He may be, we do not know; we know only that He must be more than we can conceive. It is to be expected that His creation should be, in the main, unintelligible to us.

Christians themselves have been much to blame for the misunderstanding on these matters. They have a bad habit of talking as if revelation existed to gratify curiosity by illuminating all creation so that it becomes self-explanatory and all questions are answered. But revelation appears to me to be purely practical, to be addressed to the particular animal, Fallen Man, for the relief of his urgent necessities — not to the spirit of inquiry in man for the gratification of his liberal curiosity. We know that God has visited and redeemed His people, and that tells us just as much about the general character of the creation as a dose given to one sick hen on a big farm tells it about the general character of farming in England. What we must do, which road we must take to the fountain of life, we know, and none who has seriously followed the directions complains that he has been deceived. But whether there are other creatures like ourselves, and how they are dealt with: whether inanimate matter exists only to

6 Matthew xviii. 12; Luke xv. 4.

serve living creatures or for some other reason: whether the immensity of space is a means to some end, or an illusion, or simply the natural mode in which infinite energy might be expected to create — on all these points I think we are left to our own speculations.

No. It is not Christianity which need fear the giant universe. It is those systems which place the whole meaning of existence in biological or social evolution on our own planet. It is the creative evolutionist, the Bergsonian or Shavian, or the Communist, who should tremble when he looks up at the night sky. For he really is committed to a sinking ship. He really is attempting to ignore the discovered nature of things, as though by concentrating on the possibly upward trend in a single planet he could make himself forget the inevitable downward trend in the universe as a whole, the trend to low temperatures and irrevocable disorganization. For entropy is the real cosmic wave, and evolution only a momentary tellurian ripple within it.

On these grounds, then, I submit that we Christians have as little to fear as anyone from the knowledge actually acquired. But, as I said at the beginning, that is not the fundamental answer. The endless fluctuations of scientific theory which seem today so much friendlier to us than in the last century may turn against us tomorrow. The basic answer lies elsewhere.

Let me remind you of the question we are trying to answer. It is this: How can an unchanging system survive the continual increase of knowledge? Now, in certain cases we know very well how it can. A mature scholar reading a great passage in Plato, and taking in at one glance the metaphysics, the literary beauty, and the place of both in the history of Europe, is in a very different position from a boy learning the Greek alphabet. Yet through that unchanging system of the alphabet all this vast mental and emotional activity is operating. It has not been broken by the new knowledge. It is not outworn. If it changed, all would be chaos. A great Christian statesman, considering the morality of a measure which will affect millions of lives, and which involves economic, geographical and political considerations of the utmost complexity, is in a different position from a boy first learning that one must not cheat or tell lies, or hurt innocent people. But only in so far as that first knowledge of the great moral platitudes survives unimpaired in the statesman will his deliberation be moral at all. If that goes, then there has been no progress, but only mere change. For change is not progress unless the core remains unchanged. A small oak grows into a big oak: if it became a beech, that would not be growth, but mere change. And thirdly, there is a great difference between counting apples and arriving at the mathematical formulae of modern physics. But the multiplication table is used in both and does not grow out of date.

In other words, wherever there is real progress in knowledge, there is some knowledge that is not superseded. Indeed, the very possibility of progress demands that there should be an unchanging element. New bottles for new wine, by all means: but not new palates, throats and stomachs, or it would not be, for us, 'wine' at all. I take it we should all agree to find this sort of unchanging element in the simple rules of mathematics. I would add to these the primary principles of morality. And I would also add the fundamental doctrines of Christianity. To put it in rather more technical language, I claim that the positive historical statements made by Christianity have the power, elsewhere found chiefly in formal principles, of receiving, without intrinsic change, the increasing complexity of meaning which increasing knowledge puts into them.

For example, it may be true (though I don't for a moment suppose it is) that when the Nicene Creed said 'He came down from Heaven', the writers had in mind a local movement from a local heaven to the surface of the earth — like a parachute descent. Others since may have dismissed the idea of a spatial heaven altogether. But neither the significance nor the credibility of what is asserted seems to be in the least affected by the change. On either view, the thing is miraculous: on either view, the mental images which attend the act of belief are inessential. When a Central African convert and a Harley Street specialist both affirm that Christ rose from the dead, there is, no doubt, a very great difference between their thoughts. To one, the simple picture of a dead body getting up is sufficient; the other may think of a whole series of biochemical and even physical processes beginning to work backwards. The Doctor knows that, in his experience, they never have worked backwards; but the negro knows that dead bodies don't get up and walk. Both are faced with miracle, and both know it. If both think miracle impossible, the only difference

45

is that the Doctor will expound the impossibility in much greater detail, will give an elaborate gloss on the simple statement that dead men don't walk about. If both believe, all the Doctor says will merely analyze and explicate the words 'He rose.' When the author of Genesis says that God made man in His own image, he may have pictured a vaguely corporeal God making man as a child makes a figure out of plasticine. A modern Christian philosopher may think of a process lasting from the first creation of matter to the final appearance on this planet of an organism fit to receive spiritual as well as biological life. But both mean essentially the same thing. Both are denying the same thing — the doctrine that matter by some blind power inherent in itself has produced spirituality.

Does this mean that Christians on different levels of general education conceal radically different beliefs under an identical form of words? Certainly not. For what they agree on is the substance, and what they differ about is the shadow. When one imagines his God seated in a local heaven above a flat earth, where another sees God and creation in terms of Professor Whitehead's philosophy,[7] this difference touches precisely what does not matter. Perhaps this seems to you an exaggeration. But is it? As regards material reality, we are now being forced to the conclusion that we know nothing about it save its mathematics. The tangible beach and pebbles of our first calculators, the imaginable atoms of Democritus, the plain man's picture of space, turn out to be the shadow: numbers are the substance of our knowledge, the sole liaison between mind and things. What nature is in herself evades us; what seem to naive perception to be the evident things about her, turn out to be the most phantasmal. It is something the same with our knowledge of spiritual reality. What God is in Himself, how He is to be conceived by philosophers, retreats continually from our knowledge. The elaborate world-pictures which accompany religion and which look each so solid while they last, turn out to be only shadows. It is religion itself — prayer and sacrament and repentance and adoration — which is here, in the long run, our sole avenue to the real. Like mathematics, religion can grow from within, or decay. The Jew

---

[7] Alfred North Whitehead (1861-1947), who wrote, among other works, *Science and the Modern World* (1925) and *Religion in the Making* (1926).

knows more than the Pagan, the Christian more than the Jew, the modern vaguely religious man less than any of the three. But, like mathematics, it remains simply itself, capable of being applied to any new theory of the material universe and out-moded by none.

When any man comes into the presence of God he will find, whether he wishes it or not, that all those things which seemed to make him so different from the men of other times, or even from his earlier self, have fallen off him. He is back where he always was, where every man always is. *Eadem sunt omnia semper.*[8] Do not let us deceive ourselves. No possible complexity which we can give to our picture of the universe can hide us from God: there is no copse, no forest, no jungle thick enough to provide cover. We read in Revelation of Him that sat on the throne 'from whose face the earth and heaven fled away'.[9] It may happen to any of us at any moment. In the twinkling of an eye, in a time too small to be measured, and in any place, all that seems to divide us from God can flee away, vanish leaving us naked before Him, like the first man, like the only man, as if nothing but He and I existed. And since that contact cannot be avoided for long, and since it means either bliss or horror, the business of life is to learn to like it. That is the first and great commandment.

[8] 'Everything is always the same.'
[9] Revelation xx. 11.

4

ANSWERS TO QUESTIONS ON CHRISTIANITY

[The answers to questions printed here were given by Lewis at a 'One Man Brains Trust' held on the 18th April 1944 at the Head Office of Electric and Musical Industries Ltd., Hayes, Middlesex. Shorthand notes were made and a typescript was sent to Lewis. He revised it a little, and it was printed in 1944. Mr H. W. Bowen was the question-master.]

Lewis:

I have been asked to open with a few words on Christianity and Modern Industry. Now Modern Industry is a subject of which I know nothing at all. But for that very reason it may illustrate what Christianity, in my opinion, does and does not do. Christianity does *not* replace the technical. When it tells you to feed the hungry it doesn't give you lessons in cookery. If you want to learn *that,* you must go to a cook rather than a Christian. If you are not a professional Economist and have no experience of Industry, simply being a Christian won't give you the answer to industrial problems. My own idea is that modern industry is a radically hopeless system. You can improve wages, hours, conditions, etc., but all that doesn't cure the deepest trouble: i.e., that numbers of people are kept all their lives doing dull repetition work which gives no full play to their faculties. How that is to be overcome, I do not know. If a single country abandoned the system it would merely fall a prey to the other countries which hadn't abandoned it. I don't know the solution: that is not the kind of thing Christianity teaches a person like me. Let's now carry on with the questions.

48

Question 1.

Christians are taught to love their neighbours. How, therefore, can they justify their attitude of supporting the war?

Lewis:

You are told to love your neighbour as yourself. How do you love yourself? When I look into my own mind, I find that I do not love myself by thinking myself a dear old chap or having affectionate feelings. I do not think that I love myself because I am particularly good, but just because I am myself and quite apart from my character. I might detest something which I have done. Nevertheless, I do not cease to love myself. In other words, that definite distinction that Christians make between hating sin and loving the sinner is one that you have been making in your own case since you were born. You dislike what you have done, but you don't cease to love yourself. You may even think that you ought to be hanged. You may even think that you ought to go to the Police and own up and be hanged. Love is not affectionate feeling, but a steady wish for the loved person's ultimate good as far as it can be obtained. It seems to me, therefore, that when the worst comes to the worst, if you cannot restrain a man by any method except by trying to kill him, then a Christian must do that. That is my answer. But I may be wrong. It is very difficult to answer, of course.

Question 2.

Supposing a factory worker asked you: 'How can I find God?' How would you reply?

Lewis:

I don't see how the problem would be different for a factory worker than for anyone else. The primary thing about any man is that he is a human being, sharing all the ordinary human temptations and assets. What is the special problem about the factory worker? But perhaps it is worth saying this:

Christianity really does two things about conditions here and now in this world:

(1) It tries to make them as good as possible, i.e., to reform them; but also

(2) It fortifies you against them in so far as they remain bad.

If what was in the questioner's mind was this problem of repetition work, then the factory worker's difficulty is the same as any other man confronted with any sorrow or difficulty. People will find God if they consciously seek from Him the right attitude towards all unpleasant things . . . if that is the point of the question?

Question 3.
Will you please say how you would define a practising Christian? Are there any other varieties?

Lewis:
Certainly there are a great many other varieties. It depends, of course, on what you mean by 'practising Christian'. If you mean one who has practised Christianity in every respect at every moment of his life, then there is only One on record — Christ Himself. In that sense there are no practising Christians, but only Christians who, in varying degrees, try to practise it and fail in varying degrees and then start again. A perfect practice of Christianity would, of course, consist in a perfect imitation of the life of Christ — I mean, in so far as it was applicable in one's own particular circumstances. Not in an idiotic sense — it doesn't mean that every Christian should grow a beard, or be a bachelor, or become a travelling preacher. It means that every single act and feeling, every experience, whether pleasant or unpleasant, must be referred to God. It means looking at everything as something that comes from Him, and always looking to Him and asking His will first, and saying: 'How would He wish me to deal with this?'

A kind of picture or pattern (in a very remote way) of the relation between the perfect Christian and his God, would be the relation of the good dog to its master. This is only a very imperfect picture, though, because the dog hasn't reason like its master: whereas we do share in God's reason, even if in an imperfect and interrupted way ('interrupted' because we don't think rationally for very long at a time — it's too tiring — and we haven't information to understand things fully, and our intelligence itself has certain limitations). In that way we are more like God than the dog is like us, though, of course, there are other ways in which the dog is more like us than we are like God. It is only an illustration.

Question 4.

What justification on ethical grounds and on the grounds of social expediency exists for the Church's attitude towards Venereal Disease and prophylaxis and publicity in connection with it?

Lewis:

I need further advice on that question, and then perhaps I can answer it. Can the questioner say which Church he has in mind?

Voice.

The Church concerned is the Church of England, and its attitude, though not written, is implicit in that it has more or less banned all publicity in connection with prophylactic methods of combating Venereal Disease. The view of some is that moral punishment should not be avoided.

Lewis:

I haven't myself met any clergymen of the Church of England who held that view: and I don't hold it myself. There are obvious objections to it. After all, it isn't only Venereal Disease that can be regarded as a punishment for bad conduct. Indigestion in old age may be the result of overeating in earlier life: but no one objects to advertisements for Beecham's Pills. I, at any rate, strongly dissent from the view you've mentioned.

Question 5.

Many people feel resentful or unhappy because they think they are the target of unjust fate. These feelings are stimulated by bereavement, illness, deranged domestic or working conditions, or the observation of suffering in others. What is the Christian view of this problem?

Lewis:

The Christian view is that men were created to be in a certain relationship to God (if we are in that relation to Him, the right relation to one another will follow inevitably). Christ said it was difficult for 'the rich' to enter the Kingdom of Heaven,[1] referring, no doubt, to 'riches' in the ordinary sense. But I think it really covers riches in every sense — good for-

[1] Matthew xix. 23; Mark x. 23; Luke xviii. 24.

tune, health, popularity, and all the things one wants to have. All these things tend — just as money tends — to make you feel independent of God, because if you have them you are happy already and contented in this life. You don't want to turn away to anything more, and so you try to rest in a shadowy happiness as if it could last for ever. But God wants to give you a real and eternal happiness. Consequently He may have to take all these 'riches' away from you: if He doesn't, you will go on relying on them. It sounds cruel, doesn't it? But I am beginning to find out that what people call the cruel doctrines are really the kindest ones in the long run. I used to think it was a 'cruel' doctrine to say that troubles and sorrows were 'punishments'. But I find in practice that when you are in trouble, the moment you regard it as a 'punishment', it becomes easier to bear. If you think of this world as a place intended simply for our happiness, you find it quite intolerable: think of it as a place of training and correction and it's not so bad.

Imagine a set of people all living in the same building. Half of them think it is a hotel, the other half think it is a prison. Those who think it a hotel might regard it as quite intolerable, and those who thought it was a prison might decide that it was really surprisingly comfortable. So that what seems the ugly doctrine is one that comforts and strengthens you in the end. The people who try to hold an optimistic view of this world would become pessimists: the people who hold a pretty stern view of it become optimistic.

Question 6.

Materialists and some astronomers suggest that the solar planetary system and life as we know it was brought about by an accidental stellar collision. What is the Christian view of this theory?

Lewis:

If the solar system was brought about by an accidental collision, then the appearance of organic life on this planet was also an accident, and the whole evolution of Man was an accident too. If so, then all our present thoughts are mere accidents — the accidental by-product of the movement of atoms. And this holds for the thoughts of the materialists and astronomers as well as for anyone else's. But if *their* thoughts — i.e., of Materialism and Astronomy — are merely accidental by-products, why should we believe them to be true? I see no reason for believing that one accident should be able to give me a correct account of all the other accidents. It's like expecting that the accidental shape taken by the splash when you upset a milk-jug should give you a correct account of how the jug was made and why it was upset.

Question 7.

Is it true that Christianity (especially the Protestant forms) tends to produce a gloomy, joyless condition of society which is like a pain in the neck to most people?

Lewis:

As to the distinction between Protestant and other forms of Christianity, it is very difficult to answer. I find by reading about the sixteenth century, that people like Sir Thomas More, for whom I have a great respect, always regarded Martin Luther's doctrines not as gloomy thinking, but as wishful thinking. I doubt whether we can make a distinction between Protestant and other forms in this respect. Whether Protestantism is gloomy and whether Christianity at all produces gloominess, I find it very difficult to answer, as I have never lived in a completely non-Christian society nor a completely Christian one, and I wasn't there in the sixteenth century, and only have my knowledge from reading books. I think there is about the same amount of fun and gloom in all periods. The poems, novels, letters, etc., of every period all seem to show that. But again, I don't really know the answer, of course. I wasn't there.

Question 8.

Is it true that Christians must be prepared to live a life of personal discomfort and self-sacrifice in order to qualify for 'Pie in the Sky'?

Lewis:

All people, whether Christian or not, must be prepared to live a life of discomfort. It is impossible to accept Christianity for the sake of finding comfort: but the Christian tries to lay himself open to the will of God, to do what God wants him to do. You don't know in advance whether God is going to set you to do something difficult or painful, or something that you will quite like; and some people of heroic mould are disappointed when the job doled out to them turns out to be something quite nice. But you must be prepared for the unpleasant things and the discomforts. I don't mean fasting, and things like that. They are a different matter. When you are training soldiers in manoeuvres, you practise in blank ammunition because you would like them to have practise before meeting the real enemy. So we must practise in abstaining from pleasures which are not in themselves wicked. If you don't abstain from pleasure, you won't be good when the time comes along. It is purely a matter of practise.

Voice.

Are not practices like fasting and self-denial borrowed from earlier or more primitive religions?

Lewis:

I can't say for certain which bits came into Christianity from earlier religions. An enormous amount did. I should find it hard to believe Christianity if that were not so. I couldn't believe that nine-hundred and ninety-nine religions were completely false and the remaining one true. In reality, Christianity is primarily the fulfilment of the Jewish religion, but also the fulfilment of what was vaguely hinted in all the religions at their best. What was vaguely seen in them all comes into focus in Christianity — just as God Himself comes into focus by becoming a Man. I take it that the speaker's remarks on earlier religions are based on evidence about modern savages. I don't think it is good evidence. Modern savages usually represent some decay in culture — you find them doing things which look as if they had a fairly civilized basis once, which they have forgotten. To assume that primitive man was exactly like the modern savage is unsound.

Voice.

Could you say any more on how one discovers whether a task is laid on one by God, or whether it comes in some other way? If we cannot distinguish between the pleasant and the unpleasant things, it is a complicated matter.

Lewis:

We are guided by the ordinary rules of moral behaviour, which I think are more or less common to the human race and quite reasonable and demanded by the circumstances. I don't mean anything like sitting down and waiting for a supernatural vision.

Voice.

We don't qualify for heaven by practice, but salvation is obtained at the Cross. We do nothing to obtain it, but follow Christ. We may have pain or tribulation, but nothing we do qualifies us for heaven, but Christ.

Lewis:

The controversy about faith and works is one that has gone on for a very long time, and it is a highly technical matter. I personally rely on the paradoxical text: 'Work out your own salvation . . . for it is God that worketh in you.'[2] It looks as if in one sense we do nothing, and in another case we do a damned lot. 'Work out your own salvation with fear and trembling,'[3] but you must have it in you before you can work it out. But I have no wish to go further into it, as it would interest no one but the Christians present, would it?

Question 9.

Would the application of Christian standards bring to an end or greatly reduce scientific and material progress? In other words, is it wrong for a Christian to be ambitious and strive for personal success?

Lewis:

It is easiest to think of a simplified example. How would the application of Christianity affect anyone on a desert island? Would he be less likely to build a comfortable hut? The answer is 'No.' There might come a particular moment, of course, when Christianity would tell him to bother less about the hut, i.e., if he were in danger of coming to think that the hut was the most important thing in the universe. But there is no evidence that Christianity would prevent him from building it.

Ambition! We must be careful what we mean by it. If it means the desire to get ahead of other people — which is what I think it does mean — then it is bad. If it means simply

2 Philippians ii. 12.
3 *Ibid.*

wanting to do a thing well, then it is good. It isn't wrong for an actor to want to act his part as well as it can possibly be acted, but the wish to have his name in bigger type than the other actors is a bad one.

Voice.

It's all right to be a General, but if it is one's ambition to be a General, then you shouldn't become one.

Lewis:

The mere event of becoming a General isn't either right or wrong in itself. What matters morally is your attitude towards it. The man may be thinking about winning a war; he may be wanting to be a General because he honestly thinks he has a good plan and is glad of a chance to carry it out. That's all right. But if he is thinking: 'What can I get out of the job?' or 'How can I get on the front page of the *Illustrated News?*' then it is all wrong. And what we call 'ambition' usually means the wish to be more conspicuous or more successful than someone else. It is this competitive element in it that is bad. It is perfectly reasonable to want to dance well or to look nice. But when the dominant wish is to dance better or look nicer than the others — when you begin to feel that if the others danced as well as you or looked as nice as you, that would take all the fun out of it — then you are going wrong.

Voice.

I am wondering how far we can ascribe to the work of the Devil those very legitimate desires that we indulge in. Some people have a very sensitive conception of the presence of the Devil. Others haven't. Is the Devil as real as we think he is? That doesn't trouble some people, since they have no desire to be good, but others are continually harassed by the Old Man himself.

Lewis:

No reference to the Devil or devils is included in any Christian Creeds, and it is quite possible to be a Christian without believing in them. I do believe such beings exist, but that is my own affair. Supposing there to be such beings, the degree to which humans were conscious of their presence would presumably vary very much. I mean, the more a man was in the Devil's power, the less he would be aware of it, on the principle that a man is still fairly sober as long as he knows he's drunk. It is the people who are fully awake and trying hard to be good who would be most aware of the Devil. It is when you start arming against Hitler that you first realize your country is full of Nazi agents. Of course, they don't want you to believe in the Devil. If devils exist, their first aim is to give you an anaesthetic — to put you off your guard. Only if that fails, do you become aware of them.

Voice.

Does Christianity retard scientific advancement? Or does it approve of those who help spiritually others who are on the road to perdition, by scientifically removing the environmental causes of the trouble?

Lewis:

Yes. In the abstract it is certainly so. At a particular moment, if most human beings are concentrating only on material improvements in the environment, it may be the duty of Christians to point out (and pretty loudly) that this isn't the only thing that matters. But as a general rule it is in favour of all knowledge and all that will help the human race in any way.

Question 10.

The Bible was written thousands of years ago for people in a lower state of mental development than today. Many portions seem preposterous in the light of modern knowledge. In view of this, should not the Bible be re-written with the object of discarding the fabulous and re-interpreting the remainder?

Lewis:

First of all as to the people in a lower state of mental development. I am not so sure what lurks behind that. If it means that people ten thousand years ago didn't know a good many things that we know now, of course, I agree. But if it means that there has been any advance in *intelligence* in that time, I believe there is no evidence for any such thing. The Bible can be divided into two parts — the Old and the New Testaments. The Old Testament contains fabulous elements. The New Testament consists mostly of teaching, not of narrative at all: but where it *is* narrative, it is, in my opinion, historical. As to the fabulous element in the Old Testament, I very much doubt if you would be wise to chuck it out. What you get is something *coming gradually into focus*. First you get, scattered through the heathen religions all over the world — but still quite vague and mythical — the idea of a god who is killed and broken and then comes to life again. No one knows where he is supposed to have lived and died; he's not historical. Then you get the Old Testament. Religious ideas get a bit more focused. Everything is now connected with a particular nation. And it comes still more into focus as it goes on. Jonah and the Whale,[4] Noah and his Ark,[5] are fabulous; but the Court history of King David[6] is probably as reliable as the Court history of Louis XIV. Then, in the New Testament the *thing really happens*. The dying god really appears — as a historical Person, living in a definite place and time. If we *could* sort out all the fabulous elements in the earlier stages and separate them from the historical ones, I think we might lose an essential part of the whole process. That is my own idea.

Question 11.

Which of the religions of the world gives to its followers the greatest happiness?

Lewis:

Which of the religions of the world gives to its followers the greatest happiness? While it lasts, the religion of worshipping oneself is the best.

I have an elderly acquaintance of about eighty, who has lived a life of unbroken selfishness and self-admiration from the earliest years, and is, more or less, I regret to say, one of the happiest men I know. From the moral point of view it is very difficult! I am not approaching the question from that angle. As you perhaps know, I haven't always been a Christian. I didn't go to religion to make me happy. I always knew a bottle of Port would do that. If you want a religion to make you feel really comfortable, I certainly don't recommend Christianity. I am certain there must be a patent American article

---

[4] The Book of Jonah.
[5] Genesis, chapters vi-viii.
[6] II Samuel, ch. ii — I Kings, ch. ii.

on the market which will suit you far better, but I can't give any advice on it.

Question 12.

Are there any unmistakable outward signs in a person surrendered to God? Would he be cantankerous? Would he smoke?

Lewis:

I think of the advertisements for 'White Smiles' Tooth Paste, saying that it is the best on the market. If they are true, it would follow that:

(1) Anyone who starts using it will have better teeth;

(2) Anyone using it has better teeth than he would have if he weren't using it.

But you can't test it in the case of one who has naturally bad teeth and uses it, and compare him with a healthy Negro who has never used tooth paste at all.

Take the case of a sour old maid, who is a Christian, but cantankerous. On the other hand, take some pleasant and popular fellow, but who has never been to Church. Who knows how much more cantankerous the old maid might be if she were *not* a Christian, and how much more likeable the nice fellow might be if he *were* a Christian? You can't judge Christianity simply by comparing the *product* in those two people; you would need to know what kind of raw material Christ was working on in both cases.

As an illustration, let us take a case of industrialism. Let us take two factories:

Factory A with poor and inadequate plant, and

Factory B with first-class modern plant.

You can't judge by the outside. You must consider the plant and methods by which they are run, and considering the plant at Factory A, it may be a wonder it does anything at all; and considering the new machinery at Factory B, it may be a wonder it doesn't do better.

Question 13.

What is your opinion about raffles within the plant — no matter how good the cause — which, not infrequently, is given less prominence than the alluring list of prizes?

Lewis:

Gambling ought never to be an important part of a man's

59

life. If it is a way in which large sums of money are trans-
ferred from person to person without doing any good (e.g.,
producing employment, goodwill, etc.) then it is a bad thing.
If it is carried out on a small scale, I am not sure that it is
bad. I don't know much about it, because it is about the only
vice to which I have no temptation at all, and I think it is
a risk to talk about things which are not in my own make-up,
because I don't understand them. If anyone comes to me asking to play bridge for money, I just say: 'How much do you
hope to win? Take it and go away.'

Question 14.

Many people are quite unable to understand the theological
differences which have caused divisions in the Christian Church.
Do you consider that these differences are fundamental, and
is the time now ripe for re-union?

Lewis:

The time is always ripe for re-union. Divisions between
Christians are a sin and a scandal, and Christians ought at
all times to be making contributions towards re-union, if it
is only by their prayers. I am only a layman and a recent
Christian, and I do not know much about these things, but
in all the things which I have written and thought I have
always stuck to traditional, dogmatic positions. The result is
that letters of agreement reach me from what are ordinarily
regarded as the most different kinds of Christians; for instance,
I get letters from Jesuits, monks, nuns, and also from Quakers
and Welsh Dissenters, and so on. So it seems to me that the
'extremist' elements in every Church are nearest one another
and the liberal and 'broad-minded' people in each Body could
never be united at all. The world of dogmatic Christianity is
a place in which thousands of people of quite different types
keep on saying the same thing, and the world of 'broad-mind-
edness' and watered-down 'religion' is a world where a small
number of people (all of the same type) say totally different
things and change their minds every few minutes. We shall
never get re-union from them.

Question 15.

In the past the Church used various kinds of compulsion
in attempts to force a particular brand of Christianity on the

community. Given sufficient power, is there not a danger of this sort of thing happening again?

Lewis:

Yes, I hear nasty rumours coming from Spain. Persecution is a temptation to which all men are exposed. I had a postcard signed 'M.D.' saying that anyone who expressed and published his belief in the Virgin Birth should be stripped and flogged. That shows you how easily persecution of Christians by the non-Christians might come back. Of course, they wouldn't call it Persecution: they'd call it 'Compulsory re-education of the ideologically unfit', or something like that. But, of course, I have to admit that Christians themselves have been persecutors in the past. It was worse of them, because *they* ought to have known better: they weren't worse in any other way. I detest every kind of religious compulsion: only the other day I was writing an angry letter to *The Spectator* about Church Parades in the Home Guard!

Question 16.

Is attendance at a place of worship or membership with a Christian community necessary to a Christian way of life?

Lewis:

That's a question which I cannot answer. My own experience is that when I first became a Christian, about fourteen years ago, I thought that I could do it on my own, by retiring to my rooms and reading theology, and I wouldn't go to the churches and Gospel Halls; and then later I found that it was the only way of flying your flag; and, of course, I found that this meant being a target. It is extraordinary how inconvenient to your family it becomes for you to get up early to go to Church. It doesn't matter so much if you get up early for anything else, but if you get up early to go to Church it's very selfish of you and you upset the house. If there is anything in the teaching of the New Testament which is in the nature of a command, it is that you are obliged to take the Sacrament,[7] and you can't do it without going to Church. I disliked very

[7] John vi. 53-54: 'Except ye eat the flesh of the Son of man, and drink his blood, ye have no life in you. Whoso eateth my flesh, and drinketh my blood, hath eternal life; and I will raise him up at the last day.'

much their hymns, which I considered to be fifth-rate poems set to sixth-rate music. But as I went on I saw the great merit of it. I came up against different people of quite different outlooks and different education, and then gradually my conceit just began peeling off. I realized that the hymns (which were just sixth-rate music) were, nevertheless, being sung with devotion and benefit by an old saint in elastic-side boots in the opposite pew, and then you realize that you aren't fit to clean those boots. It gets you out of your solitary conceit. It is not for me to lay down laws, as I am only a layman, and I don't know much.

Question 17.

If it is true that one has only to want God enough in order to find Him, how can I make myself want Him enough to enable myself to find Him?

Lewis:

If you don't want God, why are you so anxious to want to want Him? I think that in reality the want is a real one, and I should say that this person has in fact found God, although it may not be fully recognized yet. We are not always aware of things at the time they happen. At any rate, what is more important is that God has found this person, and that is the main thing.

5

MYTH BECAME FACT

M Y FRIEND CORINEUS HAS ADVANCED THE CHARGE THAT none of us are in fact Christians at all. According to him historic Christianity is something so barbarous that no modern man can really believe it: the moderns who claim to do so are in fact believing a modern system of thought which retains the vocabulary of Christianity and exploits the emotions inherited from it while quietly dropping its essential doctrines. Corineus compared modern Christianity with the modern English monarchy: the forms of kingship have been retained, but the reality has been abandoned.

All this I believe to be false, except of a few 'modernist' theologians who, by God's grace, become fewer every day. But for the moment let us assume that Corineus is right. Let us pretend, for purposes of argument, that *all* who now call themselves Christians have abandoned the historic doctrines. Let us suppose that modern 'Christianity' reveals a system of names, ritual, formulae and metaphors which persists although the thoughts behind it have changed. Corineus ought to be able to *explain* the persistence.

Why, on his view, do all these educated and enlightened pseudo-Christians insist on expressing their deepest thoughts in terms of an archaic mythology which must hamper and embarrass them at every turn? Why do they refuse to cut the umbilical cord which binds the living and flourishing child to its moribund mother? For, if Corineus is right, it should be a great relief to them to do so. Yet the odd thing is that even those who seem most embarrassed by the sediment of 'barbaric' Christianity in their thought become suddenly obstinate when you ask them to get rid of it altogether. They will strain the cord almost to breaking point, but they refuse to cut it. Sometimes they will take every step except the last one.

If all who professed Christianity were clergymen, it would be easy (though uncharitable) to reply that their livelihood depends on *not* taking that last step. Yet even if this were the true cause of their behaviour, even if all clergymen are intellectual prostitutes who preach for pay — and usually starvation pay — what they secretly believe to be false, surely so widespread a darkening of conscience among thousands of men not otherwise known to be criminal, itself demands explanation? And of course the profession of Christianity is not confined to the clergy. It is professed by millions of women and laymen who earn thereby contempt, unpopularity, suspicion, and the hostility of their own families. How does this come to happen?

Obstinacies of this sort are interesting. 'Why not cut the cord?' asks Corineus. 'Everything would be much easier if you would free your thought from this vestigial mythology.' To be sure: far easier. Life would be far easier for the mother of an invalid child if she put it into an Institution and adopted someone else's healthy baby instead. Life would be far easier to many a man if he abandoned the woman he has actually fallen in love with and married someone else because she is more suitable. The only defect of the healthy baby and the suitable woman is that they leave out the patient's only reason for bothering about a child or wife at all. 'Would not conversation be much more rational than dancing?' said Jane Austen's Miss Bingley. 'Much more rational,' replied Mr Bingley, 'but much less like a ball.'[1]

In the same way, it would be much more rational to abolish the English monarchy. But how if, by doing so, you leave out the one element in our State which matters most? How if the monarchy is the channel through which all the *vital* elements of citizenship — loyalty, the consecration of secular life, the hierarchical principle, splendour, ceremony, continuity — still trickle down to irrigate the dust-bowl of modern economic Statecraft?

The real answer of even the most 'modernist' Christianity to Corineus is the same. Even assuming (which I most constantly deny) that the doctrines of historic Christianity are merely mythical, it is the myth which is the vital and nourishing element in the whole concern. Corineus wants us to move with

[1] *Pride and Prejudice,* ch. xi.

the times. Now, we know where times move. They move *away*. But in religion we find something that does not move away. It is what Corineus calls the myth, that abides; it is what he calls the modern and living thought that moves away. Not only the thought of theologians, but the thought of anti-theologians. Where are the predecessors of Corineus? Where is the epicureanism of Lucretius,[2] the pagan revival of Julian the Apostate?[3] Where are the Gnostics, where is the monism of Averroës,[4] the deism of Voltaire, the dogmatic materialism of the great Victorians? They have moved with the times. But the thing they were all attacking remains: Corineus finds it still there to attack. The myth (to speak his language) has outlived the thoughts of all its defenders and of all its adversaries. It is the myth that gives life. Those elements even in modernist Christianity which Corineus regards as vestigial, are the substance: what he takes for the 'real modern belief' is the shadow.

To explain this we must look a little closer at myth in general, and at this myth in particular. Human intellect is incurably abstract. Pure mathematics is the type of successful thought. Yet the only realities we experience are concrete — this pain, this pleasure, this dog, this man. While we are loving the man, bearing the pain, enjoying the pleasure, we are not intellectually apprehending Pleasure, Pain or Personality. When we begin to do so, on the other hand, the concrete realities sink to the level of mere instances or examples: we are no longer dealing with them, but with that which they exemplify. This is our dilemma — either to taste and not to know or to know and not to taste — or, more strictly, to lack one kind of knowledge because we are in an experience or to lack another kind because we are outside it. As thinkers we are cut off from what we think about; as tasting, touching, willing, loving, hating, we do not clearly understand. The more lucidly we think, the more we are cut off: the more deeply we enter into reality, the less we can think. You cannot *study* Pleasure in the moment of the nuptial embrace, nor repentance while repenting, nor analyse the nature of humour while roaring with

2 Titus Lucretius Carus (c. 99-55), the Roman poet.
3 Roman emperor, A.D. 361-3.
4 Averroës (1126-98), of Cordova, believed that only one intellect exists for the whole human race in which every individual participates, to the exclusion of personal immortality.

65

laughter. But when else can you really know these things? 'If only my toothache would stop, I could write another chapter about Pain.' But once it stops, what do I know about pain?

Of this tragic dilemma myth is the partial solution. In the enjoyment of a great myth we come nearest to experiencing as a concrete what can otherwise be understood only as an abstraction. At this moment, for example, I am trying to understand something very abstract indeed — the fading, vanishing of tasted reality as we try to grasp it with the discursive reason. Probably I have made heavy weather of it. But if I remind you, instead, of Orpheus and Eurydice, how he was suffered to lead her by the hand but, when he turned round to look at her, she disappeared, what was merely a principle becomes imaginable. You may reply that you never till this moment attached that 'meaning' to that myth. Of course not. You are not looking for an abstract 'meaning' at all. If that was what you were doing the myth would be for you no true myth but a mere allegory. You were not knowing, but tasting; but what you were tasting turns out to be a universal principle. The moment we *state* this principle, we are admittedly back in the world of abstraction. It is only while receiving the myth as a story that you experience the principle concretely.

When we translate we get abstraction — or rather, dozens of abstractions. What flows into you from the myth is not truth but reality (truth is always *about* something, but reality is that *about which* truth is), and, therefore, every myth becomes the father of innumerable truths on the abstract level. Myth is the mountain whence all the different streams arise which become truths down here in the valley; *in hac valle abstractionis*.[5] Or, if you prefer, myth is the isthmus which connects the peninsular world of thought with that vast continent we really belong to. It is not, like truth, abstract; nor is it, like direct experience, bound to the particular.

Now as myth transcends thought, Incarnation transcends myth. The heart of Christianity is a myth which is also a fact. The old myth of the Dying God, *without ceasing to be myth,* comes down from the heaven of legend and imagination to the earth of history. It *happens* — at a particular date, in a particular place, followed by definable historical consequences. We pass from a Balder or an Osiris, dying nobody knows

[5] 'In this valley of separation.'

when or where, to a historical Person crucified (it is all in order) *under Pontius Pilate.* By becoming fact it does not cease to be myth: that is the miracle. I suspect that men have sometimes derived more spiritual sustenance from myths they did not believe than from the religion they professed. To be truly Christian we must both assent to the historical fact and also receive the myth (fact though it has become) with the same imaginative embrace which we accord to all myths. The one is hardly more necessary than the other.

A man who disbelieved the Christian story as fact but continually fed on it as myth would, perhaps, be more spiritually alive than one who assented and did not think much about it. The modernist — the extreme modernist, infidel in all but name — need not be called a fool or hypocrite because he obstinately retains, even in the midst of his intellectual atheism, the language, rites, sacraments, and story of the Christians. The poor man may be clinging (with a wisdom he himself by no means understands) to that which is his life. It would have been better that Loisy[6] should have remained a Christian: it would not necessarily have been better that he should have purged his thought of vestigial Christianity.

Those who do not know that this great myth became Fact when the Virgin conceived are, indeed, to be pitied. But Christians also need to be reminded — we may thank Corineus for reminding us — that what became Fact was a Myth, that it carries with it into the world of Fact all the properties of a myth. God is more than a god, not less; Christ is more than Balder, not less. We must not be ashamed of the mythical radiance resting on our theology. We must not be nervous about 'parallels' and 'Pagan Christs': they *ought* to be there — it would be a stumbling block if they weren't. We must not, in false spirituality, withhold our imaginative welcome. If God chooses to be mythopoeic — and is not the sky itself a myth — shall we refuse to be *mythopathic?* For this is the marriage of heaven and earth: Perfect Myth and Perfect Fact: claiming not only our love and our obedience, but also our wonder and delight, addressed to the savage, the child, and the poet in each one of us no less than to the moralist, the scholar, and the philosopher.

[6] Alfred Loisy (1857-1940), a French theologian and founder of the Modernist Movement.

6

'HORRID RED THINGS'

MANY THEOLOGIANS AND SOME SCIENTISTS ARE NOW READY to proclaim that the nineteenth century 'conflict between science and religion' is over and done with. But even if this is true, it is a truth known only to real theologians and real scientists — that is, to a few highly educated men. To the man in the street the conflict is still perfectly real, and in his mind it takes a form which the learned hardly dream of.

The ordinary man is not thinking of particular dogmas and particular scientific discoveries. What troubles him is an all-pervading difference of atmosphere between what he believes Christianity to be and that general picture of the universe which he has picked up from living in a scientific age. He gathers from the Creed that God has a 'Son' (just as if God were a god, like Odin or Jupiter): that this Son 'came down' (like a parachutist) from 'Heaven', first to earth and later to some land of the dead situated beneath the earth's surface: that, still later, He ascended into the sky and took His seat in a decorated chair placed a little to the right of His Father's throne. The whole thing seems to imply a local and material heaven — a palace in the stratosphere — a flat earth and all the rest of those archaic misconceptions.

The ordinary man is well aware that we should deny all the beliefs he attributes to us and interpret our creed in a different sense. But this by no means satisfies him. 'No doubt', he thinks, 'once those articles of belief are there, they can be allegorised or spiritualised away to any extent you please. But is it not plain that they would never have been there at all if the first generation of Christians had had any notion of what the real universe is like? A historian who has based his work on the misreading of a document may afterwards (when his mistake has been exposed) exercise great ingenuity in showing that his account of a certain battle can still be reconciled with what the document records. But the point is that none of these ingenious explanations would ever have come into existence if he had read his documents correctly at the outset. They are therefore really a waste of labour; it would be manlier of him to admit his mistake and begin all over again.'

I think there are two things that Christians must do if they wish to convince this 'ordinary' modern man. In the first place, they must make it quite clear that what will remain of the Creed after all their explanations and reinterpretations will still be something quite unambiguously supernatural, miraculous, and shocking. We may not believe in a flat earth and a sky-palace. But we must insist from the beginning that we believe, as firmly as any savage or theosophist, in a spirit-world which can, and does, invade the natural or phenomenal universe. For the plain man suspects that when we start explaining, we are going to explain away: that we have mythology for our ignorant hearers and are ready, when cornered by educated hearers, to reduce it to innocuous moral platitudes which no one ever dreamed of denying. And there are theologians who justify this suspicion. From them we must part company absolutely. If nothing remains except what could be equally well stated without Christian formulae, then the honest thing is to admit that Christianity is untrue and to begin over again without it.

In the second place, we must try to teach something about the difference between thinking and imagining. It is, of course, a historical error to suppose that all, or even most, early Christians believed in the sky-palace in the same sense in which we believe in the solar system. Anthropomorphism was condemned by the Church as soon as the question was explicitly before her. But some early Christians may have done this; and probably thousands never thought of their faith without anthropomorphic imagery. That is why we must distinguish the core of belief from the attendant imagining.

When I think of London I always see a picture of Euston

Station. But I do not believe that London *is* Euston Station. That is a simple case, because there the thinker *knows* the imagery to be false. Now let us take a more complex one. I once heard a lady tell her daughter that if you ate too many aspirin tablets you would die. 'But why?' asked the child. 'If you squash them you don't find any horrid red things inside them.' Obviously, when this child thought of poison she not only had an attendant image of 'horrid red things', but she actually believed that poison was red. And this is an error. But how far does it invalidate her thinking about poison? She learned that an overdose of aspirin would kill you; her belief was true. She knew, within limits, which of the substances in her mother's house were poisonous. If I, staying in the house, had raised a glass of what looked like water to my lips, and the child had said, 'Don't drink that. Mummie says it's poisonous,' I should have been foolish to disregard the warning on the ground that 'This child has an archaic and mythological idea of poison as horrid red things.'

There is thus a distinction not only between thought and imagination in general, but even between thought and those images which the thinker (falsely) believes to be true. When the child learned later that poison is not always red, she would not have felt that anything essential in her beliefs about poison had been altered. She would still know, as she had always known, that poison is what kills you if you swallow it. That is the essence of poison. The erroneous beliefs about colour drop away without affecting it.

In the same way an early peasant Christian might have thought that Christ's sitting at the right hand of the Father really implied two chairs of state, in a certain spatial relation, inside a sky-palace. But if the same man afterwards received a philosophical education and discovered that God has no body, parts, or passions, and therefore neither a right hand nor a palace, he would not have felt that the essentials of his belief had been altered. What had mattered to him, even in the days of his simplicity, had not been supposed details about celestial furniture. It had been the assurance that the once crucified Master was now the supreme Agent of the unimaginable Power on whom the whole universe depends. And he would recognise that in this he had never been deceived.

The critic may still ask us why the imagery — which we

admit to be untrue — should be used at all. But he has not
noticed that any language we attempt to substitute for it would
involve imagery that is open to all the same objections. To say
that God 'enters' the natural order involves just as much spatial
imagery as to say that He 'comes down'; one has simply sub-
stituted horizontal (or undefined) for vertical movement. To
say that He is 're-absorbed' into the Noumenal is better than
to say He 'ascended' into Heaven, only if the picture of something dissolving in warm fluid, or being sucked into a throat,
is less misleading than the picture of a bird, or a balloon,
going up. All language, except about objects of sense, is metaphorical through and through. To call God a 'Force' (that is,
something like a wind or a dynamo) is as metaphorical as to
call Him a Father or a King. On such matters we can make
our language more polysyllabic and duller: we cannot make it
more literal. The difficulty is not peculiar to theologians. Scientists, poets, psychoanalysts, and metaphysicians are all in the
same boat —

>   Man's reason is in such deep insolvency to sense.

Where, then, do we draw the line between explaining and
'explaining away'? I do not think there is much difficulty. All
that concerns the un-incarnate activities of God — His operation on that plane of being where sense cannot enter — must
be taken along with imagery which we know to be, in the
literal sense, untrue. But there can be no defence for applying
the same treatment to the miracles of the Incarnate God. They
are recorded as events on this earth which affected human
senses. They are the sort of thing we can describe literally.
If Christ turned water into wine, and we had been present, we
could have seen, smelled, and tasted. The story that He did
so is not of the same order as His 'sitting at the right hand
of the Father'. It is either fact, or legend, or lie. You must
take it or leave it.

7

RELIGION AND SCIENCE

M IRACLES', SAID MY FRIEND. 'OH, COME. SCIENCE HAS knocked the bottom out of all that. We know that Nature is governed by fixed laws.'

'Didn't people always know that?' said I.

'Good Lord, no,' said he. 'For instance, take a story like the Virgin Birth. We know now that such a thing couldn't happen. We know there *must* be a male spermatozoon.'

'But look here', said I, 'St Joseph —'

'Who's he?' asked my friend.

'He was the husband of the Virgin Mary. If you'll read the story in the Bible you'll find that when he saw his fiancée was going to have a baby he decided to cry off the marriage. Why did he do that?'

'Wouldn't most men?'

'Any man would', said I, 'provided he knew the laws of Nature — in other words, provided he knew that a girl doesn't ordinarily have a baby unless she's been sleeping with a man. But according to your theory people in the old days didn't know that Nature was governed by fixed laws. I'm pointing out that the story shows that St Joseph knew *that* law just as well as you do.'

'But he came to believe in the Virgin Birth afterwards, didn't he?'

'Quite. But he didn't do so because he was under any illusion as to where babies came from in the ordinary course of Nature. He believed in the Virgin Birth as something *super-natural*. He knew Nature works in fixed, regular ways: but he also believed that there existed something *beyond* Nature which could interfere with her workings — from outside, so to speak.'

'But modern science has shown there's no such thing.'

'Really,' said I. 'Which of the sciences?'

'Oh, well, that's a matter of detail,' said my friend. 'I can't give you chapter and verse from memory.'

'But, don't you see', said I, 'that science never could show anything of the sort?'

'Why on earth not?'

'Because science studies Nature. And the question is whether anything *besides* Nature exists — anything "outside". How could you find that out by studying simply Nature?'

'But don't we find out that Nature *must* work in an absolutely fixed way? I mean, the laws of Nature tell us not merely how things *do* happen, but how they *must* happen. No power could possibly alter them.'

'How do you mean?' said I.

'Look here,' said he. 'Could this "something outside" that you talk about make two and two five?'

'Well, no,' said I.

'All right,' said he. 'Well, I think the laws of Nature are really like two and two making four. The idea of their being altered is as absurd as the idea of altering the laws of arithmetic.'

'Half a moment,' said I. 'Suppose you put sixpence into a drawer today, and sixpence into the same drawer tomorrow. Do the laws of arithmetic make it certain you'll find a shilling's worth there the day after?'

'Of course', said he, 'provided no one's been tampering with your drawer.'

'Ah, but that's the whole point,' said I. 'The laws of arithmetic can tell you what you'll find, with absolute certainty, *provided that* there's no interference. If a thief has been at the drawer of course you'll get a different result. But the thief won't have broken the laws of arithmetic — only the laws of England. Now, aren't the laws of Nature much in the same boat? Don't they all tell you what will happen *provided* there's no interference?'

'How do you mean?'

'Well, the laws will tell you how a billiard ball will travel on a smooth surface if you hit it in a particular way — but

73

only provided no one interferes. If, after it's already in motion, someone snatches up a cue and gives it a biff on one
side — why, then, you won't get what the scientist predicted.'

'No, of course not. He can't allow for monkey-tricks like
that.'

'Quite, and in the same way, if there was anything outside
Nature, and if it interfered — then the events which the scientist expected wouldn't follow. That would be what we call
a miracle. In one sense it wouldn't break the laws of Nature.
The laws tell you what will happen if nothing interferes. They
can't tell you whether something *is* going to interfere. I mean,
it's not the expert at arithmetic who can tell you how likely
someone is to interfere with the pennies in my drawer; a
detective would be more use. It isn't the physicist who can tell
you how likely I am to catch up a cue and spoil his experiment with the billiard ball; you'd better ask a psychologist.
And it isn't the scientist who can tell you how likely Nature
is to be interfered with from outside. You must go to the
metaphysician.'

'These are rather niggling points,' said my friend. 'You see,
the real objection goes far deeper. The whole picture of the
universe which science has given us makes it such rot to
believe that the Power at the back of it all could be interested
in us tiny little creatures crawling about on an unimportant
planet! It was all so obviously invented by people who believed in a flat earth with the stars only a mile or two away.'

'When did people believe that?'

'Why, all those old Christian chaps you're always telling
about did. I mean Boethius and Augustine and Thomas Aquinas
and Dante.'

'Sorry', said I, 'but this is one of the few subjects I do
know something about.'

I reached out my hand to a bookshelf. 'You see this book',
I said, 'Ptolemy's *Almagest*. You know what it is?'

'Yes,' said he. 'It's the standard astronomical handbook
used all through the Middle Ages.'

'Well, just read that,' I said, pointing to Book I, chapter 5.

'The earth,' read out my friend, hesitating a bit as he translated the Latin, 'the earth, in relation to the distance of the
fixed stars, has no appreciable size and must be treated as a
mathematical point!'

There was a moment's silence.

'Did they really know that *then?*' said my friend. 'But —
but none of the histories of science — none of the modern
encyclopedias — ever mention the fact.'

'Exactly,' said I. 'I'll leave you to think out the reason. It
almost looks as if someone was anxious to hush it up, doesn't
it? I wonder why.'

There was another short silence.

'At any rate', said I, 'we can now state the problem accurately. People usually think the problem is how to reconcile
what we now know about the size of the universe with our
traditional ideas of religion. That turns out not to be the
problem at all. The real problem is this. The enormous size
of the universe and the insignificance of the earth were known
for centuries, and no one ever dreamed that they had any
bearing on the religious question. Then, less than a hundred
years ago, they are suddenly trotted out as an argument against
Christianity. And the people who trot them out carefully hush
up the fact that they were known long ago. Don't you think
that all you atheists are strangely unsuspicious people?'

8

THE LAWS OF NATURE

Poor woman,' said my friend. 'One hardly knows what to say when they talk like that. She thinks her son survived Arnhem because she prayed for him. It would be heartless to explain to her that he really survived because he was standing a little to the left or a little to the right of some bullet. That bullet was following a course laid down by the laws of Nature. It couldn't have hit him. He just happened to be standing off its line . . . and so all day long as regards every bullet and every splinter of shell. His survival was simply due to the laws of Nature.'

At that moment my first pupil came in and the conversation was cut short, but later in the day I had to walk across the Park to a committee meeting and this gave me time to think the matter over. It was quite clear that once a bullet had been fired from Point A in direction B, the wind being C, and so forth, it would pursue a certain path. But might our young friend have been standing somewhere else? And might the German have fired at a different moment or in a different direction? If men have free will it would appear that they might. On that view we get a rather more complicated picture of the battle of Arnhem. The total course of events would be a kind of amalgam derived from two sources — on the one hand, from acts of human will (which might presumably have been otherwise), and, on the other, from the laws of physical nature. And this would seem to provide all that is necessary for the mother's belief that her prayers had some place among the causes of her son's preservation. God might continually influence the wills of all the combatants so as to allot death, wounds, and survival in the way He thought best, while leaving the behaviour of the projectile to follow its normal course.

But I was still not quite clear about the physical side of this picture. I had been thinking (vaguely enough) that the bullet's flight was *caused* by the laws of Nature. But is this really so? Granted that the bullet is set in motion, and granted the wind and the earth's gravitation and all the other relevant factors, then it is a 'law' of Nature that the bullet must take the course it did. But then the pressing of the trigger, the side wind, and even the earth, are not exactly *laws*. They are facts or events. They are not laws but things that obey laws. Obviously, to consider the pressing of the trigger would only lead us back to the free-will side of the picture. We must, therefore, choose a simpler example.

The laws of physics, I understand, decree that when one billiards ball (A) sets another billiards ball (B) in motion, the momentum lost by A exactly equals the momentum gained by B. This is a *Law*. That is, this is the pattern to which the movement of the two billiards balls must conform. Provided, of course, that something sets ball A in motion. And here comes the snag. The *law* won't set it in motion. It is usually a man with a cue who does that. But a man with a cue would send us back to free-will, so let us assume that it was lying on a table in a liner and that what set it in motion was a lurch of the ship. In that case it was not the law which produced the movement; it was a wave. And that wave, though it certainly moved *according* to the laws of physics, was not moved by them. It was shoved by other waves, and by winds, and so forth. And however far you traced the story back you would never find the *laws* of Nature causing anything.

The dazzlingly obvious conclusion now arose in my mind: *in the whole history of the universe the laws of Nature have never produced a single event.* They are the pattern to which every event must conform, provided only that it can be induced to happen. But how do you get it to do that? How do you get a move on? The laws of Nature can give you no help there. All events obey them, just as all operations with money obey the laws of arithmetic. Add six pennies to six and the result will certainly be a shilling. But arithmetic by itself won't put one farthing into your pocket. Up till now I

77

had had a vague idea that the laws of Nature could make things happen. I now saw that this was exactly like thinking that you could increase your income by doing sums about it. The *laws* are the pattern to which events conform: the source of events must be sought elsewhere.

This may be put in the form that the laws of Nature explain everything except the source of events. But this is rather a formidable exception. The laws, in one sense, cover the whole of reality except — well, except that continuous cataract of real events which makes up the actual universe. They explain everything except what we should ordinarily call 'everything'. The only thing they omit is — the whole universe. I do not mean that a knowledge of these laws is useless. Provided we can take over the actual universe as a going concern, such knowledge is useful and indeed indispensable for manipulating it; just as, if only you have some money arithmetic is indispensable for managing it. But the events themselves, the money itself — that is quite another affair.

Where, then, do actual events come from? In one sense the answer is easy. Each event comes from a previous event. But what happens if you trace this process backwards? To ask this is not exactly the same as to ask where *things* come from — how there came to be space and time and matter at all. Our present problem is not about things but about events; not, for example, about particles of matter but about this particle colliding with that. The mind can perhaps acquiesce in the idea that the 'properties' of the universal drama somehow 'just happen to be there': but whence comes the play, the story?

Either the stream of events had a beginning or it had not. If it had, then we are faced with something like creation. If it had not (a supposition, by the way, which some physicists find difficult), then we are faced with an everlasting impulse which, by its very nature, is opaque to scientific thought. Science, when it becomes perfect, will have explained the connection between each link in the chain and the link before it. But the actual existence of the chain will remain wholly unaccountable. We learn more and more about the pattern. We learn nothing about that which 'feeds' real events into the pattern. If it is not God, we must at the very least call it Destiny — the immaterial, ultimate, one-way pressure which keeps the universe on the move.

The smallest event, then, if we face the fact that it occurs (instead of concentrating on the pattern into which, if it can be persuaded to occur, it must fit), leads us back to a mystery which lies outside natural science. It is certainly a possible supposition that behind this mystery some mighty Will and Life is at work. If so, any contrast between His acts and the laws of Nature is out of the question. It is His act alone that gives the laws any events to apply to. The laws are an empty frame; it is He who fills that frame — not now and then on specially 'providential' occasions, but at every moment. And He, from His vantage point above Time, can, if He pleases, take all prayers into account in ordaining that vast complex event which is the history of the universe. For what we call 'future' prayers have always been present to Him.

In *Hamlet* a branch breaks and Ophelia is drowned. Did she die because the branch broke or because Shakespeare wanted her to die at that point in the play? Either — both — whichever you please. The alternative suggested by the question is not a real alternative at all — once you have grasped that Shakespeare is making the whole play.

9

THE GRAND MIRACLE

O NE IS VERY OFTEN ASKED AT PRESENT WHETHER WE could not have a Christianity stripped, or, as people who ask it say, 'freed' from its miraculous elements, a Christianity with the miraculous elements suppressed. Now, it seems to me that precisely the one religion in the world, or, at least, the only one I know, with which you could not do that is Christianity. In a religion like Buddhism, if you took away the miracles attributed to Gautama Buddha in some very late sources, there would be no loss; in fact, the religion would get on very much better without them because in that case the miracles largely contradict the teaching. Or even in the case of a religion like Mohammedanism, nothing essential would be altered if you took away the miracles. You could have a great prophet preaching his dogmas without bringing in any miracles; they are only in the nature of a digression, or illuminated capitals. But you cannot possibly do that with Christianity, because the Christian story is precisely the story of one grand miracle, the Christian assertion being that what is beyond all space and time, what is uncreated, eternal, came into nature, into human nature, descended into His own universe, and rose again, bringing nature up with Him. It is precisely one great miracle. If you take that away there is nothing specifically Christian left. There may be many admirable human things which Christianity shares with all other systems in the world, but there would be nothing specifically Christian. Conversely, once you have accepted that, then you will see that all other well-established Christian miracles —

because, of course, there are ill-established Christian miracles; there are Christian legends just as much as there are heathen legends, or modern journalistic legends — you will see that all the well-established Christian miracles are part of it, that they all either prepare for, or exhibit, or result from the Incarnation. Just as every natural event exhibits the total character of the natural universe at a particular point and space of time; so every miracle exhibits the character of the Incarnation.

Now, if one asks whether that central grand miracle in Christianity is itself probable or improbable, of course, quite clearly you cannot be applying Hume's kind of probability. You cannot mean a probability based on statistics according to which the more often a thing has happened, the more likely it is to happen again (the more often you get indigestion from eating a certain food, the more probable it is, if you eat it again, that you will again have indigestion). Certainly the Incarnation cannot be probable in that sense. It is of its very nature to have happened only once. But then it is of the very nature of the history of this world to have happened only once; and if the Incarnation happened at all, it is the central chapter of that history. It is improbable in the same way in which the whole of nature is improbable, because it is only there once, and will happen only once. So one must apply to it a quite different kind of standard.

I think we are rather in this position. Supposing you had before you a manuscript of some great work, either a symphony or a novel. There then comes to you a person, saying, 'Here is a new bit of the manuscript that I found; it is the central passage of that symphony, or the central chapter of that novel. The text is incomplete without it. I have got the missing passage which is really the centre of the whole work.' The only thing you could do would be to put this new piece of the manuscript in that central position, and then see how it reacted on the whole of the rest of the work. If it constantly brought out new meanings from the whole of the rest of the work, if it made you notice things in the rest of the work which you had not noticed before, then I think you would decide that it was authentic. On the other hand, if it failed to do that, then, however attractive it was in itself, you would reject it.

Now, what is the missing chapter in this case, the chapter

81

which Christians are offering? The story of the Incarnation is the story of a descent and resurrection. When I say 'resurrection' here, I am not referring simply to the first few hours, or the first few weeks of the Resurrection. I am talking of this whole, huge pattern of descent, down, down, and then up again. What we ordinarily call the Resurrection being just, so to speak, the point at which it turns. Think what that descent is. The coming down, not only into humanity, but into those nine months which precede human birth, in which they tell us we all recapitulate strange pre-human, sub-human forms of life, and going lower still into being a corpse, a thing which, if this ascending movement had not begun, would presently have passed out of the organic altogether, and have gone back into the inorganic, as all corpses do. One has a picture of someone going right down and dredging the sea-bottom. One has a picture of a strong man trying to lift a very big, complicated burden. He stoops down and gets himself right under it so that he himself disappears; and then he straightens his back and moves off with the whole thing swaying on his shoulders. Or else one has the picture of a diver, stripping off garment after garment, making himself naked, then flashing for a moment in the air, and then down through the green, and warm, and sunlit water into the pitch black, cold, freezing water, down into the mud and slime, then up again, his lungs almost bursting, back again to the green and warm and sunlit water, and then at last out into the sunshine, holding in his hand the dripping thing he went down to get. This thing is human nature; but, associated with it, all nature, the new universe. That indeed is a point I cannot go into tonight, because it would take a whole sermon — this connexion between human nature and nature in general. It sounds startling, but I believe it can be fully justified.

Now, as soon as you have thought of this, this pattern of the huge dive down to the bottom, into the depths of the universe and coming up again into the light, everyone will see at once how that is imitated and echoed by the principles of the natural world; the descent of the seed into the soil, and its rising again in the plants. There are also all sorts of things in our own spiritual life where a thing has to be killed, and broken, in order that it may then become bright, and strong, and splendid. The analogy is obvious. In that sense the doctrine fits in very well, so well in fact that immediately there comes the suspicion, Is it not fitting in a great deal too well? In other words, does not the Christian story show this pattern of descent and re-ascent because that is part of all the nature religions of the world? We have read about it in *The Golden Bough*.[1] We all know about Adonis, and the stories of the rest of those rather tedious people; is not this one more instance of the same thing, 'the dying God'? Well, yes it is. That is what makes the question subtle. What the anthropological critic of Christianity is always saying is perfectly true. Christ *is* a figure of that sort. And here comes a very curious thing. When I first, after childhood, read the Gospels, I was full of that stuff about the dying God, *The Golden Bough,* and so on. It was to me then a very poetic, and mysterious, and quickening idea; and when I turned to the Gospels never will I forget my disappointment and repulsion at finding hardly anything about it at all. The metaphor of the seed dropping into the ground in this connexion occurs (I think) twice in the New Testament,[2] and for the rest hardly any notice is taken; it seemed to me extraordinary. You had a dying God, Who was always representative of the corn: you see Him holding the corn, that is, bread, in His hand, and saying, 'This is My Body',[3] and from my point of view, as I then was, He did not seem to realize what He was saying. Surely there, if anywhere, this connexion between the Christian story and the corn must have come out; the whole context is crying out for it. But everything goes on as if the principal actor, and still more, those about Him, were totally ignorant of what they were doing. It is as if you got very good evidence concerning the sea-serpent, but the men who brought this good evidence seemed never to have heard of sea-serpents. Or to put it in another way, why was it that the only case of the 'dying God' which might conceivably have been historical occurred among a people (and the only people in the whole Mediterranean world) who had not got any trace of this nature religion, and indeed seemed to know nothing about it? Why is it among *them* the thing suddenly appears to happen?

[1] By Sir James George Frazer.
[2] John xii. 24; I Corinthians xv. 36.
[3] Matthew xxvi. 26; Mark xiv. 22; Luke xxii. 19; I Corinthians xi. 24.

The principal actor, humanly speaking, hardly seems to know of the repercussions His words (and sufferings) would have in any pagan mind. Well, that is almost inexplicable, except on one hypothesis. How if the corn king is not mentioned in that Book, because He is here of whom the corn king was an image? How if the representation is absent because here, at last, the thing represented is present? If the shadows are absent because the thing of which they were shadows is here? The corn itself is in its far-off way an imitation of the supernatural reality; the thing dying, and coming to life again, descending, and re-ascending beyond all nature. The principle is there in nature because it was first there in God Himself. Thus one is getting in behind the nature religions, and behind nature to Someone Who is not explained by, but explains, not, indeed, the nature religions directly, but that whole characteristic behaviour of nature on which nature religions were based. Well, that is one way in which it surprised me. It seemed to fit in a very peculiar way, showing me something about nature more fully than I had seen it before, while itself remaining quite outside and above the nature religions.

Then another thing. We, with our modern democratic 'and arithmetical presuppositions would so have liked and expected all men to start equal in their search for God. One has the picture of great centripetal roads coming from all directions, with well-disposed people, all meaning the same thing, and getting closer and closer together. How shockingly opposite to that is the Christian story! One people picked out of the whole earth; that people purged and proved again and again. Some are lost in the desert before they reach Palestine; some stay in Babylon; some becoming indifferent. The whole thing narrows and narrows, until at last it comes down to a little point, small as the point of a spear — a Jewish girl at her prayers. That is what the whole of human nature has narrowed down to before the Incarnation takes place. Very unlike what we expected, but, of course, not in the least unlike what seems, in general, as shown by nature, to be God's way of working. The universe is quite a shockingly selective, undemocratic place out of apparently infinite space, a relatively tiny proportion occupied by matter of any kind. Of the stars perhaps only one has planets: of the planets only one is at all likely to sustain organic life. Of the animals only one species is rational. Selection as seen in nature, and the appalling waste which it involves, appears a horrible and an unjust thing by human standards. But the selectiveness in the Christian story is not quite like that. The people who are selected are, in a sense, unfairly selected for a supreme honour; but it is also a supreme burden. The People of Israel come to realize that it is their woes which are saving the world. Even in human society, though, one sees how this inequality furnishes an opportunity for every kind of tyranny and servility. Yet, on the other hand, one also sees that it furnishes an opportunity for some of the very best things we can think of — humility, and kindness, and the immense pleasures of admiration. (I cannot conceive how one would get through the boredom of a world in which you never met anyone more clever, or more beautiful, or stronger than yourself. The very crowds who go after the football celebrities and film-stars know better than to desire that kind of equality!) What the story of the Incarnation seems to be doing is to flash a new light on a principle in nature, and to show for the first time that this principle of inequality in nature is neither good nor bad. It is a common theme running through both the goodness and badness of the natural world, and I begin to see how it can survive as a supreme beauty in a redeemed universe.

And with that I have unconsciously passed over to the third point. I have said that the selectiveness was not unfair in the way in which we first suspect, because those selected for the great honour are also selected for the great suffering, and their suffering heals others. In the Incarnation we get, of course, this idea of vicariousness of one person profiting by the earning of another person. In its highest form that is the very centre of Christianity. And we also find this same vicariousness to be a characteristic, or, as the musician would put it, a *leit-motif* of nature. It is a law of the natural universe that no being can exist on its own resources. Everyone, everything, is hopelessly indebted to everyone and everything else. In the universe, as we now see it, this is the source of many of the greatest horrors: all the horrors of carnivorousness, and the worse horrors of the parasites, those horrible animals that live under the skin of other animals, and so on. And yet, suddenly seeing it in the light of the Christian story, one realizes that vicariousness is not in itself bad; that all these animals, and insects, and horrors are merely that principle of vicariousness twisted in one way. For when you think it out, nearly everything good in nature also comes from vicariousness. After all, the child, both before and after birth, lives on its mother, just as the parasite lives on its host, the one being a horror, the other being the source of almost every natural goodness in the world. It all depends upon what you do with this principle. So that I find in that third way also, that what is implied by the Incarnation just fits in exactly with what I have seen in nature, and (this is the important point) each time it gives it a new twist. If I accept this supposed missing chapter, the Incarnation, I find it begins to illuminate the whole of the rest of the manuscript. It lights up nature's pattern of death and rebirth; and, secondly, her selectiveness; and, thirdly, her vicariousness.

Now I notice a very odd point. All other religions in the world, as far as I know them, are either nature religions, or anti-nature religions. The nature religions are those of the old, simple pagan sort that you know about. You actually got drunk in the temple of Bacchus. You actually committed fornication in the temple of Aphrodite. The more modern form of nature religion would be the religion started, in a sense, by Bergson[4] (but he repented, and died Christian), and carried on in a more popular form by Mr Bernard Shaw. The anti-nature religions are those like Hinduism and Stoicism, where men say, 'I will starve my flesh. I care not whether I live or die.' All natural things are to be set aside: the aim is Nirvana, apathy, negative spirituality. The nature religions simply affirm my natural desires. The anti-natural religions simply contradict them. The nature religions simply give a new sanction to what I already always thought about the universe in my moments of rude health and cheerful brutality. The anti-nature religions merely repeat what I always thought about it in my moods of lassitude, or delicacy, or compassion.

But here is something quite different. Here is something telling me — well, what? Telling me that I must never, like the Stoics, say that death does not matter. Nothing is less

---

[4] Henri Bergson (1859-1941). His 'nature religion' is particularly evident in his *Matière et Mémoire* (1896) and *L'Evolution Créatrice* (1907).

Christian than that. Death which made Life Himself shed tears at the grave of Lazarus,[5] and shed tears of blood in Gethsemane.[6] This is an appalling horror; a stinking indignity. (You remember Thomas Browne's splendid remark: 'I am not so much afraid of death, as ashamed of it.')[7] And yet, somehow or other, infinitely good. Christianity does not simply affirm or simply deny the horror of death; it tells me something quite new about it. Again, it does not, like Nietzsche, simply confirm my desire to be stronger, or cleverer than other people. On the other hand, it does not allow me to say, 'Oh, Lord, won't there be a day when everyone will be as good as everyone else?' In the same way, about vicariousness. It will not, in any way, allow me to be an exploiter, to act as a parasite on other people; yet it will not allow me any dream of living on my own. It will teach me to accept with glad humility the enormous sacrifice that others make for me, as well as to make sacrifices for others.

That is why I think this Grand Miracle is the missing chapter in this novel, the chapter on which the whole plot turns; that is why I believe that God really has dived down into the bottom of creation, and has come up bringing the whole redeemed nature on His shoulder. The miracles that have already happened are, of course, as Scripture so often says, the first fruits of that cosmic summer which is presently coming on.[8] Christ has risen, and so we shall rise. St Peter for a few seconds walked on the water;[9] and the day will come when there will be a re-made universe, infinitely obedient to the will of glorified and obedient men, when we can do all things, when we shall be those gods that we are described as being in Scripture. To be sure, it feels wintry enough still: but often in the very early spring it feels like that. Two thousand years are only a day or two by this scale. A man really ought to say, 'The Resurrection happened two thousand years ago' in the same spirit in which he says, 'I saw a crocus yesterday.' Be-

[5] John xi. 35.

[6] Luke xxii. 44.

[7] Browne's actual words are 'I am not so much afraid of death, as ashamed thereof.' *Religio Medici*, First Part, Section 40.

[8] Romans viii. 23; xi. 16; xvi. 5; I Corinthians xv. 20; James i. 18; Revelation xiv. 4.

[9] Matthew xiv. 29.

cause we know what is coming behind the crocus. The spring cames slowly down this way; but the great thing is that the corner has been turned. There is, of course, this difference, that in the natural spring the crocus cannot choose whether it will respond or not. We can. We have the power either of withstanding the spring, and sinking back into the cosmic winter, or of going on into those 'high mid-summer pomps' in which our Leader, the Son of man, already dwells, and to which He is calling us. It remains with us to follow or not, to die in this winter, or to go on into that spring and that summer.

10

CHRISTIAN APOLOGETICS

Some of you are priests and some are leaders of youth organizations.[1] I have little right to address either. It is for priests to teach me, not for me to teach them. I have never helped to organize youth, and while I was young myself I successfully avoided being organized. If I address you it is in response to a request so urged that I came to regard compliance as a matter of Obedience.

I am to talk about Apologetics. Apologetics means of course Defence. The first question is — what do you propose to defend? Christianity, of course: and Christianity as understood by the Church in Wales. And here at the outset I must deal with an unpleasant business. It seems to the layman that in the Church of England we often hear from our priests doctrine which is not Anglican Christianity. It may depart from Anglican Christianity in either of two ways: (1) It may be so 'broad' or 'liberal' or 'modern' that it in fact excludes any real Supernaturalism and thus ceases to be Christian at all. (2) It may, on the other hand, be Roman. It is not, of course, for me to define to you what Anglican Christianity is — I am your pupil, not your teacher. But I insist that wherever you draw the lines, bounding lines must exist, beyond which your doctrine will cease either to be Anglican or to be Christian: and I suggest also that the lines come a great deal sooner than many modern priests think. I think it is your duty

[1] This paper was read to an assembly of Anglican priests and youth leaders at the 'Carmarthen Conference for Youth Leaders and Junior Clergy' of the Church in Wales at Carmarthen during Easter 1945.

to fix the lines clearly in your own minds: and if you wish to go beyond them you must change your profession.

This is your duty not specially as Christians or as priests but as honest men. There is a danger here of the clergy developing a special professional conscience which obscures the very plain moral issue. Men who have passed beyond these boundary lines in either direction are apt to protest that they have come by their unorthodox opinions honestly. In defence of those opinions they are prepared to suffer obloquy and to forfeit professional advancement. They thus come to feel like martyrs. But this simply misses the point which so gravely scandalizes the layman. We never doubted that the unorthodox opinions were honestly held: what we complain of is your continuing your ministry after you have come to hold them. We always knew that a man who makes his living as a paid agent of the Conservative Party may honestly change his views and honestly become a Communist. What we deny is that he can honestly continue to be a Conservative agent and to receive money from one party while he supports the policy of another.

Even when we have thus ruled out teaching which is in direct contradiction to our profession, we must define our task still further. We are to defend Christianity itself — the faith preached by the Apostles, attested by the Martyrs, embodied in the Creeds, expounded by the Fathers. This must be clearly distinguished from the whole of what any one of us may think about God and Man. Each of us has his individual emphasis: each holds, in addition to the Faith, many opinions which seem to him to be consistent with it and true and important. And so perhaps they are. But as apologists it is not our business to defend *them*. We are defending Christianity; not 'my religion'. When we mention our personal opinions we must always make quite clear the difference between them and the Faith itself. St Paul has given us the model in I Corinthians vii. 25: on a certain point he has 'no commandment of the Lord' but gives 'his judgement'. No one is left in doubt as to the difference in *status* implied.

This distinction, which is demanded by honesty, also gives the apologist a great tactical advantage. The great difficulty is to get modern audiences to realize that you are preaching Christianity solely and simply because you happen to think it *true;* they always suppose you are preaching it because you like it or think it good for society or something of that sort. Now a clearly maintained distinction between what the Faith actually says and what you would like it to have said or what you understand or what you personally find helpful or think probable, forces your audience to realize that you are tied to your data just as the scientist is tied by the results of the experiments; that you are not just saying what you like. This immediately helps them to realize that what is being discussed is a question about objective fact — not gas about ideals and points of view.

Secondly, this scrupulous care to preserve the Christian message as something distinct from one's own ideas, has one very good effect upon the apologist himself. It forces him, again and again, to face up to those elements in original Christianity which he personally finds obscure or repulsive. He is saved from the temptation to skip or slur or ignore what he finds disagreeable. And the man who yields to that temptation will, of course, never progress in Christian knowledge. For obviously the doctrines which one finds easy are the doctrines which give Christian sanction to truths you already knew. The new truth which you do not know and which you need must, in the very nature of things, be hidden precisely in the doctrines you least like and least understand. It is just the same here as in science. The phenomenon which is troublesome, which doesn't fit in with the current scientific theories, is the phenomenon which compels reconsideration and thus leads to new knowledge. Science progresses because scientists, instead of running away from such troublesome phenomena or hushing them up, are constantly seeking them out. In the same way, there will be progress in Christian knowledge only as long as we accept the challenge of the difficult or repellent doctrines. A 'liberal' Christianity which considers itself free to alter the Faith whenever the Faith looks perplexing or repellent *must* be completely stagnant. Progress is made only into a *resisting* material.

From this there follows a corollary about the Apologist's private reading. There are two questions he will naturally ask himself. (1) Have I been 'keeping up', keeping abreast of recent movements in theology? (2) Have I *stood firm (super monstratas vias*)² amidst all these 'winds of doctrine'?³ I want to say emphatically that the second question is far the more important of the two. Our upbringing and the whole atmosphere of the world we live in make it certain that our main temptation will be that of yielding to winds of doctrine, not that of ignoring them. We are not at all likely to be hidebound: we are very likely indeed to be the slaves of fashion. If one has to choose between reading the new books and reading the old, one must choose the old: not because they are necessarily better but because they contain precisely those truths of which our own age is neglectful. The standard of permanent Christianity must be kept clear in our minds and it is against that standard that we must test all contemporary thought. In fact, we must at all costs *not* move with the times. We serve One who said 'Heaven and Earth shall move with the times, but my words shall not move with the times.'⁴

I am speaking, so far, of theological reading. Scientific reading is a different matter. If you know any science it is very desirable that you should keep it up. We have to answer the current scientific attitude towards Christianity, not the attitude which scientists adopted one hundred years ago. Science is in continual change and we must try to keep abreast of *it*. For the same reason, we must be very cautious of snatching at any scientific theory which, for the moment, seems to be in our favour. We may *mention* such things; but we must mention them lightly and without claiming that they are more than 'interesting'. Sentences beginning 'Science has now proved' should be avoided. If we try to base our apologetic on some recent development in science, we shall usually find that just as we have put the finishing touches to our argument science has changed its mind and quietly withdrawn the theory we have been using as our foundation stone. *Timeo Danaos et dona ferentes*⁵ is a sound principle.

---

² The source of this is, I believe, Jeremiah vi. 16: '*State super vias et videte, et interrogate de semitis antiquis quae sit via bona, et ambulate in ea*' which is translated "Stand ye in the ways, and see, and ask for the old paths, where is the good way, and walk therein.'

³ Ephesians iv. 14.

⁴ Matthew xxiv. 35; Mark xiii. 31; Luke xxi. 33.

⁵ 'I fear the Greeks even when they bear gifts', Virgil, *Aeneid*, bk. II, line 49.

While we are on the subject of science, let me digress for a moment. I believe that any Christian who is qualified to write a good popular book on any science may do much more by that than by any directly apologetic work. The difficulty we are up against is this. We can make people (often) attend to the Christian point of view for half an hour or so; but the moment they have gone away from our lecture or laid down our article, they are plunged back into a world where the opposite position is taken for granted. As long as that situation exists, widespread success is simply impossible. We must attack the enemy's line of communication. What we want is not more little books about Christianity, but more little books by Christians on other subjects — with their Christianity *latent*. You can see this most easily if you look at it the other way round. Our Faith is not very likely to be shaken by any book on Hinduism. But if whenever we read an elementary book on Geology, Botany, Politics, or Astronomy, we found that its implications were Hindu, that would shake us. It is not the books written in direct defence of Materialism that make the modern man a materialist; it is the materialistic assumptions in all the other books. In the same way, it is not books on Christianity that will really trouble him. But he would be troubled if, whenever he wanted a cheap popular introduction to some science, the best work on the market was always by a Christian. The first step to the re-conversion of this country is a series, produced by Christians, which can beat the *Penguin* and the *Thinkers Library* on their own ground. Its Christianity would have to be latent, not explicit: and *of course* its science perfectly honest. Science *twisted* in the interests of apologetics would be sin and folly. But I must return to my immediate subject.

Our business is to present that which is timeless (the same yesterday, today, and tomorrow)[6] in the particular language of our own age. The bad preacher does exactly the opposite: he takes the ideas of our own age and tricks them out in the traditional language of Christianity. Thus, for example, he may think about the Beveridge Report[7] and *talk* about the coming

[6] Hebrews xiii. 8.

[7] Sir William H. Beveridge, *Social Insurance and Allied Services,* Command Paper 6404, Parliamentary Session 1942-43 (London: H. M. Stationery Office, 1942). The 'Beveridge Report' is a plan for the present Social Security system in Britain.

of the Kingdom. The core of his thought is merely contemporary; only the superficies is traditional. But your teaching must be timeless at its heart and wear a modern dress.

This raises the question of Theology and Politics. The nearest I can get to a settlement of the frontier problem between them is this: — that Theology teaches us what ends are desirable and what means are lawful, while Politics teaches what means are effective. Thus Theology tells us that every man ought to have a decent wage. Politics tells by what means this is likely to be attained. Theology tells us which of these means are consistent with justice and charity. On the political question guidance comes not from Revelation but from natural prudence, knowledge of complicated facts and ripe experience. If we have these qualifications we may, of course, state our political opinions: but then we must make it quite clear that we are giving our personal judgement and have no command from the Lord. Not many priests have these qualifications. Most political sermons teach the congregation nothing except what newspapers are taken at the Rectory.

Our great danger at present is lest the Church should continue to practise a merely missionary technique in what has become a missionary situation. A century ago our task was to edify those who had been brought up in the Faith: our present task is chiefly to convert and instruct infidels. Great Britain is as much part of the mission field as China. Now if you were sent to the Bantus you would be taught their language and traditions. You need similar teaching about the language and mental habits of your own uneducated and unbelieving fellow countrymen. Many priests are quite ignorant on this subject. What I know about it I have learned from talking in R.A.F.[8] camps. They were mostly inhabited by Englishmen and, therefore, some of what I shall say may be irrelevant to the situation in Wales. You will sift out what does not apply.

(1) I find that the uneducated Englishman is an almost total sceptic about History. I had expected he would disbelieve the Gospels because they contain miracles: but he really disbelieves them because they deal with things that happened 2000 years ago. He would disbelieve equally in the battle of Actium if he heard of it. To those who have had our kind

[8] The Royal Air Force.

94

of education, his state of mind is very difficult to realize. To us the Present has always appeared as one section in a huge continuous process. In his mind the Present occupies almost the whole field of vision. Beyond it, isolated from it, and quite unimportant, is something called 'The Old Days' — a small, comic jungle in which highwaymen, Queen Elizabeth, knights-in-armour etc. wander about. Then (strangest of all) beyond The Old Days comes a picture of 'Primitive Man'. He is 'Science', not 'history', and is therefore felt to be much more real than The Old Days. In other words, the Pre-historic is much more believed in than the Historic.

(2) He has a distrust (very rational in the state of his knowledge) of ancient texts. Thus a man has sometimes said to me 'These records were written in the days before printing, weren't they? and you haven't got the original bit of paper, have you? So what it comes to is that someone wrote something and someone else copied it and someone else copied *that* and so on. Well, by the time it comes to us, it won't be in the least like the original.' This is a difficult objection to deal with because one cannot, there and then, start teaching the whole science of textual criticism. But at this point their real religion (i.e. faith in 'science') has come to my aid. The assurance that there is a 'Science' called 'Textual Criticism' and that its results (not only as regards the New Testament, but as regards ancient texts in general) are generally accepted, will usually be received without objection. (I need hardly point out that the word 'text' must not be used, since to your audience it means only 'a scriptural quotation'.)

(3) A sense of sin is almost totally lacking. Our situation is thus very different from that of the Apostles. The Pagans (and still more the *metuentes*[9]) to whom they preached were haunted by a sense of guilt and to them the Gospel was, therefore, 'good news'. We address people who have been trained to believe that whatever goes wrong in the world is someone else's fault — the Capitalists', the Government's, the Nazis', the Generals' etc. They approach God Himself as His *judges*. They want to know, not whether they can be acquitted for sin, but whether He can be acquitted for creating such a world.

[9] The *metuentes* or 'god-fearers' were a class of Gentiles who worshipped God without submitting to circumcision and the other ceremonial obligations of the Jewish Law. See Psalm cxviii. 4 and Acts x. 2.

In attacking this fatal insensibility it is useless to direct attention (a) To sins your audience do not commit, or (b) To things they do, but do not regard as sins. They are usually not drunkards. They are mostly fornicators, but then they do not feel fornication to be wrong. It is, therefore, useless to dwell on either of these subjects. (Now that contraceptives have removed the obviously *uncharitable* element in fornication I do not myself think we can expect people to recognize it as sin until they have accepted Christianity as a whole.)

I cannot offer you a water-tight technique for awakening the sense of sin. I can only say that, in my experience, if one begins from the sin that has been one's own chief problem during the last week, one is very often surprised at the way this shaft goes home. But whatever method we use, our continual effort must be to get their mind away from public affairs and 'crime' and bring them down to brass tacks — to the whole network of spite, greed, envy, unfairness and conceit in the lives of 'ordinary decent people' like themselves (and ourselves).

(4) We must learn the language of our audience. And let me say at the outset that it is no use at all laying down *a priori* what the 'plain man' does or does not understand. You have to find out by experience. Thus most of us would have supposed that the change from 'may truly and indifferently minister justice' to 'may truly and impartially'[10] made that place easier to the uneducated; but a priest of my acquaintance discovered that his sexton saw no difficulty in *indifferently* ('It means making no difference between one man and another' he said) but had no idea what *impartially* meant.

On this question of language the best thing I can do is to make a list of words which are used by the people in a sense different from ours.

ATONEMENT. Does not really exist in a spoken modern English, though it would be recognized as 'a religious word'. In so far as it conveys any meaning to the unedu-

---

[10] The first quotation is from the prayer for the 'Whole state of Christ's Church' in the service of Holy Communion, Prayer Book (1662). The second is the revised form of that same phrase as found in the 1928 Prayer Book.

cated I think it means *compensation*. No one word will express to them what Christians mean by *Atonement*: you must paraphrase.

BEING. (Noun) Never means merely 'entity' in popular speech. Often it means what we should call a 'personal being' (e.g. a man said to me 'I believe in the Holy Ghost but I don't think He is a being!').

CATHOLIC means Papistical.

CHARITY. Means (a) Alms (b) A 'charitable organization' (c) Much more rarely — Indulgence (i.e. a 'charitable' attitude towards a man is conceived as one that denies or condones his sins, not as one that loves the sinner in spite of them).

CHRISTIAN. Has come to include almost no idea of *belief*. Usually a vague term of approval. The question 'What do you call a Christian?' has been asked of me again and again. The answer they *wish* to receive is 'A Christian is a decent chap who's unselfish etc.'.

CHURCH. Means (a) A sacred building, (b) The clergy. Does *not* suggest to them the 'company of all faithful people'.[11] Generally used in a bad sense. Direct defence of the Church is part of our duty: but use of the word *Church* where there is no time to defend it alienates sympathy and should be avoided where possible.

CREATIVE. Now means merely 'talented', 'original'. The idea of creation in the theological sense is absent from their minds.

CREATURE means 'beast', 'irrational animal'. Such an expression as 'We are only creatures' would almost certainly be misunderstood.

CRUCIFIXION, CROSS etc. Centuries of hymnody and religious cant have so exhausted these words that they now very faintly — if at all — convey the idea of execution by torture. It is better to paraphrase; and, for the same reason, to say *flogged* for New Testament *scourged*.[12]

DOGMA. Used by the people only in a bad sense to mean 'unproved assertion delivered in an arrogant manner'.

---

[11] A phrase which occurs in the prayer of 'Thanksgiving' at the end of the service of Holy Communion.
[12] Matthew xxvii. 26; Mark xv. 15; John xix. 1.

IMMACULATE CONCEPTION. In the mouth of an uneducated speaker *always* means *Virgin Birth*.

MORALITY means *chastity*.

PERSONAL. I had argued for at least ten minutes with a man about the existence of a 'personal devil' before I discovered that *personal* meant to him *corporeal*. I suspect this of being widespread. When they say they don't believe in a 'personal' God they may often mean only that they are not anthropomorphists.

POTENTIAL. When used at all is used in an engineering sense: *never* means 'possible'.

PRIMITIVE. Means crude, clumsy, unfinished, inefficient. 'Primitive Christianity' would not mean to them at all what it does to you.

SACRIFICE. Has no associations with temple and altar. They are familiar with this word only in the journalistic sense ('The Nation must be prepared for heavy sacrifices.').

SPIRITUAL. Means primarily *immaterial, incorporeal,* but with serious confusions from the Christian uses of $\pi\nu\varepsilon\hat{\upsilon}\mu\alpha$.[13] Hence the idea that whatever is 'spiritual' in the sense of 'non-sensuous' is somehow *better* than anything sensuous: e.g., they don't really believe that envy could be as bad as drunkenness.

VULGARITY. Usually means obscenity or 'smut'. There are bad confusions (and not only in uneducated minds) between: (a) The obscene or lascivious: what is calculated to provoke lust. (b) The indecorous: what offends against good taste or propriety. (c) The vulgar proper: what is socially 'low'. 'Good' people tend to think (b) as sinful as (a) with the result that others feel (a) to be just as innocent as (b).

To conclude — you must translate every bit of your Theology into the vernacular. This is very troublesome and it means you can say very little in half an hour, but it is essential. It is also of the greatest service to your own thought. I have come to the conviction that if you cannot translate your thoughts into uneducated language, then your thoughts were confused. Power to translate is the test of having really understood one's own meaning. A passage from some theological

13 Which means 'spirit', as in I Corinthians xiv. 12.

work for translation into the vernacular ought to be a compulsory paper in every Ordination examination.

I turn now to the question of the actual attack. This may be either emotional or intellectual. If I speak only of the intellectual kind, that is not because I undervalue the other but because, not having been given the gifts necessary for carrying it out, I cannot give advice about it. But I wish to say most emphatically that where a speaker has that gift, the direct evangelical appeal of the 'Come to Jesus' type can be as overwhelming today as it was a hundred years ago. I have seen it done, preluded by a religious film and accompanied by hymn singing, and with very remarkable effect. I cannot do it: but those who can ought to do it with all their might. I am not sure that the ideal missionary team ought not to consist of one who argues and one who (in the fullest sense of the word) preaches. Put up your arguer first to undermine their intellectual prejudices; then let the evangelist proper launch his appeal. I have seen this done with great success. But here I must concern myself only with the intellectual attack. *Non omnia possumus omnes.*[14]

And first, a word of encouragement. Uneducated people are not irrational people. I have found that they will endure, and can follow, quite a lot of sustained argument if you go slowly. Often, indeed, the novelty of it (for they have seldom met it before) delights them.

Do not attempt to water Christianity down. There must be no pretence that you can have it with the Supernatural left out. So far as I can see Christianity is precisely the one religion from which the miraculous cannot be separated. You must frankly argue for supernaturalism from the very outset.

The two popular 'difficulties' you will probably have to deal with are these. (1) 'Now that we know how huge the universe is and how insignificant the Earth, it is ridiculous to believe that the universal God should be specially interested in our concerns.' In answer to this you must first correct their error about *fact*. The insignificance of Earth in relation to the universe is not a modern discovery: nearly 2000 years ago Ptolemy (*Almagest,* bk. 1, ch. v) said that in relation to the distance of the fixed stars Earth must be treated as a mathematical point without magnitude. Secondly, you should

[14] 'Not all things can we all do', Virgil, *Eclogues,* bk. VIII, line 63.

point out that Christianity says what God has done for Man; it doesn't say (because it doesn't know) what He has or has not done in other parts of the universe. Thirdly, you might recall the parable of the one lost sheep.[15] If Earth has been specially sought by God (which we don't know) that may not imply that it is the most important thing in the universe, but only that it has *strayed*. Finally, challenge the whole tendency to identify size and importance. Is an elephant more important than a man, or a man's leg than his brain?

(2) 'People believed in miracles in the Old Days because they didn't then know that they were contrary to the Laws of Nature.' But they did. If St Joseph didn't know that a virgin birth was contrary to Nature (i.e. if he didn't know the normal origin of babies) why, on discovering his wife's pregnancy, was he 'minded to put her away'?[16] Obviously, no event would be recorded as a wonder *unless* the recorders knew the natural order and saw that this was an exception. If people didn't yet know that the Sun rose in the East they wouldn't be even interested in its once rising in the West. They would not record it as a *miraculum* — nor indeed record it at all. The very idea of 'miracle' presupposes knowledge of the Laws of Nature; you can't have the idea of an exception until you have the idea of a rule.

It is very difficult to produce arguments on the popular level for the existence of God. And many of the most popular arguments seem to me invalid. Some of these may be produced in discussion by friendly members of the audience. This raises the whole problem of the 'embarrassing supporter'. It is brutal (and dangerous) to repel him; it is often dishonest to agree with what he says. I usually try to avoid saying anything about the validity of his argument *in itself* and reply, 'Yes. That may do for you and me. But I'm afraid if we take that line our friend here on my left might say etc. etc.'

Fortunately, though very oddly, I have found that people are usually disposed to hear the divinity of Our Lord discussed *before* going into the existence of God. When I began I used, if I were giving two lectures, to devote the first to mere Theism; but I soon gave up this method because it

15 Matthew xviii. 11-14; Luke xv. 4-7.
16 Matthew i. 19.

seemed to arouse little interest. The number of clear and determined atheists is apparently not very large.

When we come to the Incarnation itself, I usually find that some form of the *aut Deus aut malus homo*[17] can be used. The majority of them start with the idea of the 'great human teacher' who was deified by His superstitious followers. It must be pointed out how very improbable this is among Jews and how different to anything that happened with Plato, Confucius, Buddha, Mohammed. The Lord's own words and claims (of which many are quite ignorant) must be forced home. (The whole case, on a popular level, is very well put indeed in Chesterton's *The Everlasting Man.*)

Something will usually have to be said about the historicity of the Gospels. You who are trained theologians will be able to do this in ways which I could not. My own line was to say that I was a professional literary critic and I thought I did know the difference between legend and historical writing: that the Gospels were certainly not legends (in one sense they're not *good* enough): and that if they are not history then they are realistic prose fiction of a kind which actually never existed before the eighteenth century. Little episodes such as Jesus writing in the dust when they brought Him the woman taken in adultery[18] (which have no *doctrinal* significance at all) are the mark.

One of the great difficulties is to keep before the audience's mind the question of Truth. They always think you are recommending Christianity not because it is *true* but because it is *good*. And in the discussion they will at every moment try to escape from the issue 'True — or False' into stuff about a good society, or morals, or the incomes of Bishops, or the Spanish Inquisition, or France, or Poland — or anything whatever. You have to keep forcing them back, and again back, to the real point. Only thus will you be able to undermine (a) Their belief that a certain amount of 'religion' is desirable but one mustn't carry it too far. One must keep on pointing out that Christianity is a statement which, if false, is of *no* importance, and, if true, of infinite importance. The one thing it cannot be is moderately important. (b) Their firm disbelief

[17] 'Either God or a bad man.'
[18] John viii. 3-8.

101

of Article XVIII.[19] Of course it should be pointed out that, though all salvation is through Jesus, we need not conclude that He cannot save those who have not explicitly accepted Him in this life. And it should (at least in my judgement) be made clear that we are not pronouncing all other religions to be totally false, but rather saying that in Christ whatever is true in all religions is consummated and perfected. But, on the other hand, I think we must attack wherever we meet it the nonsensical idea that mutually exclusive propositions about God can both be true.

For my own part, I have sometimes told my audience that the only two things really worth considering are Christianity and Hinduism. (Islam is only the greatest of the Christian heresies, Buddhism only the greatest of the Hindu heresies. Real Paganism is dead. All that was best in Judaism and Platonism survives in Christianity.) There isn't really, for an adult mind, this infinite variety of religions to consider. We may *salva reverentia*[20] divide religions, as we do soups, into 'thick' and 'clear'. By Thick I mean those which have orgies and ecstasies and mysteries and local attachments: Africa is full of Thick religions. By Clear I mean those which are philosophical, ethical and universalizing: Stoicism, Buddhism, and the Ethical Church are Clear religions. Now if there is a true religion it must be both Thick and Clear: for the true God must have made both the child and the man, both the savage and the citizen, both the head and the belly. And the only two religions that fulfil this condition are Hinduism and Christianity. But Hinduism fulfils it imperfectly. The Clear religion of the Brahmin hermit in the jungle and the Thick religion of the neighbouring temple go on *side by side*. The Brahmin hermit doesn't bother about the temple prostitution nor the worshipper in the temple about the hermit's metaphysics. But Christianity really breaks down the middle wall of the partition. It takes a convert from central Africa and

---

[19] Article XVIII in the Prayer Book: *Of obtaining eternal Salvation only by the Name of Christ,* which says 'They also are to be had accursed that presume to say, That every man shall be saved by the Law or Sect which he professeth, so that he be diligent to frame his life according to that Law, and the light of Nature. For holy Scripture doth set out unto us only the Name of Jesus Christ, whereby men must be saved.'

[20] 'Without outraging reverence.'

tells him to obey an enlightened universalist ethic: it takes a twentieth-century academic prig like me and tells me to go fasting to a Mystery, to drink the blood of the Lord. The savage convert has to be Clear: I have to be Thick. That is how one knows one has come to the real religion.

One last word. I have found that nothing is more dangerous to one's own faith than the work of an apologist. No doctrine of that Faith seems to me so spectral, so unreal as one that I have just successfully defended in a public debate. For a moment, you see, it has seemed to rest on oneself: as a result, when you go away from that debate, it seems no stronger than that weak pillar. That is why we apologists take our lives in our hands and can be saved only by falling back continually from the web of our own arguments, as from our intellectual counters, into the Reality — from Christian apologetics into Christ Himself. That also is why we need one another's continual help — *oremus pro invicem*.[21]

[21] 'Let us pray for each other.'

11

WORK AND PRAYER

E VEN IF I GRANT YOUR POINT AND ADMIT THAT ANSWERS to prayer are theoretically possible, I shall still think they are infinitely improbable. I don't think it at all likely that God requires the ill-informed (and contradictory) advice of us humans as to how to run the world. If He is all-wise, as you say He is, doesn't He know already what is best? And if He is all-good won't He do it whether we pray or not?'

This is the case against prayer which has, in the last hundred years, intimidated thousands of people. The usual answer is that it applies only to the lowest sort of prayer, the sort that consists in asking for things to happen. The higher sort, we are told, offers no advice to God; it consists only of 'communion' or intercourse with Him; and those who take this line seem to suggest that the lower kind of prayer really is an absurdity and that only children or savages would use it.

I have never been satisfied with this view. The distinction between the two sorts of prayer is a sound one; and I think on the whole (I am not quite certain) that the sort which asks for nothing is the higher or more advanced. To be in the state in which you are so at one with the will of God that you wouldn't want to alter the course of events even if you could is certainly a very high or advanced condition.

But if one simply rules out the lower kind two difficulties follow. In the first place, one has to say that the whole historical tradition of Christian prayer (including the Lord's Prayer itself) has been wrong; for it has always admitted prayers for our daily bread, for the recovery of the sick, for protection from enemies, for the conversion of the outside world, and the like. In the second place, though the other kind of prayer may be 'higher' if you restrict yourself to it because you have got beyond the desire to use any other, there is nothing specially 'high' or 'spiritual' about abstaining from prayers that make requests simply because you think they're no good. It might be a very pretty thing (but, again, I'm not absolutely certain) if a little boy never asked for cake because he was so high-minded and spiritual that he didn't want any cake. But there's nothing specially pretty about a little boy who doesn't ask because he has learned that it is no use asking. I think that the whole matter needs reconsideration.

The case against prayer (I mean the 'low' or old-fashioned kind) is this. The thing you ask for is either good — for you and for the world in general — or else it is not. If it is, then a good and wise God will do it anyway. If it is not, then He won't. In neither case can your prayer make any difference. But if this argument is sound, surely it is an argument not only against praying, but against doing anything whatever?

In every action, just as in every prayer, you are trying to bring about a certain result; and this result must be good or bad. Why, then, do we not argue as the opponents of prayer argue, and say that if the intended result is good God will bring it to pass without your interference, and that if it is bad He will prevent it happening whatever you do? Why wash your hands? If God intends them to be clean, they'll come clean without your washing them. If He doesn't, they'll remain dirty (as Lady Macbeth found)[1] however much soap you use. Why ask for the salt? Why put on your boots? Why do anything?

We know that we can act and that our actions produce results. Everyone who believes in God must therefore admit (quite apart from the question of prayer) that God has not chosen to write the whole of history with His own hand. Most of the events that go on in the universe are indeed out of our control, but not all. It is like a play in which the scene and the general outline of the story is fixed by the author, but certain minor details are left for the actors to improvise.

[1] Shakespeare, *Macbeth*, V, i, 34-57.

It may be a mystery why He should have allowed us to cause real events at all; but it is no odder that He should allow us to cause them by praying than by any other method.

Pascal says that God 'instituted prayer in order to allow His creatures the dignity of causality'. It would perhaps be truer to say that He invented both prayer and physical action for that purpose. He gave us small creatures the dignity of being able to contribute to the course of events in two different ways. He made the matter of the universe such that we can (in those limits) do things to it; that is why we can wash our own hands and feed or murder our fellow creatures. Similarly, He made His own plan or plot of history such that it admits a certain amount of free play and can be modified in response to our prayers. If it is foolish and impudent to ask for victory in a war (on the ground that God might be expected to know best), it would be equally foolish and impudent to put on a mackintosh — does not God know best whether you ought to be wet or dry?

The two methods by which we are allowed to produce events may be called work and prayer. Both are alike in this respect — that in both we try to produce a state of affairs which God has not (or at any rate not yet) seen fit to provide 'on His own'. And from this point of view the old maxim *laborare est orare* (work is prayer) takes on a new meaning. What we do when we weed a field is not quite different from what we do when we pray for a good harvest. But there is an important difference all the same.

You cannot be sure of a good harvest whatever you do to a field. But you can be sure that if you pull up one weed that one weed will no longer be there. You can be sure that if you drink more than a certain amount of alcohol you will ruin your health or that if you go on for a few centuries more wasting the resources of the planet on wars and luxuries you will shorten the life of the whole human race. The kind of causality we exercise by work is, so to speak, divinely guaranteed, and therefore ruthless. By it we are free to do ourselves as much harm as we please. But the kind which we exercise by prayer is not like that; God has left Himself a discretionary power. Had He not done so, prayer would be an activity too dangerous for man and we should have the horrible state of things envisaged by Juvenal: 'Enormous prayers which Heaven in anger grants.'[2]

Prayers are not always — in the crude, factual sense of the word — 'granted'. This is not because prayer is a weaker kind of causality, but because it is a stronger kind. When it 'works' at all it works unlimited by space and time. That is why God has retained a discretionary power of granting or refusing it; except on that condition prayer would destroy us. It is not unreasonable for a headmaster to say, 'Such and such things you may do according to the fixed rules of this school. But such and such other things are too dangerous to be left to general rules. If you want to do them you must come and make a request and talk over the whole matter with me in my study. And then — we'll see.'

[2] *Satires*, Bk. IV, Satire x, line 111.

12

MAN OR RABBIT?

C AN'T YOU LEAD A GOOD LIFE WITHOUT BELIEVING IN Christianity?' This is the question on which I have been asked to write, and straight away, before I begin trying to answer it, I have a comment to make. The question sounds as if it were asked by a person who said to himself, 'I don't care whether Christianity is in fact true or not. I'm not interested in finding out whether the real universe is more like what the Christians say than what the Materialists say. All I'm interested in is leading a good life. I'm going to choose beliefs not because I think them true but because I find them helpful.' Now frankly, I find it hard to sympathise with this state of mind. One of the things that distinguishes man from the other animals is that he wants to know things, wants to find out what reality is like, simply for the sake of knowing. When that desire is completely quenched in anyone, I think he has become something less than human. As a matter of fact, I don't believe any of you have really lost that desire. More probably, foolish preachers, by always telling you how much Christianity will help you and how good it is for society, have actually led you to forget that Christianity is not a patent medicine. Christianity claims to give an account of *facts* —to tell you what the real universe is like. Its account of the universe may be true, or it may not, and once the question is really before you, then your natural inquisitiveness must make you want to know the answer. If Christianity is untrue, then no honest man will want to believe it, however helpful it might be: if it is true, every honest man will want to believe it, even if it gives him no help at all.

As soon as we have realised this, we realise something else. If Christianity should happen to be true, then it is quite impossible that those who know this truth and those who don't should be equally well equipped for leading a good life. Knowledge of the facts must make a difference to one's actions. Suppose you found a man on the point of starvation and wanted to do the right thing. If you had no knowledge of medical science, you would probably give him a large solid meal; and as a result your man would die. That is what comes of working in the dark. In the same way a Christian and a non-Christian may both wish to do good to their fellow men. The one believes that men are going to live for ever, that they were created by God and so built that they can find their true and lasting happiness only by being united to God, that they have gone badly off the rails, and that obedient faith in Christ is the only way back. The other believes that men are an accidental result of the blind workings of matter, that they started as mere animals and have more or less steadily improved, that they are going to live for about seventy years, that their happiness is fully attainable by good social services and political organisations, and that everything else (e.g., vivisection, birth-control, the judicial system, education) is to be judged to be 'good' or 'bad' simply in so far as it helps or hinders that kind of 'happiness'.

Now there are quite a lot of things which these two men could agree in doing for their fellow citizens. Both would approve of efficient sewers and hospitals and a healthy diet. But sooner or later the difference of their beliefs would produce differences in their practical proposals. Both, for example, might be very keen about education: but the kinds of education they wanted people to have would obviously be very different. Again, where the Materialist would simply ask about a proposed action 'Will it increase the happiness of the majority?', the Christian might have to say, 'Even if it does increase the happiness of the majority, we can't do it. It is unjust.' And all the time, one great difference would run through their whole policy. To the Materialist things like nations, classes, civilizations must be more important than individuals, because the individuals live only seventy odd years each and the group may last for centuries. But to the Christian, individuals are more important, for they live eternally; and races, civilizations and the like, are in comparison the creatures of a day.

The Christian and the Materialist hold different beliefs about the universe. They can't both be right. The one who is wrong will act in a way which simply doesn't fit the real universe. Consequently, with the best will in the world, he will be helping his fellow creatures to their destruction.

With the best will in the world . . . then it won't be his fault. Surely God (if there is a God) will not punish a man for honest mistakes? But was *that* all you were thinking about? Are we ready to run the risk of working in the dark all our lives and doing infinite harm, provided only someone will assure us that our own skins will be safe, that no one will punish us or blame us? I will not believe that the reader is quite on that level. But even if he were, there is something to be said to him.

The question before each of us is not 'Can *someone* lead a good life without Christianity?' The question is, 'Can *I?'* We all know there have been good men who were not Christians; men like Socrates and Confucius who had never heard of it, or men like J. S. Mill who quite honestly couldn't believe it. Supposing Christianity to be true, these men were in a state of honest ignorance or honest error. If their intentions were as good as I suppose them to have been (for of course I can't read their secret hearts) I hope and believe that the skill and mercy of God will remedy the evils which their ignorance, left to itself, would naturally produce both for them and for those whom they influenced. But the man who asks me, 'Can't I lead a good life without believing in Christianity?' is clearly not in the same position. If he hadn't heard of Christianity he would not be asking this question. If, having heard of it, and having seriously considered it, he had decided that it was untrue, then once more he would not be asking the question. The man who asks this question has heard of Christianity and is by no means certain that it may not be true. He is really asking, 'Need I bother about it? Mayn't I just evade the issue, just let sleeping dogs lie, and get on with being "good"? Aren't good intentions enough to keep me safe and blameless without knocking at that dreadful door and making sure whether there is, or isn't someone inside?'

To such a man it might be enough to reply that he is really asking to be allowed to get on with being 'good' before he has done his best to discover what *good* means. But that is not the whole story. We need not inquire whether God will punish him for his cowardice and laziness; they will punish themselves. The man is shirking. He is deliberately trying not to know whether Christianity is true or false, because he foresees endless trouble if it should turn out to be true. He is like the man who deliberately 'forgets' to look at the notice board because, if he did, he might find his name down for some unpleasant duty. He is like the man who won't look at his bank account because he's afraid of what he might find there. He is like the man who won't go to the doctor when he first feels a mysterious pain, because he is afraid of what the doctor may tell him.

The man who remains an unbeliever for such reasons is not in a state of honest error. He is in a state of dishonest error, and that dishonesty will spread through all his thoughts and actions: a certain shiftiness, a vague worry in the background, a blunting of his whole mental edge, will result. He has lost his intellectual virginity. Honest rejection of Christ, however mistaken, will be forgiven and healed — 'Whosoever shall speak a word against the Son of man, it shall be forgiven him.'[1] But to *evade* the Son of Man, to look the other way, to pretend you haven't noticed, to become suddenly absorbed in something on the other side of the street, to leave the receiver off the telephone because it might be He who was ringing up, to leave unopened certain letters in a strange handwriting bcause they might be from Him — this is a different matter. You may not be certain yet whether you ought to be a Christian; but you do know you ought to be a Man, not an ostrich, hiding its head in the sand.

But still — for intellectual honour has sunk very low in our age — I hear someone whimpering on with his question, 'Will it help me? Will it make me happy? Do you really think I'd be better if I became a Christian?' Well, if you must have it, my answer is 'Yes.' But I don't like giving an answer at all at this stage. Here is a door, behind which, according to

[1] Luke xii. 10.

111

some people, the secret of the universe is waiting for you. Either that's true, or it isn't. And if it isn't, then what the door really conceals is simply the greatest fraud, the most colossal 'sell' on record. Isn't it obviously the job of every man (that is a man and not a rabbit) to try to find out which, and then to devote his full energies either to serving this tremendous secret or to exposing and destroying this gigantic humbug? Faced with such an issue, can you really remain wholly absorbed in your own blessed 'moral development'?

All right, Christianity will do you good — a great deal more good than you ever wanted or expected. And the first bit of good it will do you is to hammer into your head (you won't enjoy *that*!) the fact that what you have hitherto called 'good' — all that about 'leading a decent life' and 'being kind' — isn't quite the magnificent and all-important affair you supposed. It will teach you that in fact you can't be 'good' (not for twenty-four hours) on your own moral efforts. And then it will teach you that even if you were, you still wouldn't have achieved the purpose for which you were created. Mere *morality* is not the end of life. You were made for something quite different from that. J. S. Mill and Confucius (Socrates was much nearer the reality) simply didn't know what life is about. The people who keep on asking if they can't lead a decent life without Christ, don't know what life is about; if they did they would know that 'a decent life' is mere machinery compared with the thing we men are really made for. Morality is indispensable: but the Divine Life, which gives itself to us and which calls us to be gods, intends for us something in which morality will be swallowed up. We are to be re-made. All the rabbit in us is to disappear — the worried, conscientious, ethical rabbit as well as the cowardly and sensual rabbit. We shall bleed and squeal as the handfuls of fur come out; and then, surprisingly, we shall find underneath it all a thing we have never yet imagined: a real Man, an ageless god, a son of God, strong, radiant, wise, beautiful, and drenched in joy.

'When that which is perfect is come, then that which is in part shall be done away.'[2] The idea of reaching 'a good life' without Christ is based on a double error. Firstly, we cannot do it; and secondly, in setting up 'a good life' as our final

[2] I Cor. xiii. 10.

goal, we have missed the very point of our existence. Morality is a mountain which we cannot climb by our own efforts; and if we could we should only perish in the ice and unbreathable air of the summit, lacking those wings with which the rest of the journey has to be accomplished. For it is *from* there that the real ascent begins. The ropes and axes are 'done away' and the rest is a matter of flying.

13

ON THE TRANSMISSION OF CHRISTIANITY[1]

DURING THE WAR WE TURN WITH QUICKENED INTEREST from the newspaper accounts of the fighting to the report of any man who has just returned from taking part in it himself. The manuscript of this little book when it was first put into my hands gave me a similar excitement. Discussions on education and on religious education are admirable things; but here we have something different — a first-hand record of the results which the existing system is actually producing while we discuss. Its value is enhanced by the fact that the author is not a minister of education, nor a headmaster, nor a clergyman, nor even a professional teacher. The facts he records are facts against which he ran his head unexpectedly, almost (you might say) accidentally, while doing a particular war-time job.

There are, of course, other things besides this in the book. But I emphasize its purely documentary value because that seems to me to be far the most important thing about it — the thing on which public attention ought to be focused. The abstracts of the author's lectures — or rather openings of discussions — are indeed full of interest, and many will wish

---

[1] This paper was originally published as a Preface to B. G. Sandhurst's book, *How Heathen is Britain?* (London, 1946), in which Mr Sandhurst describes his work with a group of young men in an attempt to discover what their views were about Man and the Godhead of Christ.

114

to comment on them. They are the part of the book which it is easiest to discuss. But I insist that to concentrate on that part is an evasion.

When every allowance has been made for the possibility (delightfully unsuspected by himself) that the author has unusual talents as a teacher, two facts still emerge from his record unshaken. Firstly, that the content of, and the case for, Christianity, are not put before most schoolboys under the present system; and secondly, that when they are so put a majority find them acceptable. The importance of these two facts is that between them they blow away a whole fog of 'reasons for the decline of religion' which are often advanced and often believed. If we had noticed that the young men of the present day found it harder and harder to get the right answers to sums, we should consider that this had been adequately explained the moment we discovered that schools had for some years ceased to teach arithmetic. After that discovery we should turn a deaf ear to people who offered explanations of a vaguer and larger kind — people who said that the influence of Einstein had sapped the ancestral belief in fixed numerical relations, or that gangster films had undermined the desire to get right answers, or that the evolution of consciousness was now entering on its post-arithmetical phase. Where a clear and simple explanation completely covers the facts no other explanation is in court. If the younger generation have never been told what the Christians say and never heard any arguments in defence of it, then their agnosticism or indifference is fully explained. There is no need to look any further: no need to talk about the general intellectual climate of the age, the influence of mechanistic civilization on the character of urban life. And having discovered that the cause of their ignorance is lack of instruction, we have also discovered the remedy. There is nothing in the nature of the younger generation which incapacitates them for receiving Christianity. If any one is prepared to tell them, they are apparently ready to hear.

I allow, of course, that the explanation which our author has discovered merely puts the problem a generation further back. The young people today are un-Christian because their teachers have been either unwilling or unable to transmit Christianity to them. For the impotence or unbelief of their

115

teachers larger and, no doubt, vaguer explanations are to be sought. But that, be it noted, is a historical problem. The schoolmasters of today are, for the most part, the undergraduates of twenty years ago — the products of the 'postwar' period. It is the mental climate of the Twenties that now dominates the form room class. In other words, the sources of unbelief among young people today do not lie in those young people. The outlook which they have — until they are taught better — is a backwash from an earlier period. It is nothing intrinsic to themselves which holds them back from the Faith.

This very obvious fact — that each generation is taught by an earlier generation — must be kept very firmly in mind. The beliefs which boys fresh from school now hold are largely the beliefs of the Twenties. The beliefs which boys from school will hold in the Sixties will be largely those of the undergraduates of today. The moment we forget this we begin to talk nonsense about education. We talk of the views of contemporary adolescence as if some peculiarity in contemporary adolescence had produced them out of itself. In reality, they are usually a delayed result — for the mental world also has its time-bombs — of obsolete adolescence, now middle-aged and dominating its form room. Hence the futility of many schemes for education. None can give to another what he does not possess himself. No generation can bequeath to its successor what it has not got. You may frame the syllabus as you please. But when you have planned and reported *ad nauseam,* if we are sceptical we shall teach only scepticism to our pupils, if fools only folly, if vulgar only vulgarity, if saints sanctity, if heroes heroism. Education is only the most fully conscious of the channels whereby each generation influences the next. It is not a closed system. Nothing which was not in the teachers can flow from them into the pupils. We shall all admit that a man who knows no Greek himself cannot teach Greek to his form: but it is equally certain that a man whose mind was formed in a period of cynicism and disillusion, cannot teach hope or fortitude.

A society which is predominantly Christian will propagate Christianity through its schools: one which is not, will not. All the ministries of education in the world cannot alter this law. We have, in the long run, little either to hope or fear from government.

The State may take education more and more firmly under its wing. I do not doubt that by so doing it can foster conformity, perhaps even servility, up to a point; the power of the State to de-liberalize a profession is undoubtedly very great. But all the teaching must still be done by concrete human individuals. The State has to use the men who exist. Nay, as long as we remain a democracy, it is men who give the State its powers. And over these men, until all freedom is extinguished, the free winds of opinion blow. Their minds are formed by influences which government cannot control. And as they come to be, so will they teach. Let the abstract scheme of education be what it will: its actual operation will be what the men make it. No doubt, there will be in each generation of teachers a percentage, perhaps even a majority, of government tools. But I do not think it is they who will determine the actual character of the education. The boy — and perhaps especially the English boy — has a sound instinct. The teaching of one true man will carry further and print deeper than that of a dozen white Babus. A minister of education (going back, unless I am mistaken, as far as Julian the Apostate[2] for his precedent) may banish Christian clergy from the schools. But if the wind of opinion is blowing in the Christian direction, it will make no difference. It may even do us good; and the minister will have been unknowingly 'the goddes boteler'.[3]

We are often told that education is a key position. That is very false in one sense and very true in another. If it means that you can do any great thing by interfering with existing schools, altering curricula and the like, it is very false. As the teachers are, so they will teach. Your 'reform' may incommode and overwork them, but it will not radically alter the total effect of their teaching. Planning has no magic whereby it can elicit figs from thistles or choke-pears from vines. The rich, sappy, fruit-laden tree will bear sweetness and strength and spiritual health: the dry, prickly, withered tree will teach hate, jealousy, suspicion, and inferiority complex

[2] See p. 65.
[3] Chaucer, *The Hous of Fame*, bk. II, line 592.

— whatever you *tell* it to teach. They will do it unknowingly and all day long. But if we mean that to make adult Christians now and even beyond that circle, to spread the immediately sub-Christian perceptions and virtues, the rich Platonic or Virgilian *penumbra* of the Faith, and thus to alter the type who will be teachers in the future — if we mean that to do this is to perform the greatest of all services for our descendants, then it is very true.

So at least it seems to me: I do not know how far the author would agree with me. He has exposed the actual workings of modern education. To blame the schoolmasters of the last ten years for it would be ridiculous. The majority of them failed to hand on Christianity because they had it not: will you blame a eunuch because he gets no children or a stone because it yields no blood? The minority, isolated in a hostile environment, have probably done all they could, have perhaps done wonders: but little was in their power. Our author has also shown that the ignorance and incredulity of the pupils are very often removable — their roots far shallower than we had feared. I do not draw from this moral that it is now our business to 'get our teeth into the schools'. For one thing, I do not think we shall be allowed to. It is unlikely that in the next forty years England will have a government which would encourage or even tolerate any radically Christian elements in its State system of education. Where the tide flows towards increasing State control, Christianity, with its claims in one way personal and in the other way ecumenical and both ways antithetical to omnicompetent government, must always in fact (though not for a long time yet in words) be treated as an enemy. Like learning, like the family, like any ancient and liberal profession, like the common law, it gives the individual a standing ground against the State. Hence Rousseau, the father of the totalitarians, said wisely enough, from his own point of view, of Christianity, *Je ne connais rien de plus contraire à l'esprit social.*[4] In the second place, even if we were permitted to force a Christian curriculum on the existing schools with the existing teachers we should only be making masters hypocrites and hardening thereby the pupils' hearts.

[4] 'I know nothing more opposed to the social spirit.'

I am speaking, of course, of large schools on which a secular character is already stamped. If any man, in some little corner out of the reach of the omnicompetent, can make, or preserve a really Christian school, that is another matter. His duty is plain.

I do not, therefore, think that our hope of re-baptising England lies in trying to 'get at' the schools. Education is not *in that sense* a key position. To convert one's adult neighbour and one's adolescent neighbour (just free from school) is the practical thing. The cadet, the undergraduate, the young worker in the C.W.U. are obvious targets: but any one and every one is a target. If you make the adults of today Christian, the children of tomorrow will receive a Christian education. What a society has, that, be sure, and nothing else, it will hand on to its young. The work is urgent, for men perish around us. But there is no need to be uneasy about the ultimate event. As long as Christians have children and non-Christians do not, one need have no anxiety for the next century. Those who worship the Life-Force do not do much about transmitting it: those whose hopes are all based on the terrestrial future do not entrust much to it. If these processes continue, the final issue can hardly be in doubt.

14

'MISERABLE OFFENDERS'

AN INTERPRETATION OF
PRAYER BOOK LANGUAGE

O NE OF THE ADVANTAGES OF HAVING A WRITTEN AND printed service, is that it enables you to see when people's feelings and thoughts have changed. When people begin to find the words of our service difficult to join in, that is of course a sign that we do not feel about those things exactly as our ancestors. Many people have, as their immediate re-action to that situation, the simple remedy — 'Well, change the words' — which would be very sensible if you knew that we are right and our ancestors were wrong. It is always at least worth while to find out who it is that is wrong.

The Lenten season is devoted especially to what theologians call contrition, and so every day in Lent a prayer is said in which we ask God to give us 'contrite hearts'.[1] Contrite, as you know, is a word translated from Latin, meaning crushed or pulverized. Now modern people complain that there is too much of that note in our Prayer Book. They do not wish their hearts to be pulverized, and they do not feel that they can sincerely say that they are 'miserable offenders'.[2] I once knew a regular churchgoer who never repeated the words, 'the burden of them (i.e. his sins) is intolerable',[3] because he

[1] The Lenten Collect is appended at the end of this paper.
[2] From the General Confession at Morning and Evening Prayer, which is appended.
[3] The General Confession at the Holy Communion, also appended.

120

did not feel that they were intolerable. But he was not understanding the words. I think the Prayer Book is very seldom talking primarily about our feelings; that is (I think) the first mistake we're apt to make about these words 'we are miserable offenders'. I do not think whether we are feeling miserable or not matters. I think it is using the word miserable in the old sense — meaning an object of pity. That a person can be a proper object of pity when he is not feeling miserable, you can easily understand if you imagine yourself looking down from a height on two crowded express trains that are traveling towards one another along the same line at 60 miles an hour. You can see that in forty seconds there will be a head-on collision. I think it would be very natural to say about the passengers of these trains, that they were objects of pity. This would not mean that they felt miserable themselves; but they would certainly be proper objects of pity. I think that is the sense in which to take the word 'miserable'. The Prayer Book does not mean that we should feel miserable but that if we could see things from a sufficient height above we should all realize that we are in fact proper objects of pity.

As to the other one, about the burden of our sins being intolerable, it might be clearer if we said 'unbearable', because that still has two meanings: you say 'I cannot bear it,' when you mean it gives you great pain, but you also say 'That bridge will not bear that truck' — not meaning 'That bridge will feel pain,' but 'If that truck goes on to it, it will break and not be a bridge any longer, but a mass of rubble.' I wonder if that is what the Prayer Book means; that, whether we feel miserable or not, and however we feel, there is on each of us a load which, if nothing is done about it, will in fact break us, will send us from this world to whatever happens afterwards, not as souls but as broken souls.

But are we really to believe that on each of us there lies something which, if not taken off us, will in fact break us? It is very difficult. No man has any natural knowledge of his own inner state and I think that at the beginning we probably find it much easier to understand and believe this about other people than about ourselves. I wonder, would I be safe in guessing that every second person has in his life a terrible problem, conditioned by some other person; either someone you work for, or someone who works for you, either someone among your friends or your relations, or actually someone in your own house, who is making, and has for years made, your life very much more difficult than it need be? — someone who has that fatal flaw in his character, on which again and again all your efforts have been wrecked, someone whose fatal laziness or jealousy or intolerable temper, or the fact that he never tells the truth, or the fact that he will always backbite and bear tales, or whatever the fatal flaw may be, which, whether it breaks him or not, will certainly break you.

There are two stages, I think, in one's approach to this problem. One begins by thinking that if only something external happened; if only after the war you could get a better job, if only you could get a new house or if only your mother-in-law or daughter-in-law was no longer living with you; if something like that happened, then things would really be better. But after a certain age you no longer think that, because you know for a fact, that even if all this happened, your husband would still be sulky and self-centred, your wife jealous or extravagant, or your employer a bully, or someone you employ and cannot dispense with, a cheat. You know, that if the war ended and you had a better job and a new house, and your mother-in-law or your daughter-in-law no longer lived with you, there would still be that final flaw in 'so and so's' character.

Perhaps in one's misery, one lets out to an intimate friend a little of what the real trouble is, and your intimate friend says, 'Why do you not speak to him or her? Why not have the matter out? They really cannot be as bad as you think.' But you say to yourself 'Oh! He doesn't know,' for of course you have tried again and again to have the matter out, and you know by bitter experience that it will not do the slightest good. You have tried it so often, and you know that any attempt to have it out will only produce either a scene or a total failure of understanding; or, perhaps worst of all, the other person will be kind and equable, and entirely agree with you, and promise to be different. And then in twenty-four hours everything will be exactly the same as it always has been!

Supposing you are not mistaken, misled by your own anger or something of that sort. Supposing you are fairly near the truth, then you are in one sense getting a glimpse of what God

122

must see all the time, because in a certain sense He's up against these people. He is up against their problem as you are. He also has made excellent plans; He has also again and again done His part, by sending into the world prophets and wise men and at last Himself, His own Son. Again and again His plans too have been shipwrecked by that fatal flaw in people's character. And no doubt He sees much more clearly than we do; but even we can see in the case of other people, that unless something is done about their load it will break them. We can see that under the influence of nagging jealousy, or possessive selfishness, their character is day by day ceasing to be human.

Now take a step further. When God looks into your office, or parish, or school, or hospital, or factory, or home, He sees all these people like that, and of course, sees one more, the one whom you do not see. For we may be quite certain that, just as in other people, there is something on which our best endeavours have again and again been shipwrecked, so in us there is something quite equally fatal, on which their endeavours have again and again been shipwrecked. If we are beginners in the Christian life we have nothing to make the fatal flaw clear to ourselves. Does the person with a smelly breath know it smells? Or does the Club bore know he is a bore? Is there a single man or woman who believes himself or herself to be a bore or temperamentally jealous? Yet the world is pretty well sprinkled with bores and jealous people. If we are like that, everyone else will know it before we do. You ask why your friends have not told you about it. But what if they have? They may have tried again and again; but on every occasion, we thought they were being queer, that they were in a bad temper, or simply mistaken. They have tried again and again, and have probably now given it up.

What should be done about it? What is the good of my talking about the fatal flaw if one does not know about it? I think the first step is to get down to the flaws which one does know. I am speaking to Christians. Many of you, no doubt, are very far ahead of me in the Christian way. It is not for me to decide whether you should confess your sins to a priest or not (our Prayer Book leaves that free to all and demands it of none)[4] but if you do not, you should at least make a list on a piece of paper, and make a serious act of

[4] See the Exhortation in the service of Holy Communion.

penance about each one of them. There is something about the mere words, you know, provided you avoid two dangers, either of sensational exaggeration — trying to work things up and make melodramatic sins out of small matters — or the opposite danger of slurring things over. It is essential to use the plain, simple, old-fashioned words that you would use about anyone else. I mean words like theft, or fornication, or hatred, instead of 'I did not mean to be dishonest,' or 'I was only a boy then,' or 'I lost my temper.' I think that this steady facing of what one does know and bringing it before God, without excuses, and seriously asking for Forgiveness and Grace, and resolving as far as in one lies to do better, is the only way in which we can ever begin to know the fatal thing which is always there, and preventing us from becoming perfectly just to our wife or husband, or being a better employer or employee. If this process is gone through, I do not doubt that most of us will come to understand and to share these old words like 'contrite', 'miserable' and 'intolerable'.

Does that sound very gloomy? Does Christianity encourage morbid introspection? The alternative is much more morbid. Those who do not think about their own sins make up for it by thinking incessantly about the sins of others. It is healthier to think of one's own. It is the reverse of morbid. It is not even, in the long run, very gloomy. A serious attempt to repent and really to know one's own sins is in the long run a lightening and relieving process. Of course, there is bound to be a first dismay and often terror and later great pain, yet that is much less in the long run than the anguish of a mass of unrepented and unexamined sins, lurking in the background of our minds. It is the difference between the pain of the tooth about which you should go to the dentist, and the simple straight-forward pain which you know is getting less and less every moment when you have had the tooth out.

APPENDICES TO 'MISERABLE OFFENDERS'

1. *The Collect for Ash Wednesday (the first day of Lent), which is read every day in Lent after the Collect appointed for the Day:*

Almighty and everlasting God, who hatest nothing that thou hast made, and dost forgive the sins of all them that are penitent: Create and make in us new and contrite hearts, that we worthily lamenting our sins, and acknowledging our wretchedness, may obtain of thee, the God of all mercy, perfect remission and forgiveness; through Jesus Christ our Lord. *Amen.*

2. *The General Confession, which is said both at Morning and Evening Prayer:*

Almighty and most merciful Father, We have erred and strayed from thy ways like lost sheep, We have followed too much the devices and desires of our own hearts, We have offended against thy holy laws, We have left undone those things which we ought to have done, And we have done those things which we ought not to have done, And there is no health in us: But thou, O Lord, have mercy upon us miserable offenders; Spare thou them, O God, which confess their faults, Restore thou them that are penitent, According to thy promises declared unto mankind in Christ Jesus our Lord: And grant, O most merciful Father, for his sake, That we may hereafter live a godly, righteous, and sober life, To the glory of thy holy Name. *Amen.*

3. *The General Confession, which is made at Holy Communion:*

Almighty God, Father of our Lord Jesus Christ, Maker of all things, Judge of all men: We acknowledge and bewail our manifold sins and wickedness, Which we from time to time most grievously have committed, By thought, word, and deed, Against thy Divine Majesty, Provoking most justly thy wrath and indignation against us. We do earnestly repent, And are heartily sorry for these our misdoings; The remembrance of them is grievous unto us; The burden of them is intolerable. Have mercy upon us, Have mercy upon us, most merciful Father; For thy Son our Lord Jesus Christ's sake, Forgive us all that is past; And grant that we may ever hereafter Serve and please thee In newness of life, To the honour and glory of thy Name; Through Jesus Christ our Lord. *Amen.*

15

THE FOUNDING OF THE
OXFORD SOCRATIC CLUB[1]

LIKE A QUIETLY EFFICIENT NURSE ARRIVING IN A HOUSE CON-
fused by illness, or like the new general arriving at the siege
of Ismail in Byron's *Don Juan,* our Chairman[2] broke in (if she
will pardon the word) during the autumn of 1941 on that
welter of discussion which even in war-time makes up five-
eighths of the night life of the Oxford undergraduate. By stages
which must have been very swift (for I cannot remember
them), we found that a new society had been formed, that
it was attempting the difficult programme of meeting once a
week,[3] that it was actually carrying this programme out, that
its numbers were increasing, and that neither foul weather
nor crowded rooms (they were lucky who found seats even
on the floor) would reduce the size of the meetings. This was
the Socratic Club. Socrates had exhorted men to 'follow the
argument wherever it led them': the Club came into existence
to apply his principle to one particular subject-matter — the
pros and *cons* of the Christian Religion.

It is a little remarkable that, to the best of my knowledge,
no society had ever before been formed for such a purpose.

[1] This is Lewis's Preface to the first *Socratic Digest,* vol. I (Oxford,
1942-1943). What is not mentioned here is the very important fact
that Lewis was the Society's President from the time of its first meeting until he went to Cambridge in 1954.

[2] Miss Stella Aldwinckle, who is still Chairman.

[3] The first meeting was in Somerville College, Oxford, on the 26th
January 1942.

There had been plenty of organizations that were explicit-ly Christian — the S.C.M.,[4] the Ark,[5] the O.U.C.H.,[6] the O.I.C.C.U.[7]— and there had been plenty of others, scientific or political, which were, if not explicitly, yet profoundly anti-Christian in outlook. The question about Christianity arose, no doubt, often enough in private conversation, and cast its shadow over the aesthetic or philosophical debates in many societies: but an arena specially devoted to the conflict be-tween Christian and unbeliever was a novelty. Its value from a merely cultural point of view is very great. In any fairly large and talkative community such as a university there is always the danger that those who think alike should gravitate together into *coteries* where they will henceforth encounter opposition only in the emasculated form of rumour that the outsiders say thus and thus. The absent are easily refuted, complacent dogmatism thrives, and differences of opinion are embittered by group hostility. Each group hears not the best, but the worst, that the other group can say. In the Socratic all this was changed. Here a man could get the case for Christianity without all the paraphernalia of pietism and the the case against it without the irrelevant *sansculottisme* of our common anti-God weeklies. At the very least we helped to civilize one another; sometimes we ventured to hope that if our Athenian patron were allowed to be present, unseen, at our meetings he might not have found the atmosphere wholly alien.

We also learned, in those motley — and usually stifling — assemblies where English boys fresh from public schools rubbed shoulders with elderly European *Gelehrten* in exile, almost any type of opinion might turn up. Everyone found how little he had known about everyone else. We of the Christian party discovered that the weight of the sceptical attack did not always come where we expected it; our opponents had to correct what seemed to us their almost bottomless ignorance of the Faith they supposed themselves to be rejecting.

It is (theoretically) a difficulty in the British Constitution

[4] The Student Christian Movement.
[5] An Oxford Christian society.
[6] Oxford University Church Union.
[7] Oxford Intercollegiate Christian Union, now called The Christian Union.

127

that the Speaker of the House of Commons must himself be a member of one of the Parties. There is a similar difficulty about the Socratic. Those who founded it do not for one moment pretend to be neutral. It was the Christians who constructed the arena and issued the challenge. It will therefore always be possible for the lower (the less Athenian) type of unbeliever to regard the whole thing as a cunningly — or not even so very cunningly — disguised form of propaganda. The Athenian type, if he had this objection to make, would put it in a paper and read that paper to the Socratic itself. He would be welcome to do so — though I doubt whether he would have the stomach if he knew with what pains and toil the committee has scoured *Who's Who* to find intelligent atheists who had leisure or zeal to come and propagate their creed. But when all is said and done, the answer to any such suspicion lies deeper. It is not here that the honesty of the Socratic comes in. We never claimed to be impartial. But argument is. It has a life of its own. No man can tell where it will go. We expose ourselves, and the weakest of our party, to your fire no less than you are exposed to ours. Worse still, we expose ourselves to the recoil from our own shots; for if I may trust my personal experience no doctrine is, for the moment, dimmer to the eye of faith than that which a man has just successfully defended. The arena is common to both parties and cannot finally be cheated; in it you risk nothing, and we risk all.

Others may have quite a different objection to our proceedings. They may protest that intellectual discussion can neither build Christianity nor destroy it. They may feel that religion is too sacred to be thus bandied to and fro in public debate, too sacred to be talked of — almost, perhaps, too sacred for anything to be done with it at all. Clearly, the Christian members of the Socratic think differently. They know that intellectual assent is not faith, but they do not believe that religion is only 'what a man does with his solitude'. Or, if it is, then they care nothing for 'religion' and all for Christianity. Christianity is not merely what a man does with his solitude. It is not even what God does with His solitude. It tells of God descending into the coarse publicity of history and there enacting what can — and must — be talked about.

16

RELIGION WITHOUT DOGMA?[1]

IN HIS PAPER ON 'THE GROUNDS OF MODERN AGNOSTICISM',
Professor Price maintains the following positions: (1) That
the essence of religion is belief in God and immortality; (2)
that in most actual religions the essence is found in connection with 'accretions of dogma and mythology'[2] which have
been rendered incredible by the progress of science; (3) that
it would be very desirable, if it were possible, to retain the
essence purged of the accretions; but (4) that science has
rendered the essence almost as hard to believe as the accretions. For the doctrine of immortality involves the dualistic
view that man is a composite creature, a soul in a state of
symbiosis with a physical organism. But in so far as science
can successfully regard man monistically, as a single organism

---

[1] This paper was originally read to the Oxford Socratic Club on
the 20th May 1946 as 'Religion without Dogma?', and later published
in the *Phoenix Quarterly*, vol. I, No. 1 (Autumn 1946) under the
title 'A Christian Reply to Professor Price'. It is an answer to 'The
Grounds of Modern Agnosticism', a paper which Professor Price read
to the Socratic Club on the 23rd October 1944, and which was published in the same issue of the *Phoenix Quarterly*. Though Lewis's paper
was afterwards reprinted in *The Socratic Digest* [1948], it is obvious
from the fact that many errors which appear in the *Socratic* version
were corrected in the *Quarterly* version, that the *Quarterly* version represents Lewis's final revision. I have incorporated in the text given here
all the marginal emendations which Lewis made in his copy of the
Phoenix Quarterly, as well as those portions from the *Socratic* version
which he had omitted in his revision.
[2] H. H. Price, 'The Grounds of Modern Agnosticism', *Phoenix Quarterly*, vol. I, No. 1 (Autumn 1946), p. 25.

whose psychological properties all arise from his physical, the soul becomes an indefensible hypothesis. In conclusion, Professor Price found our only hope in certain empirical evidence for the soul which appears to him satisfactory; in fact, in the findings of Psychical Research.

My disagreement with Professor Price begins, I am afraid, at the threshold. I do not define the essence of religion as belief in God and immortality. Judaism in its earlier stages had no belief in immortality, and for a long time no belief which was religiously relevant. The shadowy existence of the ghost in Sheol was one of which Jehovah took no account and which took no account of Jehovah. In Sheol all things are forgotten. The religion was centred on the ritual and ethical demands of Jehovah in the present life, and also, of course, on benefits expected from Him. These benefits are often merely worldly benefits (grandchildren and peace upon Israel), but a more specifically religious note is repeatedly struck. The Jew is athirst for the living God,[3] he delights in His Laws as in honey or treasure,[4] he is conscious of himself in Jehovah's presence as unclean of lips and heart.[5] The glory or splendour of God is worshipped for its own sake. In Buddhism, on the other hand, we find that a doctrine of immortality is central, while there is nothing specifically religious. Salvation from immortality, deliverance from reincarnation, is the very core of its message. The existence of the gods is not necessarily decried, but it is of no religious significance. In Stoicism again both the religious quality and the belief in immortality are variables, but they do not vary in direct ratio. Even within Christianity itself we find a striking expression, not without influence from Stoicism, of the subordinate position of immortality. When Henry More ends a poem on the spiritual life by saying that if, after all, he should turn out to be mortal he would be

> . . . satisfide
> A lonesome mortall God t' have died.[6]

[3] Psalm xlii. 2.
[4] Psalm xix. 10.
[5] Isaiah vi. 5.
[6] 'Resolution', *The Complete Poems of Dr Henry More,* ed. Alexander B. Grosart (Edinburgh, 1878), line 117, p. 176.

From my own point of view, the example of Judaism and Buddhism is of immense importance. The system, which is meaningless without a doctrine of immortality, regards immortality as a nightmare, not as a prize. The religion which, of all ancient religions, is most specifically religious, that is, at once most ethical and most numinous, is hardly interested in the question. Believing, as I do, that Jehovah is a real being, indeed the *ens realissimum,* I cannot sufficiently admire the divine tact of thus training the chosen race for centuries in religion before even hinting the shining secret of eternal life. He behaves like the rich lover in a romance who woos the maiden on his own merits, disguised as a poor man, and only when he has won her reveals that he has a throne and palace to offer. For I cannot help thinking that any religion which begins with a thirst for immortality is damned, as a religion, from the outset. Until a certain spiritual level has been reached, the promise of immortality will always operate as a bribe which vitiates the whole religion and infinitely inflames those very self-regards which religion must cut down and uproot. For the essence of religion, in my view, is the thirst for an end higher than natural ends; the finite self's desire for, and acquiescence in, and self-rejection in favour of, an object wholly good and wholly good for it. That the self-rejection will turn out to be also a self-finding, that bread cast upon the waters will be found after many days, that to die is to live — these arc sacred paradoxes of which the human race must not be told too soon.

Differing from Professor Price about the essence of religion, I naturally cannot, in a sense, discuss whether the essence as he defines it co-exists with accretions of dogma and mythology. But I freely admit that the essence as I define it always co-exists with other things; and that some of these other things even I would call mythology. But my list of things mythological would not coincide with his, and our views of mythology itself probably differ. A great many different views on it have, of course, been held. Myths have been accepted as literally true, then as allegorically true (by the Stoics), as confused history (by Euhemerus),[7] as priestly

---

[7] A Sicilian writer (c. 315 B.C.) who developed the theory that the ancient beliefs about the gods originated from the elaboration of traditions of actual historical persons.

131

lies (by the philosophers of the enlightenment), as imitative agricultural ritual mistaken for propositions (in the days of Frazer).[8] If you start from a naturalistic philosophy, then something like the view of Euhemerus or the view of Frazer is likely to result. But I am not a naturalist. I believe that in the huge mass of mythology which has come down to us a good many different sources are mixed — true history, allegory, ritual, the human delight in story telling, etc. But among these sources I include the supernatural, both diabolical and divine. We need here concern ourselves only with the latter. If my religion is erroneous then occurrences of similar motifs in pagan stories are, of course, instances of the same, or a similar error. But if my religion is true, then these stories my well be a *preparatio evangelica,* a divine hinting in poetic and ritual form at the same central truth which was later focussed and (so to speak) historicised in the Incarnation. To me, who first approached Christianity from a delighted interest in, and reverence for, the best pagan imagination, who loved Balder before Christ and Plato before St Augustine, the anthropological argument against Christianity has never been formidable. On the contrary, I could not believe Christianity if I were forced to say that there were a thousand religions in the world of which 999 were pure nonsense and the thousandth (fortunately) true. My conversion, very largely, depended on recognizing Christianity as the completion, the actualization, the entelechy, of something that had never been wholly absent from the mind of man. And I still think that the agnostic argument from similarities between Christianity and paganism works only if you know the answer. If you start by knowing on other grounds that Christianity is false, then the pagan stories may be another nail in its coffin: just as if you started by knowing that there were no such things as crocodiles then the various stories about dragons might help to confirm your disbelief. But if the truth or falsehood of Christianity is the very question you are discussing, then the argument from anthropology is surely a *petitio.*

There are, of course, many things in Christianity which I accept as fact and which Professor Price would regard as

[8] James George Frazer, *The Golden Bough: A Study in Magic and Religion* (London, 1922).

mythology. In a word, there are miracles. The contention is that science has proved that miracles cannot occur. According to Professor Price 'a Deity who intervened miraculously and suspended natural law could never be accepted by Science';[9] whence he passes on to consider whether we cannot still believe in Theism without miracles. I am afraid I have not understood why the miracles could never be accepted by one who accepted science.

Professor Price bases his view on the nature of scientific method. He says that that method is based on two assumptions. The first is that all events are subject to laws, and he adds: 'It does not matter for our purpose whether the laws are "deterministic" or only "statistical." '[10] But I submit that it matters to the scientist's view of the miraculous. The notion that natural laws may be merely statistical results from the modern belief that the individual unit of matter obeys no laws. Statistics were introduced to explain why, despite the lawlessness of the individual unit, the behaviour of gross bodies was regular. The explanation was that, by a principle well known to actuaries, the law of averages levelled out the individual eccentricities of the innumerable units contained in even the smallest gross body. But with this conception of the lawless units the whole impregnability of nineteenth-century Naturalism has, as it seems to me, been abandoned. What is the use of saying that all events are subject to laws if you also say that every event which befalls the individual unit of matter is *not* subject to laws. Indeed, if we define nature as the system of events in space-time governed by interlocking laws, then the new physics has really admitted that something other than nature exists. For if nature means the interlocking system, then the behaviour of the individual unit is outside nature. We have admitted what may be called the sub-natural. After that admission what confidence is left us that there may not be a supernatural as well? It may be true that the lawlessness of the little events fed into nature from the sub-natural is always ironed out by the law of averages. It does not follow that great events could not be fed into her by the supernatural: nor that they also would allow themselves to be ironed out.

[9] Price, *op. cit.,* p. 20.
[10] *Ibid.*

The second assumption which Professor Price attributes to the scientific method is 'that laws can only be discovered by the study of publicly observable regularities.'[11] Of course they can. This does not seem to me to be an assumption so much as a self-evident proposition. But what is it to the purpose? If a miracle occurs it is by definition an interruption of regularity. To discover a regularity is by definition not to discover its interruptions, even if they occur. You cannot discover a railway accident from studying Bradshaw:[12] only by being there when it happens or hearing about it afterwards from someone who was. You cannot discover extra half-holidays by studying a school timetable: you must wait till they are announced. But surely this does not mean that a student of Bradshaw is logically forced to deny the possibility of railway accidents. This point of scientific method merely shows (what no one to my knowledge ever denied) that if miracles *did* occur, science, as science, could not prove, or disprove, their occurrence. What cannot be trusted to recur is not material for science: that is why history is not one of the sciences. You cannot find out what Napoleon did at the battle of Austerlitz by asking him to come and fight it again in a laboratory with the same combatants, the same *terrain,* the same weather, and in the same age. You have to go to the records. We have not, in fact, proved that science excludes miracles: we have only proved that the question of miracles, like innumerable other questions, excludes laboratory treatment.

If I thus hand over miracles from science to history (but not, of course, to historians who beg the question by beginning with materialistic assumptions) Professor Price thinks I shall not fare much better. Here I must speak with caution, for I do not profess to be a historian or a textual critic. I would refer you to Sir Arnold Lunn's book *The Third Day*.[13] If Sir Arnold is right, then the Biblical criticism which began in the nineteenth century has already shot its bolt and most of its conclusions have been successfully disputed, though it will, like nineteenth-century materialism, long continue to dominate popular thought. What I can say with more certainty

[11] *Ibid.*
[12] George Bradshaw (1801-1853), who founded *Bradshaw's Railway Guide* which was published from 1839 to 1961.
[13] (London, 1945).

is that that *kind* of criticism — the kind which discovers that every old book was made by six anonymous authors well provided with scissors and paste and that every anecdote of the slightest interest is unhistorical, has already begun to die out in the studies I know best. The period of arbitrary scepticism about the canon and text of Shakespeare is now over: and it is reasonable to expect that this method will soon be used only on Christian documents and survive only in the *Thinkers Library* and the theological colleges.

I find myself, therefore, compelled to disagree with Professor Price's second point. I do not think that science has shown, or, by its nature, could ever show that the miraculous element in religion is erroneous. I am not speaking, of course, about the psychological effects of science on those who practise it or read its results. That the continued application of scientific methods breeds a temper of mind unfavourable to the miraculous, may well be the case, but even here there would seem to be some difference among the sciences. Certainly, if we think, not of the miraculous in particular, but of religion in general there is such a difference. Mathematicians, astronomers and physicists are often religious, even mystical; biologists much less often; economists and psychologists very seldom indeed. It is as their subject matter comes nearer to man himself that their anti-religious bias hardens.

And that brings me to Professor Price's fourth point — for I would rather postpone consideration of his third. His fourth point, it will be remembered, was that science had undermined not only what he regards as the mythological accretions of religion, but also what he regards as its essence. That essence is for him Theism and immortality. In so far as natural science can give a satisfactory account of man as a purely biological entity, it excludes the soul and therefore excludes immortality. That, no doubt, is why the scientists who are most, or most nearly, concerned with man himself are the most anti-religious.

Now most assuredly if naturalism is right then it is at this point, at the study of man himself, that it wins its final victory and overthrows all our hopes: not only our hope of immortality, but our hope of finding significance in our lives here and now. On the other hand, if naturalism is wrong, it will be here that it will reveal its fatal philosophical defect, and that is what I think it does.

On the fully naturalistic view all events are determined by laws. Our logical behaviour, in other words our thoughts, and our ethical behaviour, including our ideals as well as our acts of will, are governed by biochemical laws; these, in turn, by physical laws which are themselves actuarial statements about the lawless movements of matter. These units never intended to produce the regular universe we see: the law of averages (successor to Lucretius's *exiguum clinamen*)[14] has produced it out of the collision of these random variations in movement. The physical universe never intended to produce organisms. The relevant chemicals on earth, and the sun's heat, thus juxtaposed, gave rise to this disquieting disease of matter: organization. Natural selection, operating on the minute differences between one organism and another, blundered into that sort of phosphorescence or mirage which we call consciousness — and that, in some cortexes beneath some skulls, at certain moments, still in obedience to physical laws, but to physical laws now filtered through laws of a more complicated kind, takes the form we call thought. Such, for instance, is the origin of this paper: such was the origin of Professor Price's paper. What we should speak of as his 'thoughts' were merely the last link of a causal chain in which all the previous links were irrational. He spoke as he did because the matter of his brain was behaving in a certain way: and the whole history of the universe up to that moment had forced it to behave in that way. What we called his thought was essentially a phenomenon of the same sort as his other secretions — the form which the vast irrational process of nature was bound to take at a particular point of space and time.

Of course it did not feel like that to him or to us while it was going on. He appeared to himself to be studying the nature of things, to be in some way aware of realities, even supersensuous realities, outside his own head. But if strict naturalism is right, he was deluded: he was merely enjoying the conscious reflection of irrationally determined events in his own head. It appeared to him that his thoughts (as he called them) could have to outer realities that wholly immaterial relation which we call truth or falsehood: though, in fact, being but the shadow of cerebral events, it is not easy

[14] 'small inclination', *De Rerum Natura,* bk. II, line 292.

to see that they could have any relation to the outer world except causal relations. And when Professor Price defended scientists, speaking of their devotion to truth and their constant following of the best light they knew, it seemed to him that he was choosing an attitude in obedience to an ideal. He did not feel that he was merely suffering a reaction determined by ultimately amoral and irrational sources, and no more capable of rightness or wrongness than a hiccup or a sneeze.

It would have been impossible for Professor Price to have written, or us to have read, his paper with the slightest interest if he and we had consciously held the position of strict naturalism throughout. But we can go further. It would be impossible to accept naturalism itself if we really and consistently believed naturalism. For naturalism is a system of thought. But for naturalism all thoughts are mere events with irrational causes. It is, to me at any rate, impossible to regard the thoughts which make up naturalism in that way and, at the same time, to regard them as a real insight into external reality. Bradley distinguished *idea-event* from *idea-making*,[15] but naturalism seems to me committed to regarding ideas simply as events. For meaning is a relation of a wholly new kind, as remote, as mysterious, as opaque to empirical study, as soul itself.

Perhaps this may be even more simply put in another way. Every particular thought (whether it is a judgment of fact or a judgment of value) is always and by all men discounted the moment they believe that it can be explained, without remainder, as the result of irrational causes. Whenever you know what the other man is saying is wholly due to his complexes or to a bit of bone pressing on his brain, you cease to attach any importance to it. But if naturalism were true then all thoughts whatever would be wholly the result of irrational causes. Therefore, all thoughts would be equally worthless. Therefore, naturalism is worthless. If it is true, then we can know no truths. It cuts its own throat.

I remember once being shown a certain kind of knot which was such that if you added one extra complication to make assurance doubly sure you suddenly found that the whole thing had come undone in your hands and you had only a

[15] 'Spoken and Written English', *The Collected Papers of Henry Bradley*, ed. Robert Bridges (Oxford, 1928), pp. 168-93.

bit of string. It is like that with naturalism. It goes on claiming territory after territory: first the inorganic, then the lower organisms, then man's body, then his emotions. But when it takes the final step and we attempt a naturalistic account of thought itself, suddenly the whole thing unravels. The last fatal step has invalidated all the preceding ones: for they were all reasonings and reason itself has been discredited. We must, therefore, either give up thinking altogether or else begin over again from the ground floor.

There is no reason, at this point, to bring in either Christianity or spiritualism. We do not need them to refute naturalism. It refutes itself. Whatever else we may come to believe about the universe, at least we cannot believe naturalism. The validity of rational thought, accepted in an utterly non-naturalistic, transcendental (if you will), supernatural sense, is the necessary presupposition of all other theorizing. There is simply no sense in beginning with a view of the universe and trying to fit the claims of thought in at a later stage. By thinking at all we have claimed that our thoughts are more than mere natural events. All other propositions must be fitted in as best they can round that primary claim.

Holding that science has not refuted the miraculous element in religion, much less that naturalism, rigorously taken, can refute anything except itself, I do not, of course, share Professor Price's anxiety to find a religion which can do without what he calls mythology. What he suggests is simple Theism, rendered credible by a belief in immortality which, in its turn, is guaranteed by Psychical Research. Professor Price is not, of course, arguing that immortality would of itself prove Theism: it would merely remove an obstacle to Theism. The positive source of Theism he finds in religious experience.

At this point it is very important to decide which of two questions we are asking. We may be asking: (1) whether this purged minimal religion suggested by Professor Price is capable, as a historical, social and psychological entity, of giving fresh heart to society, strengthening the moral will, and producing all those other benefits which, it is claimed, the old religions have sometimes produced. On the other hand, we may be asking: (2) whether this minimal religion will be the true one; that is, whether it contains the only true propositions we can make about ultimate questions.

The first question is not a religious question but a sociological one. The religious mind as such, like the older sort of scientific mind as such, does not care a rap about socially useful propositions. Both are athirst for reality, for the utterly objective, for that which is what it is. The 'open mind' of the scientist and the emptied and silenced mind of the mystic are both efforts to eliminate what is our own in order that the Other may speak. And if, turning aside from the religious attitude, we speak for a moment as mere sociologists, we must admit that history does not encourage us to expect much envigorating power in a minimal religion. Attempts at such a minimal religion are not new — from Akhenaten[16] and Julian the Apostate[17] down to Lord Herbert of Cherbury[18] and the late H. G. Wells. But where are the saints, the consolations, the ecstacies? The greatest of such attempts was that simplification of Jewish and Christian traditions which we call Islam. But it retained many elements which Professor Price would regard as mythical and barbaric, and its culture is by no means one of the richest or most progressive.

Nor do I see how such a religion, if it became a vital force, would long be preserved in its freedom from dogma. Is its God to be conceived pantheistically, or after the Jewish, Platonic, Christian fashion? If we are to retain the minimal religion in all its purity, I suppose the right answer would be: 'We don't know, and we must be content not to know.' But that is the end of the minimal religion as a practical affair. For the question is of pressing practical importance. If the God of Professor Price's religion is an impersonal spirituality diffused through the whole universe, equally present, and present in the same mode, at all points of space and time, then He — or it — will certainly be conceived as being beyond good and

---

[16] Akhenaten (Amenhotep IV), king of Egypt, who came to the throne about 1375 B.C. and introduced a new religion, in which the sun-god Ra (designated as 'Aten') superseded Amon.

[17] Roman emperor A.D. 361-3, who was brought up compulsorily as a Christian, but who on attaining the throne proclaimed himself a pagan, and made a great effort to revive the worship of the old gods.

[18] Edward Herbert (1583-1648). He is known as the 'Father of Deism', for he maintained that among the 'common notions' apprehended by instinct are the existence of God, the duty of worship and repentance, and future rewards and punishment. This 'natural religion', he believed, had been vitiated by superstition and dogma.

139

evil, expressed equally in the brothel or the torture chamber and in the model factory or the university common room. If, on the other hand, He is a personal Being standing outside His creation, commanding this and prohibiting that, quite different consequences follow. The choice between these two views affects the choice between courses of action at every moment both in private and public life. Nor is this the only such question that arises. Does the minimal religion know whether its god stands in the same relation to all men, or is he related to some as he is not related to others? To be true to its undogmatic character it must again say: 'Don't ask.' But if that is the reply, then the minimal religion cannot exclude the Christian view that He was present in a special way in Jesus, nor the Nazi view that He is present in a special way in the German race, nor the Hindu view that He is specially present in the Brahmin, nor the central African view that He is specially present in the thigh-bone of a dead English Tommy.

All these difficulties are concealed from us as long as the minimal religion exists only on paper. But suppose it were somehow established all over what is left of the British Empire, and let us suppose that Professor Price has (most reluctantly and solely from a sense of duty) become its supreme head on earth. I predict that one of two things must happen: (1) In the first month of his reign he will find himself uttering his first dogmatic definition — he will find himself saying, for example: 'No. God is not an amoral force diffused through the whole universe to whom suttee and temple prostitution are no more and no less acceptable than building hospitals and teaching children; he is a righteous creator, separate from his creation, who demands of you justice and mercy' or (2) Professor Price will not reply. In the second case is it not clear what will happen? Those who have come to his minimal religion from Christianity will conceive God in the Jewish, Platonic, Christian way; those who have come from Hinduism will conceive Him pantheistically; and the plain men who have come from nowhere will conceive Him as a righteous Creator in their moments of self-indulgence. And the ex-Marxist will think He is specially present in the Proletariat, and the ex-Nazi will think He is specially present in the German people. And they will hold world conferences at which they all speak the same language and reach the most edifying agreement: but they will

140

all mean totally different things. The minimal religion in fact cannot, while it remains minimal, be acted on. As soon as you *do* anything you have assumed one of the dogmas. In practice it will not be a religion at all; it will be merely a new colouring given to all the different things people were doing already.

I submit it to Professor Price, with great respect, that when he spoke of mere Theism, he was all the time unconsciously assuming a particular conception of God: that is, he was assuming a dogma about God. And I do not think he was deducing it solely, or chiefly from his own religious experience or even from a study of religious experience in general. For religious experience can be made to yield almost any sort of God. I think Professor Price assumed a certain sort of God because he has been brought up in a certain way: because Bishop Butler and Hooker and Thomas Aquinas and Augustine and St Paul and Christ and Aristotle and Plato are, as we say, 'in his blood'. He was not really starting from scratch. Had he done so, had God meant in his mind a being about whom no dogma whatever is held, I doubt whether he would have looked for even social salvation in such an empty concept. All the strength and value of the minimal religion, for him as for all others who accept it, is derived not from it, but from the tradition which he imports into it.

The minimal religion will, in my opinion, leave us all doing what we were doing before. Now it, in itself, will not be an objection from Professor Price's point of view. He was not working for unity, but for some spiritual dynamism to see us through the black night of civilization. If Psychical Research has the effect of enabling people to continue, or to return to, all the diverse religions which naturalism has threatened, and if they can thus get power and hope and discipline, he will, I fancy, be content. But the trouble is that if this minimal religion leaves Buddhists still Buddhists, and Nazis still Nazis, then it will, I believe, leave us — as Western, mechanised, democratic, secularised men — exactly where we were. In what way will a belief in the immortality vouched for by Psychical Research, and in an unknown God, restore to us the virtue and energy of our ancestors? It seems to me that both beliefs, unless reinforced by something else, will be to modern man very shadowy and inoperative. If indeed we knew that

141

God were righteous, that He had purposes for us, that He was the leader in a cosmic battle and that some real issue hung on our conduct in the field, then it would be something to the purpose. Or if, again, the utterances which purport to come from the other world ever had the accent which really *suggests* another world, ever spoke (as even the inferior actual religions do) with that voice before which our mortal nature trembles with awe or joy, then that also would be to the purpose. But the god of minimal Theism remains powerless to excite either fear or love: can be given power to do so only from those traditional resources to which, in Professor Price's conception, science will never permit our return. As for the utterances of the mediums . . . I do not wish to be offensive. But will even the most convinced spiritualist claim that one sentence from that source has ever taken its place among the golden sayings of mankind, has ever approached (much less equalled) in power to elevate, strengthen or correct even the second rank of such sayings? Will anyone deny that the vast majority of spirit messages sink pitiably below the best that has been thought and said even in this world? — that in most of them we find a banality and provincialism, a paradoxical union of the prim with the enthusiastic, of flatness and gush, which would suggest that the souls of the moderately respectable are in the keeping of Annie Besant[19] and Martin Tupper?[20]

I am not arguing from the vulgarity of the messages that their claim to come from the dead is false. If I did the spiritualist would reply that this quality is due to imperfections in the medium of communication. Let it be so. We are not here discussing the truth of spiritualism, but its power to become the starting point of a religion. And for that purpose I submit that the poverty of its contents disqualifies it. A minimal religion compounded of spirit messages and bare Theism has no power to touch any of the deepest chords in our nature, or to evoke any response which will raise us even to a higher secular level — let alone to the spiritual life. The god of whom no dogmas are believed is a mere shadow. He will not produce

[19] Annie Besant (1847-1933) was an ardent supporter of Liberal causes and became a member of the Theosophical Society in 1889.

[20] Martin Tupper (1810 89) is probably best known for his *Proverbial Philosophy* — commonplace maxims and reflections couched in a rhythmical form.

that fear of the Lord in which wisdom begins, and, therefore, will not produce that love in which it is consummated. The immortality which the messages suggest can produce in mediocre spirits only a vague comfort for our unredeemedly personal hankerings, a shadowy sequel to the story of this world in which all comes right (but right in how pitiable a sense!), while the more spiritual will feel that it has added a new horror to death — the horror of mere endless succession, of indefinite imprisonment in that which binds us all, *das Gemeine*.[21] There is in this minimal religion nothing that can convince, convert, or (in the higher sense) console; nothing, therefore, which can restore vitality to our civilization. It is not costly enough. It can never be a controller or even a rival to our natural sloth and greed. A flag, a song, an old school tie, is stronger than it; much more, the pagan religions. Rather than pin my hopes on it I would almost listen again to the drum-beat in my blood (for the blood is at least in some sense the life) and join in the song of the Maenads:

> Happy they whom the Daimons
> Have befriended, who have entered
> The divine orgies, making holy
> Their life-days, till the dance throbs
> In their heart-beats, while they romp with
> Dionysus on the mountains . . .[22]

Yes, almost; almost I'd sooner be a pagan suckled in a creed outworn.

Almost, but not, of course, quite. If one is forced to such an alternative, it is perhaps better to starve in a wholly secularised and meaningless universe than to recall the obscenities and cruelties of paganism. They attract because they are a distortion of the truth, and therefore, retain some of its flavour. But with this remark I have passed into our second question. I shall not be expected at the end of this paper to begin an apologetic for the truth of Christianity. I will only say something which in one form or another I have said perhaps too often already. If there is no God then we have no interest in the minimal religion or any other. We will not

[21] Johann Wolfgang Goethe, *Epilog zu Schillers Glocke*, 1. 32. '*das Gemeine*' means something like 'that which dominates us all'.
[22] Euripides, *Bacchae*, 1. 74.

make a lie even to save civilization. But if there is, then it is so probable as to be almost axiomatic that the initiative lies wholly on His side. If He can be known it will be by self-revelation on His part, not by speculation on ours. We, therefore, look for Him where it is claimed that He has revealed Himself by miracle, by inspired teachers, by enjoined ritual. The traditions conflict, yet the longer and more sympathetically we study them the more we become aware of a common element in many of them: the theme of sacrifice, of mystical communion through the shed blood, of death and rebirth, of redemption, is too clear to escape notice. We are fully entitled to use moral and intellectual criticism. What we are not, in my opinion, entitled to do is simply to abstract the ethical element and set that up as a religion on its own. Rather in that tradition which is at once more completely ethical and most transcends mere ethics — in which the old themes of the sacrifice and rebirth recur in a form which transcends, though there it no longer revolts, our conscience and our reason — we may still most reasonably believe that we have the consummation of all religion, the fullest message from the wholly other, the living creator, who, if He is at all, must be the God not only of the philosophers, but of mystics and savages, not only of the head and heart, but also of the primitive emotions and the spiritual heights beyond all emotion. We may still reasonably attach ourselves to the Church, to the only concrete organization which has preserved down to this present time the core of all the messages, pagan and perhaps pre-pagan, that have ever come from beyond the world, and begin to practice the only religion which rests not upon some selection of certain supposedly 'higher' elements in our nature, but on the shattering and rebuilding, the death and rebirth, of that nature in every part: neither Greek nor Jew nor barbarian, but a new creation.

[NOTE: The debate between Lewis and Professor Price did not end here. In *The Socratic Digest*, No. 4 [1948], there follows a 'Reply' to Lewis's 'Religion without Dogma?' by Professor Price (pp. 94-102). Then, at a meeting of the Socratic Club on the 2nd February 1948, Miss G. E. M. Anscombe read a paper entitled 'A Reply to Mr C. S. Lewis's Argument that "Naturalism is Self-refuting" ', afterwards published in the same issue of the *Digest* (pp. 7-15) as Professor Price's

'Reply'. Miss Anscombe criticised the argument found on pp. 136-38 of the paper printed above as well as chapter III, 'The Self-Contradiction of the Naturalist', of Lewis's book *Miracles* (London, 1947). The two short pieces that follow are (A) the Socratic minute-book account of Lewis's reply to Miss Anscombe and (B) a reply written by Lewis himself — both reprinted from the same issue of the *Digest* mentioned above (pp. 15-16). Aware that the third chapter of his *Miracles* was ambiguous, Lewis revised this chapter for the Fontana (1960) issue of *Miracles* in which chapter III is retitled 'The Cardinal Difficulty of Naturalism'.]

A

In his reply Mr C. S. Lewis agreed that the words 'cause' and 'ground' were far from synonymous but said that the recognition of a ground could be the cause of assent, and that assent was only rational when such was its cause. He denied that such words as 'recognition' and 'perception' could be properly used of a mental act among whose causes the thing perceived or recognized was not one.

Miss Anscombe said that Mr Lewis had misunderstood her and thus the first part of the discussion was confined to the two speakers who attempted to clarify their positions and their differences. Miss Anscombe said that Mr Lewis was still not distinguishing between 'having reasons' and 'having reasoned' in the causal sense. Mr Lewis understood the speaker to be making a tetrachotomy thus: (1) logical reasons; (2) having reasons (i.e. psychological); (3) historical causes; (4) scientific causes or observed regularities. The main point in his reply was that an observed regularity was only the symptom of a cause, and not the cause itself, and in reply to an interruption by the Secretary he referred to his notion of cause as 'magical'. An open discussion followed, in which some members tried to show Miss Anscombe that there was a connection between ground and cause, while others contended against the President [Lewis] that the test for the validity of reason could never in any event be such a thing as the state of the blood stream. The President finally admitted that the word 'valid' was an unfortunate one. From the discussion in general it appeared that Mr Lewis would have to turn his argument into a rigorous analytic one, if his notion of 'validity' as the effect of causes were to stand the test of all the questions put to him.

B

I admit that *valid* was a bad word for what I meant; *veridical* (or *verific* or *veriferous*) would have been better. I also admit that the cause and effect relation between events and the ground and consequent relation between propositions are distinct. Since English uses the word *because* of both, let us here use *Because* CE for the cause and effect relation ('This doll always falls on its feet *because* CE its feet are weighted') and *Because* GC for the ground and consequent relation ('A equals C *because* GC they both equal B'). But the sharper this distinction becomes the more my difficulty increases. If an argument is to be verific the conclusion must be related to the premises as consequent to ground, i.e. the conclusion is there *because* GC certain other propositions are true. On the other hand, our thinking the conclusion is an event and must be related to previous events as effect to cause, i.e. this act of thinking must occur *because* CE previous events have occurred. It would seem, therefore, that we never think the conclusion *because* GC it is the consequent of its grounds but only *because* CE certain previous events have happened. If so, it does not seem that the GC sequence makes us more likely to think the true conclusion than not. And this is very much what I meant by the difficulty in Naturalism.

17

SOME THOUGHTS

AT FIRST SIGHT NOTHING SEEMS MORE OBVIOUS THAN THAT religious persons should care for the sick; no Christian building, except perhaps a church, is more self-explanatory than a Christian hospital. Yet on further consideration the thing is really connected with the undying paradox, the blessedly two-edged character, of Christianity. And if any of us were now encountering Christianity for the first time he would be vividly aware of this paradox.

Let us suppose that such a person began by observing those Christian activities which are, in a sense, directed towards this present world. He would find that this religion had, as a mere matter of historical fact, been the agent which preserved such secular civilization as survived the fall of the Roman Empire; that to it Europe owes the salvation, in those perilous ages, of civilized agriculture, architecture, laws, and literacy itself. He would find that this same religion has always been healing the sick and caring for the poor; that it has, more than any other, blessed marriage; and that arts and philosophy tend to flourish in its neighbourhood. In a word, it is always either doing, or at least repenting with shame for not having done, all the things which secular humanitarianism enjoins. If our enquirer stopped at this point he would have no difficulty in classifying Christianity — giving it its place on a map of the 'great religions.' Obviously (he would say), this is one of the world-affirming religions like Confucianism or the agricultural religions of the great Mesopotamian city states.

But how if our enquirer began (as he well might) with quite a different series of Christian phenomena? He might notice that the central image in all Christian art was that of a Man slowly dying by torture; that the instrument of His torture was the world-wide symbol of the Faith; that martyrdom was almost a specifically Christian action; that our calendar was as full of fasts as of feasts; that we meditated constantly on the mortality not only of ourselves but of the whole universe; that we were bidden to entrust all our treasure to another world; and that even a certain disdain for the whole natural order (*contemptus mundi*) had sometimes been reckoned a Christian virtue. And here, once again, if he knew no more, the enquirer would find Christianity quite easy to classify; but this time he would classify it as one of the world-denying religions. It would be pigeon-holed along with Buddhism.

Either conclusion would be justified if a man had only the one or the other half of the evidence before him. It is when he puts both halves together and sees that Christianity cuts right across the classification he was attempting to make — it is then that he first knows what he is up against, and I think he will be bewildered.

Probably most of those who read this page have been Christians all their lives. If so, they may find it hard to sympathise with the bewilderment I refer to. To Christians the explanation of this two-edged character in their Faith seems obvious. They live in a graded or hierarchical universe where there is a place for everything and everything should be kept in its right place. The Supernatural is higher than the Natural, but each has its place; just as a man is higher than a dog, but a dog has its place. It is, therefore, to us not at all surprising that healing for the sick and provision for the poor should be less important than (when they are, as sometimes happens, alternative to) the salvation of souls; and yet very important. Because God created the Natural — invented it out of His love and artistry — it demands our reverence; because it is only a creature and not He, it is, from another point of view, of little account. And still more, because Nature, and especially human nature, is fallen it must be corrected and the evil within it must be mortified. But its essence is good; correction is something quite different from Manichaean repudiation or Stoic superiority. Hence, in all true Christian asceticism, that respect for the thing rejected which, I think, we never find in pagan asceticism. Marriage is good, though not for me; wine is good, though I must not drink it; feasts are good, though today we fast.

This attitude will, I think, be found to depend logically on the doctrines of the Creation and the Fall. Some hazy adumbrations of a doctrine of the Fall can be found in Paganism; but it is quite astonishing how rarely outside Christianity we find — I am not sure that we ever find — a real doctrine of Creation. In Polytheism the gods are usually the product of a universe already in existence — Keats' *Hyperion,* in spirit, if not in detail, is true enough as a picture of pagan theogony. In Pantheism the universe is never something that God made. It is an emanation, something that oozes out of Him, or an appearance, something He looks like to us but really is not, or even an attack of incurable schizophrenia from which He is unaccountably suffering. Polytheism is always, in the long run, nature-worship; Pantheism always, in the long run, hostility to nature. None of these beliefs really leaves you free *both* to enjoy your breakfast *and* to mortify your inordinate appetites — much less to mortify appetites recognised as innocent at present lest they should become inordinate.

And none of them leaves anyone free to do what is being done in the Lourdes Hospital every day: to fight against death as earnestly, skilfully, and calmly as if you were a secular humanitarian while knowing all the time that death is, both for better and worse, something that the secular humanitarian has never dreamed of. The world, knowing how all our real investments are beyond the grave, might expect us to be less concerned than other people who go in for what is called Higher Thought and tell us that 'death doesn't matter'; but we 'are not high minded',[1] and we follow One who stood and wept at the grave of Lazarus — not surely, because He was grieved that Mary and Martha wept, and sorrowed for their lack of faith (though some thus interpret) but because death, the punishment of sin, is even more horrible in His eyes than in ours. The nature which He had created as God,

[1] Psalm cxxxi. 1.

the nature which He had assumed as Man, lay there before Him in its ignominy; a foul smell, food for worms. Though He was to revive it a moment later, He wept at the shame; if I may here quote a writer of my own communion, 'I am not so much afraid of death as ashamed of it.'[2] And that brings us again to the paradox. Of all men, we hope most of death; yet nothing will reconcile us to — well, its *unnaturalness*. We know that we were not made for it; we know how it crept into our destiny as an intruder; and we know Who has defeated it. Because Our Lord is risen we know that on one level it is an enemy already disarmed; but because we know that the natural level also is God's creation we cannot cease to fight against the death which mars it, as against all those other blemishes upon it, against pain and poverty, barbarism and ignorance. Because we love something else more than this world we love even this world better than those who know no other.

[2] The reference is to Sir Thomas Browne's *Religio Medici,* First Part, Section 40, where he says 'I am not so much afraid of death, as ashamed thereof.'

18

'THE TROUBLE WITH "X"...'

I SUPPOSE I MAY ASSUME THAT SEVEN OUT OF TEN OF THOSE who read these lines are in some kind of difficulty about some other human being. Either at work or at home, either the people who employ you or those whom you employ, either those who share your house or those whose house you share, either your in-laws or parents or children, your wife or your husband, are making life harder for you than it need be even in these days. It is to be hoped that we do not often mention these difficulties (especially the domestic ones) to outsiders. But sometimes we do. An outside friend asks us why we are looking so glum, and the truth comes out.

On such occasions the outside friend usually says, 'But why don't you tell them? Why don't you go to your wife (or husband, or father, or daughter, or boss, or landlady, or lodger) and have it all out? People are usually reasonable. All you've got to do is to make them see things in the right light. Explain it to them in a reasonable, quiet, friendly way.' And we, whatever we say outwardly, think sadly to ourselves, 'He doesn't know "X."' We do. We know how utterly hopeless it is to make 'X' see reason. Either we've tried it over and over again — tried it till we are sick of trying it — or else we've never tried it because we saw from the beginning how useless it would be. We know that if we attempt to 'have it all out with "X"' there will either be a 'scene,' or else 'X' will stare at us in blank amazement and say 'I don't know what on earth you're talking about'; or else (which is perhaps worst of all) 'X' will quite agree with us and promise

151

to turn over a new leaf and put everything on a new footing — and then, twenty-four hours later, will be exactly the same as 'X' has always been.

You know, in fact, that any attempt to talk things over with 'X' will shipwreck on the old, fatal flaw in 'X's' character. And you see, looking back, how all the plans you have ever made always have shipwrecked on that fatal flaw — on 'X's' incurable jealousy, or laziness, or touchiness, or muddle-headedness, or bossiness, or ill temper, or changeableness. Up to a certain age you have perhaps had the illusion that some external stroke of good fortune — an improvement in health, a rise of salary, the end of the war — would solve your difficulty. But you know better now. The war is over, and you realise that even if the other things happened, 'X' would still be 'X', and you would still be up against the same old problem. Even if you became a millionaire, your husband would still be a bully, or your wife would still nag or your son would still drink, or you'd still have to have your mother-in-law to live with you.

It is a great step forward to realise that this is so; to face the fact that even if all external things went right, real happiness would still depend on the character of the people you have to live with — and that you can't alter their characters. And now comes the point. When you have seen this you have, for the first time, had a glimpse of what it must be like for God. For, of course, this is (in one way) just what God Himself is up against. He has provided a rich, beautiful world for people to live in. He has given them intelligence to show them how it can be used, and conscience to show them how it ought to be used. He has contrived that the things they need for their biological life (food, drink, rest, sleep, exercise) should be positively delightful to them. And, having done all this, He then sees all His plans spoiled — just as our little plans are spoiled — by the crookedness of the people themselves. All the things He has given them to be happy with they turn into occasions for quarrelling and jealousy, and excess and hoarding, and tomfoolery.

You may say it is very different for God because He could, if He pleased, alter people's characters, and we can't. But this difference doesn't go quite as deep as we may at first think. God has made it a rule for Himself that He won't alter people's character by force. He can and will alter them — but only if the people will let Him. In that way He has really and truly limited His power. Sometimes we wonder why He has done so, or even wish that He hadn't. But apparently He thinks it worth doing. He would rather have a world of free beings, with all its risks, than a world of people who did right like machines because they couldn't do anything else. The more we succeed in imagining what a world of perfect automatic beings would be like, the more, I think, we shall see His wisdom.

I said that when we see how all our plans shipwreck on the characters of the people we have to deal with, we are 'in *one* way' seeing what it must be like for God. But only in one way. There are two respects in which God's view must be very different from ours. In the first place, He sees (like you) how all the people in your home or your job are in various degrees awkward or difficult; but when He looks into that home or factory or office He sees one more person of the same kind — the one you never do see. I mean, of course, yourself. That is the next great step in wisdom — to realise that you also are just that sort of person. You also have a fatal flaw in your character. All the hopes and plans of others have again and again shipwrecked on your character just as your hopes and plans have shipwrecked on theirs.

It is no good passing this over with some vague, general admission such as 'Of course, I know I have my faults.' It is important to realise that there is some really fatal flaw in you: something which gives the others just that same feeling of *despair* which their flaws give you. And it is almost certainly something you don't know about — like what the advertisements call 'halitosis', which everyone notices except the person who has it. But why, you ask, don't the others tell me? Believe me, they have tried to tell you over and over again, and you just couldn't 'take it'. Perhaps a good deal of what you call their 'nagging' or 'bad temper' or 'queerness' are just their attempts to make you see the truth. And even the faults you do know you don't know fully. You say, 'I admit I lost my temper last night'; but the others know that you're always doing it, that you are a bad-tempered person. You say, 'I admit I drank too much last Saturday'; but every one else knows that you are an habitual drunkard.

153

That is one way in which God's view must differ from mine. He sees all the characters: I see all except my own. But the second difference is this. He loves the people in spite of their faults. He goes on loving. He does not let go. Don't say, 'It's all very well for Him; He hasn't got to live with them.' He has. He is inside them as well as outside them. He is *with* them far more intimately and closely and incessantly than we can ever be. Every vile thought within their minds (and ours), every moment of spite, envy, arrogance, greed and self-conceit comes right up against His patient and longing love, and grieves His spirit more than it grieves ours.

The more we can imitate God in both these respects, the more progress we shall make. We must love 'X' more; and we must learn to see ourselves as a person of exactly the same kind. Some people say it is morbid to be always thinking of one's own faults. That would be all very well if most of us could stop thinking of our own without soon beginning to think about those of other people. For unfortunately we *enjoy* thinking about other people's faults: and in the proper sense of the word 'morbid', that is the most morbid pleasure in the world.

We don't like rationing which is imposed upon us, but I suggest one form of rationing which we ought to impose on ourselves. Abstain from all thinking about other people's faults, unless your duties as a teacher or parent make it necessary to think about them. Whenever the thoughts come unnecessarily into one's mind, why not simply shove them away? And think of one's own faults instead? For there, with God's help, one *can* do something. Of all the awkward people in your house or job there is only one whom you can improve very much. That is the practical end at which to begin. And really, we'd better. The job has to be tackled some day: and every day we put it off will make it harder to begin.

What, after all, is the alternative? You see clearly enough that nothing, not even God with all His power, can make 'X' really happy as long as 'X' remains envious, self-centred, and spiteful. Be sure there is something inside you which, unless it is altered, will put it out of God's power to prevent your being eternally miserable. While that something remains there can be no Heaven for you, just as there can be no sweet smells for a man with a cold in the nose, and no music

154

for a man who is deaf. It's not a question of God 'sending' us to Hell. In each of us there is something growing up which will of itself *be Hell* unless it is nipped in the bud. The matter is serious: let us put ourselves in His hands at once — this very day, this hour.

19

WHAT ARE WE TO MAKE OF JESUS CHRIST?

WHAT ARE WE TO MAKE OF JESUS CHRIST? THIS IS A question which has, in a sense, a frantically comic side. For the real question is not what are we to make of Christ, but what is He to make of us? The picture of a fly sitting deciding what it is going to make of an elephant has comic elements about it. But perhaps the questioner meant what are we to make of Him in the sense of 'How are we to solve the historical problem set us by the recorded sayings and acts of this Man?' This problem is to reconcile two things. On the one hand you have got the almost generally admitted depth and sanity of His moral teaching, which is not very seriously questioned, even by those who are opposed to Christianity. In fact, I find when I am arguing with very anti-God people that they rather make a point of saying, 'I am entirely in favour of the moral teaching of Christianity' — and there seems to be a general agreement that in the teaching of this Man and of His immediate followers, moral truth is exhibited at its purest and best. It is not sloppy idealism, it is full of wisdom and shrewdness. The whole thing is realistic, fresh to the highest degree, the product of a sane mind. That is one phenomenon.

The other phenomenon is the quite appalling nature of this Man's theological remarks. You all know what I mean, and I want rather to stress the point that the appalling claim which this Man seems to be making is not merely made at one moment of His career. There is, of course, the one moment which led to His execution. The moment at which the High Priest said to Him, 'Who are you?' 'I am the Anointed, the Son of the uncreated God, and you shall see Me appearing at the end of all history as the judge of the Universe.' But that claim, in fact, does not rest on this one dramatic moment. When you look into His conversation you will find this sort of claim running through the whole thing. For instance, He went about saying to people, 'I forgive your sins.' Now it is quite natural for a man to forgive something you do to *him*. Thus if somebody cheats *me* out of £5 it is quite possible and reasonable for me to say, 'Well, I forgive him, we will say no more about it.' What on earth would you say if somebody had done *you* out of £5 and *I* said, 'That is all right, I forgive him'? Then there is a curious thing which seems to slip out almost by accident. On one occasion this Man is sitting looking down on Jerusalem from the hill above it and suddenly in comes an extraordinary remark — 'I keep on sending you prophets and wise men.' Nobody comments on it. And yet, quite suddenly, almost incidentally, He is claiming to be the power that all through the centuries is sending wise men and leaders into the world. Here is another curious remark: in almost every religion there are unpleasant observances like fasting. This Man suddenly remarks one day, 'No one need fast while I am here.' Who is this Man who remarks that His mere presence suspends all normal rules? Who is the person who can suddenly tell the School they can have a half-holiday? Sometimes the statements put forward the assumption that He, the Speaker, is completely without sin or fault. This is always the attitude. 'You, to whom I am talking, are all sinners,' and He never remotely suggests that this same reproach can be brought against Him. He says again, 'I am begotten of the One God, before Abraham was, I am,' and remember what the words 'I am' were in Hebrew. They were the name of God, which must not be spoken by any human being, the name which it was death to utter.

Well, that is the other side. On the one side clear, definite moral teaching. On the other, claims which, if not true, are those of a megalomaniac, compared with whom Hitler was the most sane and humble of men. There is no half-way house and there is no parallel in other religions. If you had gone to Buddha and asked him 'Are you the son of Bramah?' he would have said, 'My son, you are still in the vale of illusion.' If you had gone to Socrates and asked, 'Are you Zeus?' he would have laughed at you. If you had gone to Mohammed and asked, 'Are you Allah?' he would first have rent his clothes and then cut your head off. If you had asked Confucius, 'Are you Heaven?', I think he would have probably replied, 'Remarks which are not in accordance with nature are in bad taste.' The idea of a great moral teacher saying what Christ said is out of the question. In my opinion, the only person who can say that sort of thing is either God or a complete lunatic suffering from that form of delusion which undermines the whole mind of man. If you think you are a poached egg, when you are looking for a piece of toast to suit you, you may be sane, but if you think you are God, there is no chance for you. We may note in passing that He was never regarded as a mere moral teacher. He did not produce that effect on any of the people who actually met Him. He produced mainly three effects — Hatred — Terror — Adoration. There was no trace of people expressing mild approval.

What are we to do about reconciling the two contradictory phenomena? One attempt consists in saying that the Man did not really say these things, but that His followers exaggerated the story, and so the legend grew up that He had said them. This is difficult because His followers were all Jews; that is, they belonged to that Nation which of all others was most convinced that there was only one God — that there could not possibly be another. It is very odd that this horrible invention about a religious leader should grow up among the one people in the whole earth least likely to make such a mistake. On the contrary we get the impression that none of His immediate followers or even of the New Testament writers embraced the doctrine at all easily.

Another point is that on that view you would have to regard the accounts of the Man as being *legends*. Now, as a literary historian, I am perfectly convinced that whatever else the Gospels are they are not legends. I have read a great deal of legend and I am quite clear that they are not the same sort of thing. They are not artistic enough to be legends. From an imaginative point of view they are clumsy, they don't work up to things properly. Most of the life of Jesus

158

is totally unknown to us, as is the life of anyone else who lived at that time, and no people building up a legend would allow that to be so. Apart from bits of the Platonic dialogues, there are no conversations that I know of in ancient literature like the Fourth Gospel. There is nothing, even in modern literature, until about a hundred years ago when the realistic novel came into existence. In the story of the woman taken in adultery we are told Christ bent down and scribbled in the dust with His finger. Nothing comes of this. No one has ever based any doctrine on it. And the art of *inventing* little irrelevant details to make an imaginary scene more convincing is a purely modern art. Surely the only explanation of this passage is that the thing really happened? The author put it in simply because he had *seen* it.

Then we come to the strangest story of all, the story of the Resurrection. It is very necessary to get the story clear. I heard a man say, 'The importance of the Resurrection is that it gives evidence of survival, evidence that the human personality survives death.' On that view what happened to Christ would be what had always happened to all men, the difference being that in Christ's case we were privileged to see it happening. This is certainly not what the earliest Christian writers thought. Something perfectly new in the history of the Universe had happened. Christ had defeated death. The door which had always been locked had for the very first time been forced open. This is something quite distinct from mere ghost-survival. I don't mean that they disbelieved in ghost-survival. On the contrary, they believed in it so firmly that, on more than one occasion, Christ had had to assure them that He was *not* a ghost. The point is that while believing in survival they yet regarded the Resurrection as something totally different and new. The Resurrection narratives are not a picture of survival after death; they record how a totally new mode of being has arisen in the Universe. Something new had appeared in the Universe: as new as the first coming of organic life. This Man, after death, does not get divided into 'ghost' and 'corpse'. A new mode of being has arisen. That is the story. What are we going to make of it?

The question is, I suppose, whether any hypothesis covers the facts so well as the Christian hypothesis. That hypothesis is that God has come down into the created universe, down

159

to manhood — and come up again, pulling it up with Him. The alternative hypothesis is not legend, nor exaggeration, nor the apparitions of a ghost. It is either lunacy or lies. Unless one can take the second alternative (and I can't) one turns to the Christian theory.

'What are we to make of Christ?' There is no question of what we can make of Him, it is entirely a question of what He intends to make of us. You must accept or reject the story.

The things He says are very different from what any other teacher has said. Others say, 'This is the truth about the Universe. This is the way you ought to go,' but He says, '*I* am the Truth, and the Way, and the Life.' He says, 'No man can reach absolute reality, except through Me. Try to retain your own life and you will be inevitably ruined. Give yourself away and you will be saved.' He says, 'If you are ashamed of Me, if, when you hear this call, you turn the other way, I also will look the other way when I come again as God without disguise. If anything whatever is keeping you from God and from Me, whatever it is, throw it away. If it is your eye, pull it out. If it is your hand, cut it off. If you put yourself first you will be last. Come to Me everyone who is carrying a heavy load, I will set that right. Your sins, all of them, are wiped out, I can do that. I am Re-birth, I am Life. Eat Me, drink Me, I am your Food. And finally, do not be afraid, I have overcome the whole Universe.' That is the issue.

20

THE PAINS OF ANIMALS

A PROBLEM IN THEOLOGY[1]

The Inquiry
by
C. E. M. Joad

FOR MANY YEARS THE PROBLEM OF PAIN AND EVIL SEEMED to me to offer an insuperable objection to Christianity. Either God could abolish them but did not, in which case, since He deliberately tolerated the presence in the universe of a state of affairs which was bad, I did not see how He could be good; or He wanted to abolish them but could not, in which case I did not see how He could be all-powerful. The dilemma is as old as St Augustine, and nobody pretends that there is an easy way of escape.

Moreover, all the attempts to explain pain away, or to mitigate its stark ferocity, or to present it as other than a very great evil, perhaps the greatest of evils, are palpable failures. They are testimonies to the kindness of men's hearts or perhaps to the queasiness of their consciences, rather than to the sharpness of their wits.

[1] In his book *The Problem of Pain* one of the questions Lewis addressed himself to was: how to account for the occurrence of pain in a universe which is the creation of an all-good God, and in creatures who are not morally sinful. His chapter on 'Animal Pain' provoked a counter-inquiry from the late C. E. M. Joad, who was Head of the Department of Philosophy at the University of London. The result was this controversy.

And yet, granting pain to be an evil, perhaps the greatest of evils, I have come to accept the Christian view of pain as not incompatible with the Christian concept of the Creator and of the world that He has made. That view I take to be briefly as follows: It was of no interest to God to create a species consisting of virtuous automata, for the 'virtue' of automata who can do no other than they do is a courtesy title only; it is analogous to the 'virtue' of the stone that rolls downhill or of the water that freezes at 32°. To what end, it may be asked, should God create such creatures? That He might be praised by them? But automatic praise is a mere succession of noises. That He might love them? But they are essentially unlovable; you cannot love puppets. And so God gave man free will that he might increase in virtue by his own efforts and become, as a free moral being, a worthy object of God's love. Freedom entails freedom to go wrong: man did, in fact, go wrong, misusing God's gift and doing evil. Pain is a by-product of evil; and so pain came into the world as a result of man's misuse of God's gift of free will.

So much I can understand; so much, indeed, I accept. It is plausible; it is rational; it hangs together.

But now I come to a difficulty, to which I see no solution; indeed, it is in the hope of learning of one that this article is written. This is the difficulty of animal pain, and, more particularly, of the pain of the animal world before man appeared upon the cosmic scene. What account do theologians give of it? The most elaborate and careful account known to me is that of C. S. Lewis.

He begins by making a distinction between sentience and consciousness. When we have the sensations *a, b,* and *c,* the fact that we have them and the fact that we know that we have them imply that there is something which stands sufficiently outside them to notice that they occur and that they succeed one another. This is consciousness, the consciousness to which the sensations happen. In other words, the experience of succession, the succession of sensations, demands a self or soul which is other than the sensations which it experiences. (Mr Lewis invokes the helpful metaphor of the bed of a river along which the stream of sensations flows.) Consciousness, therefore, implies a continuing *ego* which recognizes the succession of sensations; sentience is their mere succession. Now animals have sentience but not consciousness. Mr Lewis illustrates as follows:

> This would mean that if you give such a creature two blows with a whip, there are, indeed, two pains: but there is no co-ordinating self which can recognise that 'I have had two pains.' Even in the single pain there is no self to say 'I am in pain' — for if it could distinguish itself from the sensation — the bed from the stream — sufficiently to say 'I am in pain', it would also be able to connect the two sensations as *its* experience.[2]

(*a*) I take Mr Lewis's point — or, rather, I take it without perceiving its relevance. The question is how to account for the occurrence of pain (i) in a universe which is the creation of an all-good God; (ii) in creatures who are not morally sinful. To be told that the creatures are not really creatures, since they are not conscious in the sense of consciousness defined, does not really help matters. If it be true, as Mr Lewis says, that the right way to put the matter is not 'This animal is feeling pain' but 'Pain is taking place in this animal',[3] pain is nevertheless taking place. Pain is felt even if there is no continuing *ego* to feel it and to relate it to past and to future pains. Now it is the fact that pain is felt, no matter who or what feels it, or whether any continuing consciousness feels it, in a universe planned by a good God, that demands explanation.

(*b*) Secondly, the theory of sentience as mere succession of sensations presupposes that there is no continuing consciousness. No continuing consciousness presupposes no memory. It seems to me to be nonsense to say that animals do not remember. The dog who cringes at the sight of the whip by which he has been constantly beaten *behaves* as if he remembers, and behaviour is all that we have to go by. In general, we all act upon the assumption that the horse, the cat, and the dog with which we are acquainted remember very well, remember sometimes better than we do. Now I do not see how it is possible to explain the fact of memory without a continuing consciousness.

Mr Lewis recognizes this and concedes that the higher ani-

[2] *The Problem of Pain* (London, 1940), ch. ix, p. 120.
[3] *Ibid.*, pp. 120-21.

mals — apes, elephants, dogs, cats, and so on — have a self which connects experiences; have, in fact, what he calls a soul.[4] But this assumption presents us with a new set of difficulties.

(*a*) If animals have souls, what is to be done about their immortality? The question, it will be remembered, is elaborately debated in Heaven at the beginning of Anatole France's *Penguin Island* after the short-sighted St Mael has baptized the penguins, but no satisfactory solution is offered.

(*b*) Mr Lewis suggests that the higher domestic animals achieve immortality as members of a corporate society of which the head is man. It is, apparently, 'The-goodman-and-the-goodwife-ruling-their-children-and-their-beasts-in-the-good-homestead'[5] who survive. 'If you ask', he writes, 'concerning an animal thus raised as a member of the whole Body of the homestead, where its personal identity resides, I answer, "Where its identity always did reside even in the earthly life — in its relation to the Body and, specially, to the master who is the head of that Body." In other words, the man will know his dog: the dog will know its master and, in knowing him, will *be* itself.'[6]

Whether this is good theology, I do not know, but to our present inquiry it raises two difficulties.

(i) It does not cover the case of the higher animals who do not know man — for example, apes and elephants — but who are yet considered by Mr Lewis to have souls.

(ii) If one animal may attain good immortal selfhood in and through a good man, he may attain bad immortal selfhood in and through a bad man. One thinks of the overnourished lapdogs of idle overnourished women. It is a little hard that when, through no fault of their own, animals fall to selfish, self-indulgent, or cruel masters, they should through eternity form part of selfish, self-indulgent, or cruel superpersonal wholes and perhaps be punished for their participation in them.

(*c*) If the animals have souls and, presumably, freedom, the same sort of explanation must be adopted for pain in animals as is offered for pain in men. Pain, in other words, is one of the evils consequent upon sin. The higher animals,

4 *Ibid.*, p. 121.
5 *Ibid.*, p. 127.
6 *Ibid.*, p. 128.

then, are corrupt. The question arises, who corrupted them? There seem to be two possible answers: (1) The Devil; (2) Man.

(1) Mr Lewis considers this answer. The animals, he says, may originally all have been herbivorous. They became carnivorous — that is to say, they began to prey upon, to tear, and to eat one another because 'some mighty created power had already been at work for ill on the material universe, or the solar system, or, at least, the planet Earth, before ever man came on the scene . . . If there is such a power . . . it may well have corrupted the animal creation before man appeared.'[7]

I have three comments to make: —

(i) I find the supposition of Satan tempting monkeys frankly incredible. This, I am well aware, is not a logical objection. It is one's imagination — or is it perhaps one's common sense? — that revolts against it.

(ii) Although most animals fall victims to the redness of Nature's 'tooth and claw', many do not. The sheep falls down the ravine, breaks its leg, and starves; hundreds of thousands of migrating birds die every year of hunger; creatures are struck and not killed by lightning, and their seared bodies take long to die. Are these pains due to corruption?

(iii) The case of animals without souls cannot, on Mr Lewis's own showing, be brought under the 'moral corruption' explanation. Yet consider just one instance of nature's arrangements. The wasps, Ichneumonidae, sting their caterpillar prey in such a way as to paralyze its nerve centres. They then lay their eggs on the helpless caterpillar. When the grubs hatch from the eggs, they immediately proceed to feed upon the living but helpless flesh of their incubators, the paralyzed but still sentient caterpillars.

It is hard to suppose that the caterpillar feels no pain when slowly consumed; harder still to ascribe the pain to moral corruption; hardest of all to conceive how such an arrangement could have been planned by an all-good and all-wise Creator.

(2) The hypothesis that the animals were corrupted by man does not account for animal pain during the hundreds

[7] *Ibid.,* pp. 122-23.

of million years (probably about 900 million) when the earth contained living creatures but did not contain man.

In sum, either animals have souls or they have no souls. If they have none, pain is felt for which there can be no moral responsibility, and for which no misuse of God's gift of moral freedom can be invoked as an excuse. If they have souls, we can give no plausible account (a) of their immortality — how draw the line between animals with souls and men with souls? — or (b) of their moral corruption, which would enable Christian apologists to place them in respect of their pain under the same heading of explanation as that which is proposed and which I am prepared to accept for man?

It may well be that there is an answer to this problem. I would be grateful to anyone who would tell me what it is.

THE REPLY
by
C. S. Lewis

Though there is pleasure as well as danger in encountering so sincere and economical a disputant as Dr Joad, I do so with no little reluctance. Dr Joad writes not merely as a controversialist who demands, but as an inquirer who really desires, an answer. I come into the matter at all only because my answers have already failed to satisfy him. And it is embarrassing to me, and possibly depressing to him, that he should, in a manner, be sent back to the same shop which has once failed to supply the goods. If it were wholly a question of defending the original goods, I think I would let it alone. But it is not exactly that. I think he has perhaps slightly misunderstood what I was offering for sale.

Dr Joad is concerned with the ninth chapter of my *Problem of Pain*. And the first point I want to make is that no one would gather from his article how confessedly speculative that chapter was. This was acknowledged in my preface and repeatedly emphasized in the chapter itself. This, of course, can bring no ease to Dr Joad's difficulties; unsatisfactory answers do not become satisfactory by being tentative. I mention the character of the chapter to underline the fact that it

166

stands on a rather different level from those which preceded it. And that difference suggests the place which my 'guesswork' about Beasts (so I called it at the time and call it still) had in my own thought, and which I would like this whole question to have in Dr Joad's thought too.

The first eight chapters of my book attempted to meet the *prima facie* case against theism based on human pain. They were the fruit of a slow change of mind not at all unlike that which Dr Joad himself has undergone and to which, when it had been completed, he at once bore honourable and (I expect) costly witness. The process of his thought differed at many points (very likely for the better) from the process of mine. But we came out, more or less, at the same place. The position of which he says in his article 'So much I understand; so much, indeed, I accept' is very close to that which I reached in the first eight chapters of my *Problem*.

So far, so good. Having 'got over' the problem of human pain, Dr Joad and I both find ourselves faced with the problem of animal pain. We do not at once part company even then. We both (if I read him correctly) turn with distaste from 'the easy speeches that comfort cruel men',[8] from theologians who do not seem to see that there is a real problem, who are content to say that animals are, after all, only animals. To us, pain without guilt or moral fruit, however low and contemptible the sufferer may be, is a very serious matter.

I now ask Dr Joad to observe rather closely what I do at this point, for I doubt if it is exactly what he thinks. I do not advance a doctrine of animal sentience as proved and thence conclude 'Therefore beasts are not sacrificed without recompense, and therefore God is just.' If he will look carefully at my ninth chapter he will see that it can be divided into two very unequal parts: Part One consisting of the first paragraph, and Part Two of all the rest. They might be summarized as follows: —

Part One. The data which God has given us enable us in some degree to understand human pain. We lack such data about beasts. We know neither what they are nor why they are. All that we can say for certain is that if God is good (and I think we have grounds for saying that He is) then the

[8] G. K. Chesterton, 'A Hymn', line 11. The first line begins 'O God of earth and altar'.

167

appearance of divine cruelty in the animal world must be a false appearance. What the reality behind the false appearance may be we can only guess.

Part Two. And here are some of my own guesses.

Now it matters far more whether Dr Joad agrees with Part One than whether he approves any of the speculations in Part Two. But I will first deal, so far as I can, with his critique of the speculations.

(1) Conceding *(positionis causa)*[9] my distinction between sentience and consciousness, Dr Joad thinks it irrelevant. 'Pain is felt', he writes, 'even if there is no continuing *ego* to feel it and to relate it to past and future pain,' and 'it is the fact that pain is felt, no matter who or what feels it . . . that demands explanation.' I agree that in one sense it does not (for the present purpose) matter 'who or what' feels it. That is, it does not matter how humble, or helpless, or small, or how removed from our spontaneous sympathies, the sufferer is. But it surely does matter how far the sufferer is capable of what we can recognize as misery, how far the genuinely pitiable is consistent with its mode of existence. It will hardly be denied that the more coherently conscious the subject is, the more pity and indignation its pains deserve. And this seems to me to imply that the less coherently conscious, the less they deserve. I still think it possible for there to be a pain so instantaneous (through the absence of all perception of succession) that its 'unvalue', if I may coin the word, is indistinguishable from zero. A correspondent has instanced shooting pains in our own experience on those occasions when they are unaccompanied by fear. They may be intense: but they are gone as we recognize their intensity. In my own case I do not find anything in them which demands pity; they are, rather, comical. One tends to laugh. A series of such pains is, no doubt, terrible; but then the contention is that the series could not exist for sentience without consciousness.

(2) I do not think that behaviour 'as if from memory' proves memory in the conscious sense. A non-human observer might suppose that if we blink our eyes at the approach of an object we are 'remembering' pains received on previous occasions. But no memories, in the full sense, are involved. (It is, of course, true that the behaviour of the organism is

[9] 'for the sake of argument'.

modified by past experiences, and we may thus by metonymy say that the nerves remember what the mind forgets; but that is not what Dr Joad and I are talking of.) If we are to suppose memory in all cases where behaviour adapts itself to a probable recurrence of past events, shall we not have to assume in some insects an inherited memory of their parents' breeding habits? And are we prepared to believe this?

(3) Of course my suggested theory of the tame animals' resurrection 'in' its human (and therefore, indirectly, divine) context does not cover wild animals or ill-treated tame ones. I had made the point myself, and added 'it is intended only as an illustration . . . of the general principles to be observed in framing a theory of animal resurrection.'[10] I went on to make an alternative suggestion, observing, I hope, the same principles. My chief purpose at this stage was at once to liberate imagination and to confirm a due agnosticism about the meaning and destiny of brutes. I had begun by saying that if our previous assertion of divine goodness was sound, we might be sure that *in some way or other* 'all would be well, and all manner of thing would be well'.[11] I wanted to reinforce this by indicating how little we knew and, therefore, how many things one might keep in mind as possibilities.

(4) If Dr Joad thinks I pictured Satan 'tempting monkeys', I am myself to blame for using the word 'encouraged'. I apologize for the ambiguity. In fact, I had not supposed that 'temptation' (that is, solicitation of the will) was the only mode in which the Devil could corrupt or impair. It is probably not the only mode in which he can impair even human beings; when Our Lord spoke of the deformed woman as one 'bound by Satan',[12] I presume He did not mean that she had been tempted into deformity. Moral corruption is not the only kind of corruption. But the word *corruption* was perhaps ill-chosen and invited misunderstanding. *Distortion* would have been safer.

(5) My correspondent writes 'That even the severest injuries in most invertebrate animals are almost if not quite painless in the view of most biologists. Loeb collected much

10 *The Problem of Pain*, p. 128.
11 Lady Julian of Norwich, *Sixteen Revelations of Divine Love*, ch. xxvii.
12 Luke xiii. 16.

169

evidence to show that animals without cerebral hemispheres were indistinguishable from plants in every psychological respect. The instance readily occurs of the caterpillars which serenely go on eating though their interiors are being devoured by the larvae of some ichneumon fly. The Vivisection Act does not apply to invertebrates; which indicates the views of those who framed it.'

(6) Though Dr Joad does not raise the point, I cannot forbear adding some most interesting suggestions about animal fear from the same correspondent. He points out that human fear contains two elements: (a) the physical sensations, due to the secretions, etc.; (b) the mental images of what will happen if one loses hold, or if the bomb falls here, or if the train leaves the rails. Now (a), in itself, is so far from being an unmixed grief, that when we can get it without (b), or with unbelieved (b), or even with subdued (b), vast numbers of people like it: hence switchbacks, water-shoots, fast motoring, mountain climbing.

But all this is nothing to a reader who does not accept Part One in my ninth chapter. No man in his senses is going to start building up a theodicy with speculations about the minds of beasts as his foundation. Such speculations are in place only, as I said, to open the imagination to possibilities and to deepen and confirm our inevitable agnosticism about the reality, and only after the ways of God *to Man* have ceased to seem unjustifiable. We do not know the answer: these speculations were guesses at what it might possibly be. What really matters is the argument that there must be an answer: the argument that if, in our own lives, where alone (if at all) we know Him, we come to recognize the *pulchritudo tam antiqua et tam nova*,[13] then, in other realms where we cannot know Him *(connaître)*, though we may know *(savoir)* some few things about Him — then, despite appearances to the contrary, He cannot be a power of darkness. For there were appearances to the contrary in our own realm too; yet, for Dr Joad as for me, they have somehow been got over.

I know that there are moments when the incessant continuity and desperate helplessness of what at least seems to be animal suffering make every argument for theism sound hol-

[13] St Augustine, *Confessions,* bk. X, ch. 27. 'Beauty so ancient and so new'.

low, and when (in particular) the insect world appears to be Hell itself visibly in operation around us. Then the old indignation, the old pity arises. But how strangely ambivalent this experience is: I need not expound the ambivalence at much length, for I think I have done so elsewhere and I am sure that Dr Joad had long discerned it for himself. If I regard this pity and indignation simply as subjective experiences of my own with no validity beyond their strength at the moment (which next moment will change), I can hardly use them as standards whereby to arraign the creation. On the contrary, they become strong as arguments against God just in so far as I take them to be transcendent illumination to which creation must conform or be condemned. They are arguments against God only if they are themselves the voice of God. The more Shelleyan, the more Promethean my revolt, the more surely it claims a divine sanction. That the mere contingent Joad or Lewis, born in an era of secure and liberal civilization and imbibing from it certain humanitarian sentiments, should happen to be offended by suffering — what is that to the purpose? How will one base an argument for or against God on such an historical accident!

No. Not in so far as we feel these things, but in so far as we claim to be right in feeling them, in so far as we are sure that these standards have an empire *de jure* over all possible worlds, so far, and so far only, do they become a ground for disbelief — and at the same moment, for belief. God within us steals back at the moment of our condemning the apparent God without. Thus in Tennyson's poem the man who had become convinced that the God of his inherited creed was evil exclaimed: 'If there be such a God, may the Great God curse him and bring him to nought.'[14] For if there is no 'Great God' behind the curse, who curses? Only a puppet of the little apparent 'God'. His very curse is poisoned at the root: it is just the same sort of event as the very cruelties he is condemning, part of the meaningless tragedy.

From this I see only two exits: either that there is a Great God, and also a 'God of this world',[15] a prince of the powers of the air, whom the Great God does curse, and sometimes curses through us; or else that the operations of the Great God are not what they seem to me to be.

[14] 'Despair', xix, 106.
[15] II Corinthians iv. 4.

21

IS THEISM IMPORTANT?[1]

I HAVE LOST THE NOTES OF WHAT I ORIGINALLY SAID IN RE-plying to Professor Price's paper and cannot now remember what it was, except that I welcomed most cordially his sympathy with the Polytheists. I still do. When grave persons express their fear that England is relapsing into Paganism, I am tempted to reply, 'Would that she were.' For I do not think it at all likely that we shall ever see Parliament opened by the slaughtering of a garlanded white bull in the House of Lords or Cabinet Ministers leaving sandwiches in Hyde Park as an offering for the Dryads. If such a state of affairs came about, then the Christian apologist would have something to work on. For a Pagan, as history shows, is a man eminently convertible to Christianity. He is essentially the pre-Christian, or sub-Christian, religious man. The post-Christian man of our day differs from him as much as a *divorcée* differs from a virgin. The Christian and the Pagan have much more in common with one another than either has with the writers of the *New Statesman;* and those writers would of course agree with me. For the rest, what now occurs to me after re-reading Professor Price's paper is something like this.

1. I think we must introduce into the discussion a distinction between two senses of the word *Faith*. This may mean (a) a settled intellectual assent. In that sense faith (or 'be-

[1] This is a reply to a paper Professor H. H. Price read to the Oxford Socratic Club. Professor Price's paper was published under the same title in *The Socratic Digest,* No. 5 (1962), pp. 39-47, and Lewis's answer was originally published in the same periodical.

lief') in God hardly differs from faith in the uniformity of Nature or in the consciousness of other people. This is what, I think, has sometimes been called a 'notional' or 'intellectual' or 'carnal' faith. It may also mean (b) a trust, or confidence, in the God whose existence is thus assented to. This involves an attitude of the will. It is more like our confidence in a friend. It would be generally agreed that Faith in sense A is not a religious state. The devils who 'believe and tremble'[2] have Faith-A. A man who curses or ignores God may have Faith-A. Philosophical arguments for the existence of God are presumably intended to produce Faith-A. No doubt those who construct them are anxious to produce Faith-A because it is a necessary pre-condition of Faith-B, and in that sense their ultimate intention is religious. But their immediate object, the conclusion they attempt to prove, is not. I therefore think they cannot be justly accused of trying to get a religious conclusion out of non-religious premises. I agree with Professor Price that this cannot be done: but I deny that the religious philosophers are trying to do it.

I also think that in some ages, what claim to be Proofs of Theism have had much more efficacy in producing Faith-A than Professor Price suggests. Nearly everyone I know who has embraced Christianity in adult life has been influenced by what seemed to him to be at least probable arguments for Theism. I have known some who were completely convinced by Descartes' Ontological Proof:[3] that is, they received Faith-A from Descartes first and then went on to seek and to find, Faith-B. Even quite uneducated people who have been Christians all their lives not infrequently appeal to some simplified form of the Argument from Design. Even acceptance of tradition implies an argument which sometimes becomes explicit in the form 'I reckon all those wise men wouldn't have believed in it if it weren't true.'

Of course Faith-A usually involves a degree of subjective certitude which goes beyond the logical certainty, or even the supposed logical certainty, of the arguments employed. It may retain this certitude for a long time, I expect, even without the support of Faith-B. This excess of certitude in a settled

[2] James ii. 19.

[3] This is briefly summed up in René Descartes' *Discours de la Méthode,* Part iv, in which he says 'I think, therefore I am.'

assent is not at all uncommon. Most of those who believe in Uniformity of Nature, Evolution, or the Solar System, share it.

2. I doubt whether religious people have ever supposed that Faith-B follows automatically on the acquisition of Faith-A. It is described as a 'gift'.[4] As soon as we have Faith-A in the existence of God, we are instructed to ask from God Himself the gift of Faith-B. An odd request, you may say, to address to a First Cause, an *Ens Realissimum,* or an *Unmoved Mover.* It might be argued, and I think I would argue myself, that even such an aridly philosophical God rather fails to invite than actually repels a personal approach. It would, at any rate, do no harm to try it. But I fully admit that most of those who, having reached Faith-A, pray for Faith-B, do so because they have already had something like religious experience. Perhaps the best way of putting it would be to say that Faith-A converts into religious experience what was hitherto only potentially or implicitly religious. In this modified form I would accept Professor Price's view that philosophical proofs never, by themselves, lead to religion. Something at least *quasi*-religious uses them before, and the 'proofs' remove an inhibition which was preventing their development into religion proper.

This is not exactly *fides quaerens intellectum*,[5] for these quasi-religious experiences were not *fides.* In spite of Professor Price's rejection, I still think Otto's account of the Numinous[6] is the best analysis of them we have. I believe it is a mistake to regard the Numinous as merely an affair of 'feeling'. Admittedly, Otto can describe it only by referring to the emotions it arouses in us; but then nothing can be described except in terms of its effects in consciousness. We have in English an exact name for the emotion aroused by the Numinous, which Otto, writing in German, lacked; we have the word Awe — an emotion very like fear, with the important difference that it need imply no estimate of danger. When we fear a tiger, we fear that it may kill us: when we fear a ghost — well, we just fear the ghost, not this or that mischief which it may do us. The Numinous or Awful is that of which we

[4] e.g. I Corinthians xii. 1-11; Ephesians ii. 8.
[5] 'faith seeking understanding'.
[6] Rudolf Otto, *The Idea of the Holy,* trans. John W. Harvey (London, 1923).

have this, as it were, objectless or disinterested fear — this awe. And 'the Numinous' is not a name for our own feeling of Awe, any more than 'the Contemptible' is a name for contempt. It is the answer to the question 'of what do you feel awe'. And what we feel awe of is certainly not itself awe.

With Otto and, in a sense, with Professor Price, I would find the seed of religious experience in our experience of the Numinous. In an age like our own such experience does occur but, until religion comes and retrospectively transforms it, it usually appears to the subject to be a special form of aesthetic experience. In ancient times I think experience of the Numinous developed into the Holy only in so far as the Numinous (not in itself at all necessarily moral) came to be connected with the morally good. This happened regularly in Israel, sporadically elsewhere. But even in the higher Paganism, I do not think this process led to anything exactly like *fides*. There is nothing credal in Paganism. In Israel we do get *fides* but this is always connected with certain historical affirmations. Faith is not simply in the numinous *Elohim,* nor even simply in the holy *Jahweh,* but in the God 'of our fathers', the God who called Abraham and brought Israel out of Egypt. In Christianity this historical element is strongly re-affirmed. The object of faith is at once the *ens entium*[7] of the philosophers, the Awful Mystery of Paganism, the Holy Law given of the moralists, and Jesus of Nazareth who was crucified under Pontius Pilate and rose again on the third day.

Thus we must admit that Faith, as we know it, does not flow from philosophical argument alone; nor from experience of the Numinous alone; nor from moral experience alone; nor from history alone; but from historical events which at once fulfil and transcend the moral category, which link themselves with the most numinous elements in Paganism, and which (as it seems to us) demand as their pre-supposition the existence of a Being who is more, but not less, than the God whom many reputable philosophers think they can establish.

Religious experience, as we know it, really involves all these elements. We may, however, use the word in a narrower sense to denote moments of mystical, or devotional, or merely numinous experience; and we may then ask, with Professor Price, how such moments, being a kind of *visio,* are related to faith,

[7] 'being of beings.'

175

which by definition is 'not sight'. This does not seem to me one of the hardest questions. 'Religious experience' in the narrower sense comes and goes: especially goes. The operation of Faith is to retain, so far as the will and intellect are concerned, what is irresistible and obvious during the moments of special grace. By Faith we believe always what we hope hereafter to see always and perfectly and have already seen imperfectly and by flashes. In relation to the philosophical premises a Christian's faith is of course excessive: in relation to what is sometimes shown him, it is perhaps just as often defective. My faith even in an earthly friend goes beyond all that could be demonstratively proved; yet in another sense I may often trust him less than he deserves.

22

REJOINDER TO
DR PITTENGER

To ONE OF THE CHARGES DR NORMAN PITTENGER MAKES
in his 'Critique' in the October 1 *Christian Century*,[1] I must
with shame plead guilty. He has caught me using the word
'literally' where I did not really mean it, a vile journalistic
cliché which he cannot reprobate more severely than I now
do myself.[2]

I must also admit some truth in his charge of Apollinarian-
ism; there is a passage in my *Problem of Pain* which would
imply, if pressed, a shockingly crude conception of the Incarnation. I corrected it by a footnote to the French edition
but have not been able to do so elsewhere, save in so far as
Mere Christianity, bk. IV, ch. 3, may provide an antidote.

This must not be taken to mean that my present conception
would fully satisfy Dr Pittenger. He speaks about 'the validity
of our Lord's unique place in Christian faith as that One in
whom God was so active and so present that he may be called
"God-Man" '.[3] I am not quite sure what this means. May I

[1] W. Norman Pittenger, 'A Critique of C. S. Lewis', *Christian Century*, vol. LXXV (1 October 1958), pp. 1104-07.

[2] In *Broadcast Talks* (London, 1942), Part II, ch. 5, p. 60, Lewis
had written that 'the whole mass of Christians are literally the physical
organism through which Christ acts — that we are His fingers and
muscles, the cells of His body.' The word 'literally', however, was de-
leted when *Broadcast Talks* was reprinted with two other short books
as *Mere Christianity* (London, 1952) in which the phrase quoted above
is found in bk. II, ch. 5, p. 51.

[3] Pittenger, p. 1106.

translate it, 'our Lord's actually unique place in the structure of utter reality, the unique mode, as well as degree, of God's presence and action in Him, make the formula "God-Man" the objectively true description of Him'? If so, I think we are very nearly agreed. Or must I translate it, 'the unique place which Christians (subjectively, in their own thoughts) gave to our Lord as One in whom God was present and active to a unique degree made it reasonable for them to call Him God-Man'? If so, I must demur. In other words, if Dr Pittenger's 'may be called' means anything less or other than 'is', I could not accept his formula. For I think that Jesus Christ is (in fact) the only Son of God — that is, the only original Son of God, through whom others are enabled to 'become sons of God'.[4] If Dr Pittenger wishes to attack that doctrine, I wonder he should choose me as its representative. It has had champions far worthier of his steel.

I turn next to my book *Miracles* and am sorry to say that I here have to meet Dr Pittenger's charges with straight denials. He says that this book 'opens with a definition of miracle as the "violation" of the laws of nature'.[5] He is mistaken. The passage (chapter 2) really runs: 'I use the word *Miracle* to mean an interference with Nature by supernatural power.'[6] If Dr Pittenger thinks the difference between the true text and his mis-quotation merely verbal, he has misunderstood nearly the whole book. I never equated nature (the spatio-temporal system of facts and events) with the laws of nature (the patterns into which these facts and events fall). I would as soon equate an actual speech with the rules of grammar. In chapter 8 I say in so many words that no miracle either can or need break the laws of Nature; that 'it is . . . inaccurate to define a miracle as something that breaks the laws of Nature';[7] and that 'The divine art of miracle is not an art of suspending the pattern to which events conform but of feeding new events into that pattern.'[8] How many times does a

4 John i. 12.
5 Pittenger, p. 1105.
6 *Miracles: A Preliminary Study* (London, 1947). Because Lewis later revised chapter III of this book, all my text-references are to the 're-vised' paperback edition of *Miracles* (Fontana Books, London, 1960), p. 9.
7 *Ibid.*, p. 63.
8 *Ibid.*, p. 64.

man need to say something before he is safe from the accusation of having said exactly the opposite? (I am not for a moment imputing dishonesty to Dr Pittenger; we all know too well how difficult it is to grasp or retain the substance of a book one finds antipathetic.)

Again, Dr Pittenger contrasts my view with that which makes miracles a sign of God's action and presence in creation. Yet in chapter 15 I say that the miracle at Cana manifests 'the God of Israel who has through all these centuries given us wine' and that in the miraculous feedings God 'does close and small . . . what He has always been doing in the seas, the lakes and the little brooks'.[9] Surely this is just what Dr Pittenger wanted me to say, and what Athanasius says *(De Incarnatione* xiv. 8, edited by F. L. Cross, 1939)?

It is very true that I make no use of the different words *(semeia, terata* and the rest) which New Testament writers use for miracles. But why should I? I was writing for people who wanted to know whether the things could have happened rather than what they should be called; whether we could without absurdity believe that Christ rose from the emptied tomb. I am afraid most of my readers, if once convinced that He did not, would have felt it of minor importance to decide whether, if He had done so, this nonexistent event would have been a *teras* or a *dunamis*. And (in certain moods) one does, after all, see their point.

Dr Pittenger thinks the Naturalist whom I try to refute in chapter 3 is a man of straw. He may not be found in the circles Dr Pittenger frequents. He is quite common where I come from; and, presumably, in Moscow. There is indeed a really serious hitch in that chapter (which ought to be rewritten), but Dr Pittenger has not seen it or has charitably kept silent about it.[10]

I now turn to the more difficult and interesting question of the Fourth Gospel. It is difficult because, here again, I do not quite understand what Dr Pittenger writes. He blames me for putting all four Gospels in the same category and especially for believing that Jesus claimed deity because the Fourth Gospel says He did. But this does not mean that Dr

[9] *Ibid.*, pp. 140, 141.
[10] Lewis did, as just mentioned in a footnote above, revise chapter III of *Miracles*.

Pittenger rejects the fourth as simply untrue. According to him it gives that 'interpretation' of our Lord's 'significance' which the early Christians 'found', and 'rightly' found, 'to be true'.[11] Now in my language that significance of anything which is 'rightly found to be true' would be its true significance and those who found it would have found what the thing really meant. If the Fourth Gospel gives us what Jesus Christ really meant, why am I blamed for accepting it? But I am, and therefore Dr Pittenger's words must bear some other sense. Does he mean that what they 'rightly found to be true' was not true? Or that the significance which was rightly found to be true by them would be 'wrongly found' to be true by us? Or did they get the 'significance' right and go wrong about the 'interpretation of the significance'? I give it up.

I confess, however, that the problem of the Fourth Gospel raises in me a conflict between authority and private judgment: the authority of all those learned men who think that Gospel unhistorical, and my judgment as a literary critic which constrains me to think it at least as close to the facts as Boswell's *Johnson*. If I venture here to follow judgment in the teeth of authority, this is partly because I could never see how one escaped the dilemma *aut deus aut malus homo*[12] by confining oneself to the Synoptics. Moderns do not seem startled, as contemporaries were, by the claim Jesus there makes to forgive sins; not sins against Himself, just sins. Yet surely, if they actually met it, they would feel differently. If Dr Pittenger told me that two of his colleagues had lost him a professorship by telling lies about his character and I replied, 'I freely forgive them both', would he not think this an impertinence (both in the old and in the modern sense) bordering on insanity? And of course all three Synoptics tell the story of One who, at his trial, sealed His fate by saying He was the Son of God.

I am accused of attributing 'almost spatial transcendence' to God and of denying His continued presence within Nature because I speak of Him as 'invading' or 'intruding into' her.[13] This is really very hard of the Doctor. Of course the very word 'transcendence' contains a spatial image. So does 'im-

11 Pittenger, p. 1106.
12 'Either God or a bad man.'
13 Pittenger, p. 1105.

180

manence'. So does Dr Pittenger's 'God's action and *presence in* the creation'.[14] We must, after all, speak the language of men. (I have got much light on this problem from Edwyn Bevan's *Symbolism and Belief.*) But I freely admit that, believing both, I have stressed the transcendence of God more than His immanence. I thought, and think, that the present situation demands this. I see around me no danger of Deism but much of an immoral, naïve and sentimental pantheism. I have often found that it was in fact the chief obstacle to conversion.

Dr Pittenger says that I base the Faith on authority (which has 'grown up in the Church and won the assent of great doctors').[15] So does he; his authority is 'the total consentient witness of all Christians from the Apostles' time'.[16] I am not sure why he calls my authority 'mechanical'. Surely it differs from his mainly by being discoverable? The 'total consentient witness' would be grand if we had it. But of course the overwhelming majority of Christians, as of other men, have died, and are dying while I write, without recording their 'witness'. How does Dr Pittenger consult his authority?

Where he really hurt me was in the charge of callousness to animals. Surprised me too; for the very same passage is blamed by others for extreme sentimentality.[17] It is hard to please all. But if the Patagonians think me a dwarf and the Pygmies a giant, perhaps my stature is in fact fairly unremarkable.

The statement that I do not 'care much for' the Sermon on the Mount but 'prefer' the 'Pauline ethic' of man's sinfulness and helplessness[18] carries a suggestion of alternatives between which we may choose, where I see successive stages through which we must proceed. Most of my books are evangelistic, addressed to *tous exo*. It would have been inept to preach forgiveness and a Saviour to those who did not know they were in need of either. Hence St Paul's and the Baptist's

14 *Ibid.*
15 Pittenger, p. 1106, quoting Lewis's *Problem of Pain* (London, 1940), ch. v, p. 60.
16 Pittenger, p. 1106.
17 The reference is to the chapter on 'Animal Pain' in *The Problem of Pain.*
18 Pittenger, p. 1106.

diagnosis (would you call it exactly an *ethic?*) had to be pressed. Nor am I aware that our Lord revised it ('if ye, being evil . . .').[19] As to 'caring for' the Sermon on the Mount, if 'caring for' here means 'liking' or enjoying, I suppose no one 'cares for' it. Who can *like* being knocked flat on his face by a sledge-hammer? I can hardly imagine a more deadly spiritual condition than that of the man who can read that passage with tranquil pleasure. This is indeed to be 'at ease in Zion'.[20] Such a man is not yet ripe for the Bible; he had better start by learning sense from Islam: 'The heaven and the earth and all between, thinkest thou I made them *in jest?*'

And this illustrates what appears to me to be a weakness in the Doctor's critical method. He judges my books *in vacuo,* with no consideration of the audience to whom they were addressed or the prevalent errors they were trying to combat. The Naturalist becomes a straw man because he is not found among 'first-rate scientists' and readers of Einstein. But I was writing *ad populum,* not *ad clerum.* This is relevant to my manner as well as my matter. It is true, I do not understand why it is vulgar or offensive, in speaking of the Holy Trinity, to illustrate from plane and solid geometry the conception that what is self-contradictory on one level may be consistent on another.[21] I could have understood the Doctor's being shocked if I had compared God to an unjust judge or Christ to a thief in the night; but mathematical objects seem to me as free from sordid associations as any the mind can entertain.

But let all that pass. Suppose the image is vulgar. If it gets across to the unbeliever what the unbeliever desperately needs to know, the vulgarity must be endured. Indeed, the image's very vulgarity may be an advantage; for there is much sense in the reasons advanced by Aquinas (following Pseudo-Dionysius) for preferring to present divine truths *sub figuris vilium corporum*[22] *(Summa Theologica,* Qu. I, Art. 9 *ad tertium).*

[19] Matthew vii. 11; Luke xi. 13.
[20] Amos vi. 1.
[21] In *Mere Christianity,* bk. iv, ch. 2, p. 128, Lewis says 'In God's dimension, so to speak, you find a being who is three Persons while remaining one Being, just as a cube is six squares while remaining one cube.'
[22] 'under the figures of vile bodies.'

182

When I began, Christianity came before the great mass of my unbelieving fellow-countrymen either in the highly emotional form offered by revivalists or in the unintelligible language of highly cultured clergymen. Most men were reached by neither. My task was therefore simply that of a *translator* — one turning Christian doctrine, or what he believed to be such, into the vernacular, into language that unscholarly people would attend to and could understand. For this purpose a style more guarded, more *nuancé,* finelier shaded, more rich in fruitful ambiguities — in fact, a style more like Dr Pittenger's own — would have been worse than useless. It would not only have failed to enlighten the common reader's understanding; it would have aroused his suspicion. He would have thought, poor soul, that I was facing both ways, sitting on the fence, offering at one moment what I withdrew the next, and generally trying to trick him. I may have made theological errors. My manner may have been defective. Others may do better hereafter. I am ready, if I am young enough, to learn. Dr Pittenger would be a more helpful critic if he advised a cure as well as asserting many diseases. How does he himself do such work? What methods, and with what success, does he employ when he is trying to convert the great mass of storekeepers, lawyers, realtors, morticians, policemen and artisans who surround him in his own city?

One thing at least is sure. If the real theologians had tackled this laborious work of translation about a hundred years ago, when they began to lose touch with the people (for whom Christ died), there would have been no place for me.[23]

[23] See Letter 11.

183

23

MUST OUR IMAGE OF GOD GO?[1]

THE BISHOP OF WOOLWICH WILL DISTURB MOST OF US CHRIStian laymen less than he anticipates. We have long abandoned belief in a God who sits on a throne in a localized heaven. We call that belief anthropomorphism, and it was officially condemned before our time. There is something about this in Gibbon. I have never met any adult who replaced 'God up there' by 'God out there' in the sense 'spatially external to the universe'. If I said God is 'outside' or 'beyond' space-time, I should mean 'as Shakespeare is outside *The Tempest*'; i.e. its scenes and persons do not exhaust his being. We have always thought of God as being not only 'in' 'above', but also 'below' us: as the depth of ground. We can imaginatively speak of Father 'in heaven' yet also of the everlasting arms that are 'beneath'. We do not understand why the Bishop is so anxious to canonize the one image and forbid the other. We admit his freedom to use which he prefers. We claim our freedom to use both.

His view of Jesus as a 'window' seems wholly orthodox ('he that hath seen me hath seen the Father').[2] Perhaps the real novelty is in the Bishop's doctrine about God. But we

[1] This article, which first appeared in *The Observer* (24 March 1963), is a reply to the then Bishop of Woolwich, Dr J. A. T. Robinson's article 'Our Image of God Must Go', *The Observer* (17 March 1963), which is a summary of Dr Robinson's book *Honest to God* (London, 1963).
[2] John xiv. 9.

184

can't be certain, for here he is very obscure. He draws a sharp distinction between asking 'Does God exist as a person?' and asking whether ultimate reality is personal. But surely he who says yes to the second question has said yes to the first? Any entity describable without gross abuse of language as God must be ultimate reality, and if ultimate reality is personal, then God is personal. Does the Bishop mean that something which is not 'a person' could yet be 'personal'? Even this could be managed if 'not a person' were taken to mean 'a person and more' — as is provided for by the doctrine of the Trinity. But the Bishop does not mention this.

Thus, though sometimes puzzled, I am not shocked by his article. His heart, though perhaps in some danger of bigotry, is in the right place. If he has failed to communicate why the things he is saying move him so deeply as they obviously do, this may be primarily a literary failure. If I were briefed to defend his position I should say 'The image of the Earth-Mother gets in something which that of the Sky-Father leaves out. Religions of the Earth-Mother have hitherto been spiritually inferior to those of the Sky-Father, but, perhaps, it is now time to readmit some of their elements.' I shouldn't believe it very strongly, but some sort of case could be made out.

PART II

PART I

1

DANGERS OF
NATIONAL REPENTANCE

THE IDEA OF NATIONAL REPENTANCE SEEMS AT FIRST SIGHT
to provide such an edifying contrast to that national self-right-
eousness of which England is so often accused and with which
she entered (or is said to have entered) the last war, that a
Christian naturally turns to it with hope. Young Christians
especially — last-year undergraduates and first-year curates —
are turning to it in large numbers. They are ready to believe
that England bears part of the guilt for the present war, and
ready to admit their own share in the guilt of England. What
that share is, I do not find it easy to determine. Most of these
young men were children, and none of them had a vote or the
experience which would enable them to use a vote wisely, when
England made many of those decisions to which the present
disorders could plausibly be traced. Are they, perhaps, repenting what they have in no sense done?

If they are, it might be supposed that their error is very
harmless: men fail so often to repent their real sins that the
occasional repentance of an imaginary sin might appear almost
desirable. But what actually happens (I have watched it happening) to the youthful national penitent is a little more
complicated than that. England is not a natural agent, but
a civil society. When we speak of England's actions we mean
the actions of the British Government. The young man who
is called upon to repent of England's foreign policy is really
being called upon to repent the acts of his neighbour; for a

189

Foreign Secretary or a Cabinet Minister is certainly a neighbour. And repentance presupposes condemnation. The first and fatal charm of national repentance is, therefore, the encouragement it gives us to turn from the bitter task of repenting our own sins to the congenial one of bewailing — but, first, of denouncing — the conduct of others. If it were clear to the young that this is what he is doing, no doubt he would remember the law of charity. Unfortunately the very terms in which national repentance is recommended to him conceal its true nature. By a dangerous figure of speech, he calls the Government not 'they' but 'we'. And since, as penitents, we are not encouraged to be charitable to our own sins, nor to give ourselves the benefit of any doubt, a Government which is called 'we' is *ipso facto* placed beyond the sphere of charity or even of justice. You can say anything you please about it. You can indulge in the popular vice of detraction without restraint, and yet feel all the time that you are practising contrition. A group of such young penitents will say, 'Let us repent our national sins'; what they mean is, 'Let us attribute to our neighbour (even our Christian neighbour) in the Cabinet, whenever we disagree with him, every abominable motive that Satan can suggest to our fancy.'

Such an escape from personal repentance into that tempting region

> Where passions have the privilege to work
> And never hear the sound of their own names,[1]

would be welcome to the moral cowardice of anyone. But it is doubly attractive to the young intellectual. When a man over forty tries to repent the sins of England and to love her enemies, he is attempting something costly; for he was brought up to certain patriotic sentiments which cannot be mortified without a struggle. But an educated man who is now in his twenties usually has no such sentiment to mortify. In art, in literature, in politics, he has been, ever since he can remember, one of an angry and restless minority; he has drunk in almost with his mother's milk a distrust of English statesmen and a contempt for the manners, pleasures, and enthusiasms of his less-educated fellow countrymen. All Christians know that they must forgive their enemies. But 'my enemy' pri-

[1] Wordsworth, *The Prelude*, bk. XI, line 230.

marily means the man whom I am really tempted to hate and traduce. If you listen to young Christian intellectuals talking, you will soon find out who their real enemy is. He seems to have two names — Colonel Blimp and 'the business-man'. I suspect that the latter usually means the speaker's father, but that is speculation. What is certain is that in asking such people to forgive the Germans and Russians and to open their eyes to the sins of England, you are asking them, not to mortify, but to indulge, their ruling passion. I do not mean that what you are asking them is not right and necessary in itself; we must forgive all our enemies or be damned. But it is emphatically not the exhortation which your audience needs. The communal sins which they should be told to repent are those of their own age and class — its contempt for the uneducated, its readiness to suspect evil, its self-righteous provocations of public obloquy, its breaches of the Fifth Commandment.[2] Of these sins I have heard nothing among them. Till I do, I must think their candour towards the national enemy a rather inexpensive virtue. If a man cannot forgive the Colonel Blimp next door whom he has seen, how shall he forgive the Dictators whom he hath not seen?

Is it not, then, the duty of the Church to preach national repentance? I think it is. But the office — like many others — can be profitably discharged only by those who discharge it with reluctance. We know that a man may have to 'hate' his mother for the Lord's sake.[3] The sight of a Christian rebuking his mother, though tragic, may be edifying; but only if we are quite sure that he has been a good son and that, in his rebuke, spiritual zeal is triumphing, not without agony, over strong natural affection. The moment there is reason to suspect that he *enjoys* rebuking her — that he believes himself to be rising above the natural level while he is still, in reality, grovelling below it in the unnatural — the spectacle becomes merely disgusting. The hard sayings of our Lord are wholesome to those only who find them hard. There is a terrible chapter in M. Mauriac's *Vie de Jésus*. When the Lord spoke

[2] 'Honour thy father and thy mother; that thy days may be long in the land which the Lord thy God giveth thee.' Exodus xx. 12.

[3] Luke xiv. 26: 'If any man come to me, and hate not his father, and mother, and wife, and children, and brethren, and sisters, yea, and his own life also, he cannot be my disciple.'

of brother and child against parent, the other disciples were horrified. Not so Judas. He took to it as a duck takes to water: '*Pourquoi cetter stupeur?, se demande Judas.... Il aime dans le Christ cette vue simple, ce regard de Dieu sur l'horreur humaine.*'[4] For there are two states of mind which face the Dominical paradoxes without flinching. God guard us from one of them.

[4] François Mauriac, *Vie de Jésus* (Paris, 1936), ch. ix. ' "Why this stupefaction?" asked Judas ... He loved in Christ his simple view of things, his divine glance at human depravity.'

2

TWO WAYS WITH THE SELF

SELF-RENUNCIATION IS THOUGHT TO BE, AND INDEED IS, very near the core of Christian ethics. When Aristotle writes in praise of a certain kind of self-love, we may feel, despite the careful distinctions which he draws between the legitimate and the illegitimate *Philautia*,[1] that here we strike something essentially sub-Christian. It is more difficult, however, to decide what we think of St François de Sales's chapter, *De la douceur envers nous-mêsmes*,[2] where we are forbidden to indulge resentment even against ourselves and advised to reprove even our own faults *avec des remonstrances douces et tranquilles*,[3] feeling more compassion than passion. In the same spirit, Lady Julian of Norwich would have us 'loving and peaceable', not only to our 'even-Christians', but to 'ourself'.[4] Even the New Testament bids me love my neighbour 'as myself',[5] which would be a horrible command if the self were simply to be hated. Yet Our Lord also says that a true disciple must 'hate his own life'.[6]

We must not explain this apparent contradiction by saying that self-love is right up to a certain point and wrong beyond that point. The question is not one of degree. There are two

[1] *Nicomachean Ethics*, bk. ix, ch. 8.

[2] Pt. III, ch. ix 'Of Meekness towards Ourselves' in the *Introduction to the Devout Life* (Lyons, 1609).

[3] 'with mild and calm remonstrances'.

[4] *The Sixteen Revelations of Divine Love*, ch. xlix.

[5] Matthew xix. 19; xxii. 39; Mark xii. 31, 33; Romans xiii. 9; Galatians v. 14; James ii. 8.

[6] Luke xiv. 26; John xii. 25.

kinds of self-hatred which look rather alike in their earlier stages, but of which one is wrong from the beginning and the other right to the end. When Shelley speaks of self-contempt as the source of cruelty, or when a later poet says that he has no stomach for the man 'who loathes his neighbour as himself', they are referring to a very real and very un-Christian hatred of the self which may make diabolical a man whom common selfishness would have have left (at least, for a while) merely animal. The hard-boiled economist or psychologist of our own day, recognizing the 'ideological taint' or Freudian motive in his own make-up, does not necessarily learn Christian humility. He may end in what is called a 'low view' of all souls, including his own, which expresses itself in cynicism or cruelty, or both. Even Christians, if they accept in certain forms the doctrine of total depravity, are not always free from the danger. The logical conclusion of the process is the worship of suffering — for others as well as for the self — which we see, if I read it aright, in Mr David Lindsay's *Voyage to Arcturus,* or that extraordinary vacancy which Shakespeare depicts at the end of *Richard III.* Richard in his agony tries to turn to self-love. But he has been 'seeing through' all emotions so long that he 'sees through' even this. It becomes a mere tautology: 'Richard loves Richard; that is, I am I.'[7]

Now, the self can be regarded in two ways. On the one hand, it is God's creature, an occasion of love and rejoicing; now, indeed, hateful in condition, but to be pitied and healed. On the other hand, it is that one self of all others which is called *I* and *me,* and which on that ground puts forward an irrational claim to preference. This claim is to be not only hated, but simply killed; 'never', as George MacDonald says, 'to be allowed a moment's respite from eternal death'. The Christian must wage endless war against the clamour of the *ego* as *ego*: but he loves and approves selves as such, though not their sins. The very self-love which he has to reject is to him a specimen of how he ought to feel to all selves; and he may hope that when he has truly learned (which will hardly be in this life) to love his neighbour as himself, he may then be able to love himself as his neighbour: that is, with charity instead of partiality. The other kind of self-hatred, on the contrary, hates selves as such. It begins by accepting the special

[7] *Richard III,* V, iii, 184.

194

value of the particular self called *me;* then, wounded in its pride to find that such a darling object should be so disappointing, it seeks revenge, first upon that self, then on all. Deeply egoistic, but now with an inverted egoism, it uses the revealing argument, 'I don't spare myself' — with the implication 'then *a fortiori* I need not spare others' — and becomes like the centurion in Tacitus, *immitior quia toleraverat.*[8]

The wrong asceticism torments the self: the right kind kills the selfness. We must die daily: but it is better to love the self than to love nothing, and to pity the self than to pity no one.

[8] *Annals,* Bk. I, sect. xx, line 14. 'More relentless because he had endured (it himself).'

3

MEDITATION ON THE
THIRD COMMANDMENT

F ROM MANY LETTERS TO *The Guardian,*[1] AND FROM MUCH
that is printed elsewhere, we learn of the growing desire for
a Christian 'party', a Christian 'front', or a Christian 'platform' in politics. Nothing is so earnestly to be wished as a
real assault by Christianity on the politics of the world: nothing, at first sight, so fitted to deliver this assault as a Christian Party. But it is odd that certain difficulties in this programme should be already neglected while the printer's ink is
hardly dry on M. Maritain's *Scholasticism and Politics.*[2]

The Christian Party must either confine itself to stating what
ends are desirable and what means are lawful, or else it must
go further and select from among the lawful means those which
it deems possible and efficacious and give to these its practical
support. If it chooses the first alternative, it will not be a
political party. Nearly all parties agree in professing ends
which we admit to be desirable — security, a living wage, and
the best adjustment between the claims of order and freedom.
What distinguishes one party from another is the championship
of means. We do not dispute whether the citizens are to be
made happy, but whether an egalitarian or a hierarchical State,

[1] *The Guardian* was a weekly Anglican newspaper founded in 1846
to uphold Tractarian principles, and to show their relevance to the
best secular thought of the day.

[2] Jacques Maritain, *Scholasticism and Politics,* trans. M. J. Adler
(London, 1950).

196

whether capitalism or socialism, whether despotism or democracy is most likely to make them so.

What, then, will the Christian Party actually do? Philarchus, a devout Christian, is convinced that temporal welfare can flow only from a Christian life, and that a Christian life can be promoted in the community only by an authoritarian State which has swept away the last vestiges of the hated 'Liberal' infection. He thinks Fascism not so much an evil as a good thing perverted, regards democracy as a monster whose victory would be a defeat for Christianity, and is tempted to accept even Fascist assistance, hoping that he and his friends will prove the leaven in a lump of British Fascists. Stativus is equally devout and equally Christian. Deeply conscious of the Fall and therefore convinced that no human creature can be trusted with more than the minimum power over his fellows, and anxious to preserve the claims of God from any infringement by those of Caesar, he still sees in democracy the only hope of Christian freedom. He is tempted to accept aid from champions of the *status quo* whose commercial or imperial motives bear hardly even a veneer of theism. Finally, we have Spartacus, also a Christian and also sincere, full of the prophetic and Dominical denunciations of riches, and certain that the 'historical Jesus', long betrayed by the Apostles, the Fathers, and the Churches, demands of us a Left revolution. And he also is tempted to accept help from unbelievers who profess themselves quite openly to be the enemies of God.

The three types represented by these three Christians presumably come together to form a Christian Party. Either a deadlock ensues (and there the history of the Christian Party ends) or else one of the three succeeds in floating a party and driving the other two, with their followers, out of its ranks. The new party — being probably a minority of the Christians who are themselves a minority of the citizens — will be too small to be effective. In practice, it will have to attach itself to the un-Christian party nearest to it in beliefs about means — to the Fascists if Philarchus has won, to the Conservatives if Stativus, to the Communists if Spartacus. It remains to ask how the resulting situation will differ from that in which Christians find themselves today.

It is not reasonable to suppose that such a Christian Party will acquire new powers of leavening the infidel organization to which it is attached. Why should it? Whatever it calls itself, it will represent, not Christendom, but a part of Christendom. The principle which divides it from its brethren and unites it to its political allies will not be theological. It will have no authority to speak for Christianity; it will have no more power than the political skill of its members gives it to control the behaviour of its unbelieving allies. But there will be a real, and most disastrous, novelty. It will be not simply a *part* of Christendom, but *a part claiming to be the whole*. By the mere act of calling itself the Christian Party it implicitly accuses all Christians who do not join it of apostasy and betrayal. It will be exposed, in an aggravated degree, to that temptation which the Devil spares none of us at any time — the temptation of claiming for our favourite opinions that kind and degree of certainty and authority which really belongs only to our Faith. The danger of mistaking our merely natural, though perhaps legitimate, enthusiasms for holy zeal, is always great. Can any more fatal expedient be devised for increasing it than that of dubbing a small band of Fascists, Communists, or Democrats 'the Christian Party'? The demon inherent in every party is at all times ready enough to disguise himself as the Holy Ghost; the formation of a Christian Party means handing over to him the most efficient make-up we can find. And when once the disguise has succeeded, his commands will presently be taken to abrogate all moral laws and to justify whatever the unbelieving allies of the 'Christian' Party wish to do. If ever Christian men can be brought to think treachery and murder the lawful means of establishing the *régime* they desire, and faked trials, religious persecution and organized hooliganism the lawful means of maintaining it, it will, surely, be by just such a process as this. The history of the late medieval pseudo-Crusader, of the Covenanters,[3] of the Orangemen,[4] should be remembered. On those who add 'Thus said the Lord' to their merely human utterances descends the doom of a conscience which seems clearer and clearer the more it is loaded with sin.

All this comes from pretending that God has spoken when

[3] The bodies of Presbyterians in Scotland who in the 16th and 17th centuries bound themselves by religious and political oaths to maintain the cause of their religion.

[4] Members of the Orange Association (founded in 1795) who defended the cause of Protestantism in Ireland.

He has not spoken. He will not settle the two brothers' in-heritance: 'Who made Me a judge or a divider over you?'[5] By the natural light He has shown us what means are lawful: to find out which one is efficacious He has given us brains. The rest He has left to us.

M. Maritain has hinted at the only way in which Christianity (as opposed to schismatics blasphemously claiming to repre-sent it) can influence politics. Nonconformity has influenced modern English history not because there was a Nonconformist Party but because there was a Nonconformist conscience which all parties had to take into account. An interdenominational Christian Voters' Society might draw up a list of assurances about ends and means which every member was expected to exact from any political party as the price of his support. Such a society might claim to represent Christendom far more truly than any 'Christian Front'; and for that reason I should be prepared, in principle, for membership and obedience to be obligatory on Christians. 'So all it comes down to is pestering M.P.'s[6] with letters?' Yes: just that. I think such pestering combines the dove and the serpent. I think it means a world where parties have to take care not to alienate Christians, in-stead of a world where Christians have to be 'loyal' to infidel parties. Finally, I think a minority can influence politics only by 'pestering' or by becoming a 'party' in the new continental sense (that is, a secret society of murderers and blackmailers) which is impossible to Christians. But I had forgotten. There is a third way — by becoming a majority. He who converts his neighbour has performed the most practical Christian-political act of all.

[5] Luke xii. 14.
[6] Members of Parliament.

4

ON THE READING
OF OLD BOOKS[1]

THERE IS A STRANGE IDEA ABROAD THAT IN EVERY SUBJECT the ancient books should be read only by the professionals, and that the amateur should content himself with the modern books. Thus I have found as a tutor in English Literature that if the average student wants to find out something about Platonism, the very last thing he thinks of doing is to take a translation of Plato off the library shelf and read the *Symposium*. He would rather read some dreary modern book ten times as long, all about 'isms' and influences and only once in twelve pages telling him what Plato actually said. The error is rather an amiable one, for it springs from humility. The student is half afraid to meet one of the great philosophers face to face. He feels himself inadequate and thinks he will not understand him. But if he only knew, the great man, just because of his greatness, is much more intelligible than his modern commentator. The simplest student will be able to understand, if not all, yet a very great deal of what Plato said; but hardly anyone can understand some modern books on Platonism. It has always therefore been one of my main endeavours as a teacher to persuade the young that first-hand knowledge is not only more worth acquiring than second-hand knowledge, but is usually much easier and more delightful to acquire.

[1] This paper was originally written and published as an Introduction to St Athanasius' *The Incarnation of the Word of God,* trans. by A. Religious of C.S.M.V. (London, 1944).

This mistaken preference for the modern books and this shyness of the old ones is nowhere more rampant than in theology. Wherever you find a little study circle of Christian laity you can be almost certain that they are studying not St Luke or St Paul or St Augustine or Thomas Aquinas or Hooker[2] or Butler,[3] but M. Berdyaev[4] or M. Maritain[5] or Mr Niebuhr[6] or Miss Sayers[7] or even myself.

Now this seems to me topsy-turvy. Naturally, since I myself am a writer, I do not wish the ordinary reader to read no modern books. But if he must read only the new or only the old, I would advise him to read the old. And I would give him this advice precisely because he is an amateur and therefore much less protected than the expert against the dangers of an exclusive contemporary diet. A new book is still on its trial and the amateur is not in a position to judge it. It has to be tested against the great body of Christian thought down the ages, and all its hidden implications (often unsuspected by the author himself) have to be brought to light. Often it cannot be fully understood without the knowledge of a good many other modern books. If you join at eleven o'clock a conversation which began at eight you will often not see the real bearing of what is said. Remarks which seem to you very ordinary will produce laughter or irritation and you will not see why — the reason, of course, being that the earlier stages of the conversation have given them a special point. In the same way sentences in a modern book which look quite ordinary may be directed 'at' some other book; in this way you may be led to accept what you would have indignantly rejected if you knew its real significance. The only safety is to have a standard of plain, central Christianity ('mere Christianity' as Baxter called it) which puts the controversies of the moment in their proper perspective. Such a standard can be acquired only from the old books. It is a good rule, after reading a new book, never to allow yourself another new one till you have read an old

2 Richard Hooker (c. 1554-1600), an Anglican divine.
3 Joseph Butler (1692-1752), Bishop of Durham.
4 Nicolas Berdyaev (1874-1948), a Russian philosopher and author.
5 Jacques Maritain (b. 1882), a French Thomist philosopher.
6 Reinhold Niebuhr (b. 1892), an American theologian.
7 Dorothy L. Sayers (1893-1957), author of several religious plays and many popular detective stories.

one in between. If that is too much for you, you should at least read one old one to every three new ones.

Every age has its own outlook. It is specially good at seeing certain truths and specially liable to make certain mistakes. We all, therefore, need the books that will correct the characteristic mistakes of our own period. And that means the old books. All contemporary writers share to some extent the contemporary outlook — even those, like myself, who seem most opposed to it. Nothing strikes me more when I read the controversies of past ages than the fact that both sides were usually assuming without question a good deal which we should now absolutely deny. They thought that they were as completely opposed as two sides could be, but in fact they were all the time secretly united — united *with* each other and *against* earlier and later ages — by a great mass of common assumptions. We may be sure that the characteristic blindness of the twentieth century — the blindness about which posterity will ask, 'But how *could* they have thought that?' — lies where we have never suspected it, and concerns something about which there is untroubled agreement between Hitler and President Roosevelt[8] or between Mr H. G. Wells and Karl Barth. None of us can fully escape this blindness, but we shall certainly increase it, and weaken our guard against it, if we read only modern books. Where they are true they will give us truths which we half knew already. Where they are false they will aggravate the error with which we are already dangerously ill. The only palliative is to keep the clean sea breeze of the centuries blowing through our minds, and this can be done only by reading old books. Not, of course, that there is any magic about the past. People were no cleverer then than they are now; they made as many mistakes as we. But not the *same* mistakes. They will not flatter us in the errors we are already committing; and their own errors, being now open and palpable, will not endanger us. Two heads are better than one, not because either is infallible, but because they are unlikely to go wrong in the same direction. To be sure, the books of the future would be just as good a corrective as the books of the past, but unfortunately we cannot get at them.

I myself was first led into reading the Christian classics, almost accidentally, as a result of my English studies. Some,

[8] This was written in 1943.

such as Hooker, Herbert,[9] Traherne,[10] Taylor[11] and Bunyan,[12] I read because they are themselves great English writers; others, such as Boethius,[13] St Augustine, Thomas Aquinas and Dante, because they were 'influences'. George MacDonald I had found for myself at the age of sixteen and never wavered in my allegiance, though I tried for a long time to ignore his Christianity. They are, you will note, a mixed bag, representative of many Churches, climates and ages. And that brings me to yet another reason for reading them. The divisions of Christendom are undeniable and are by some of these writers most fiercely expressed. But if any man is tempted to think — as one might be tempted who read only contemporaries — that 'Christianity' is a word of so many meanings that it means nothing at all, he can learn beyond all doubt, by stepping out of his own century, that this is not so. Measured against the ages 'mere Christianity' turns out to be no insipid interdenominational transparency, but something positive, self-consistent, and inexhaustible. I know it, indeed, to my cost. In the days when I still hated Christianity,[14] I learned to recognize, like some all too familiar smell, that almost unvarying *something* which met me, now in Puritan Bunyan, now in Anglican Hooker, now in Thomist Dante. It was there (honeyed and floral) in François de Sales;[15] it was there (grave and homely) in Spenser[16] and Walton;[17] it was there (grim but manful) in Pascal[18] and Johnson;[19] there again, with a mild, frightening, Paradisial flavour, in Vaughan[20] and Boehme[21]

[9] George Herbert (1593-1633), the English poet.

[10] Thomas Traherne (1637-74), an English writer of religious works.

[11] Jeremy Taylor (1613-67), an English divine, best known for his *Holy Living* and *Holy Dying*.

[12] John Bunyan (1628-88), best known for his *Pilgrim's Progress.*

[13] Boethius was born about 470 A.D. and wrote *The Consolation of Philosophy.*

[14] Those who wish to know more about this period should read Lewis's autobiography, *Surprised by Joy* (London, 1955).

[15] Francois de Sales (1567-1622) is best known for his *Introduction to the Devout Life* and the *Treatise on the Love of God.*

[16] Edmund Spenser (1552?-99), author of *The Faerie Queene.*

[17] Izaak Walton (1593-1683), best known for his *Compleat Angler.*

[18] Blaise Pascal (1623-62), especially noted for his *Pensées.*

[19] Dr Samuel Johnson (1709-84).

[20] Henry Vaughan (1622-95), an English poet.

[21] Jakob Boehme (1575-1624), a German Lutheran theosophical author.

and Traherne. In the urban sobriety of the eighteenth century one was not safe — Law[22] and Butler were two lions in the path. The supposed 'Paganism' of the Elizabethans could not keep it out; it lay in wait where a man might have supposed himself safest, in the very centre of *The Faerie Queene* and the *Arcadia*.[23] It was, of course, varied; and yet — after all — so unmistakably the same; recognizable, not to be evaded, the odour which is death to us until we allow it to become life:

> an air that kills
> From yon far country blows.[24]

We are all rightly distressed, and ashamed also, at the divisions of Christendom. But those who have always lived within the Christian fold may be too easily dispirited by them. They are bad, but such people do not know what it looks like from without. Seen from there, what is left intact, despite all the divisions, still appears (as it truly is) an immensely formidable unity. I know, for I saw it; and well our enemies know it. That unity any of us can find by going out of his own age. It is not enough, but it is more than you had thought till then. Once you are well soaked in it, if you then venture to speak, you will have an amusing experience. You will be thought a Papist when you are actually reproducing Bunyan, a Pantheist when you are quoting Aquinas, and so forth. For you have now got on to the great level viaduct which crosses the ages and which looks so high from the valleys, so low from the mountains, so narrow compared with the swamps, and so broad compared with the sheeptracks.

The present book is something of an experiment. The translation is intended for the world at large, not only for theological students. If it succeeds, other translations of other great Christian books will presumably follow. In one sense, of course, it is not the first in the field. Translations of the *Theologia Germanica*,[25] the *Imitation*,[26] the *Scale of Perfection*,[27] and

---

[22] William Law (1686-1761), whose *Serious Call to a Devout and Holy Life* much influenced Lewis.

[23] By Sir Philip Sidney (1554-86).

[24] A. E. Housman, *A Shropshire Lad* (London, 1896), stanza 40.

[25] A late 14th century anonymous mystical treatise.

[26] *The Imitation of Christ,* a manual of spiritual devotion first put into circulation in 1418. The authorship has traditionally been assigned to Thomas à Kempis (c. 1380-1471).

the *Revelations* of Lady Julian of Norwich,[28] are already on the market, and are very valuable, though some of them are not very scholarly. But it will be noticed that these are all books of devotion rather than of doctrine. Now the layman or amateur needs to be instructed as well as to be exhorted. In this age his need for knowledge is particularly pressing. Nor would I admit any sharp division between the two kinds of book. For my own part, I tend to find the doctrinal books often more helpful in devotion than the devotional books, and I rather suspect that the same experience may await many others. I believe that many who find that 'nothing happens' when they sit down, or kneel down, to a book of devotion, would find that the heart sings unbidden while they are working their way through a tough bit of theology with a pipe in their teeth and a pencil in their hand.

This is a good translation of a very great book. St Athanasius has suffered in popular estimation from a certain sentence in the 'Athanasian Creed'.[29] I will not labour the point that that work is not exactly a creed and was not by St. Athanasius, for I think it is a very fine piece of writing. The words 'Which Faith except every one do keep whole and undefiled, without doubt he shall perish everlastingly' are the offence. They are commonly misunderstood. The operative word is *keep;* not *acquire,* or even *believe,* but *keep.* The author, in fact, is not talking about unbelievers, but about deserters, not about those who have never heard of Christ, nor even those who have misunderstood and refused to accept Him, but of those who having really understood and really believed, then allow themselves, under the sway of sloth or of fashion or any other invited confusion to be drawn away into sub-Christian modes of thought. They are a warning against the curious modern assumption that all changes of belief, however brought about, are necessarily exempt from blame.[30] But this is not my immediate concern. I mention 'the creed (commonly called) of St Athanasius' only to get out of the reader's way what may have been a bogey and to put the true Athanasius in its place.

[27] By Walter Hilton (d. 1396), an English mystic.
[28] *The Sixteen Revelations of Divine Love* by Lady Julian of Norwich (c. 1342 -after 1413).
[29] A profession of faith found in the English Prayer Book.
[30] See Hebrews vi. 4 *et seq.*

His epitaph is *Athanasius contra mundum,* 'Athanasius against the world'. We are proud that our country has more than once stood against the world. Athanasius did the same. He stood for the Trinitarian doctrine, 'whole and undefiled', when it looked as if all the civilized world was slipping back from Christianity into the religion of Arius[31]— into one of those 'sensible' synthetic religions which are so strongly recommended today and which, then as now, included among their devotees many highly cultivated clergymen. It is his glory that he did not move with the times; it is his reward that he now remains when those times, as all times do, have moved away.

When I first opened his *De Incarnatione* I soon discovered by a very simple test that I was reading a masterpiece. I knew very little Christian Greek except that of the New Testament and I had expected difficulties. To my astonishment I found it almost as easy as Xenophon; and only a master mind could, in the fourth century, have written so deeply on such a subject with such classical simplicity. Every page I read confirmed this impression. His approach to the Miracles is badly needed today, for it is the final answer to those who object to them as 'arbitrary and meaningless violations of the laws of Nature'.[32] They are here shown to be rather the re-telling in capital letters of the same message which Nature writes in her crabbed cursive hand; the very operations one would expect of Him who was so full of life that when He wished to die He had to 'borrow death from others'. The whole book, indeed, is a picture of the Tree of Life — a sappy and golden book, full of buoyancy and confidence. We cannot, I admit, appropriate all its confidence today. We cannot point to the high virtue of Christian living and the gay, almost mocking courage of Christian martyrdom, as a proof of our doctrines with quite that assurance which Athanasius takes as a matter of course. But whoever may be to blame for that it is not Athanasius.

The translator knows so much more Christian Greek than I that it would be out of place for me to praise her version. But it seems to me to be in the right tradition of English trans-

[31] Arius (c. 250-c. 336), a champion of subordinationist teaching about the Person of Christ.

[32] A few years after this was written, Lewis himself wrote an admirable defence of Miracles in his *Miracles: A Preliminary Study* (London, 1947).

lation. I do not think the reader will find here any of that sawdusty quality which is so common in modern renderings from the ancient languages. That is as much as the English reader will notice; those who compare the version with the original will be able to estimate how much wit and talent is presupposed in such a choice, for example, as 'those wiseacres' on the very first page.

5

TWO LECTURES

AND SO', SAID THE LECTURER, 'I END WHERE I BEGAN.
Evolution, development, the slow struggle upwards and on-
wards from crude and inchoate beginnings towards ever-
increasing perfection and elaboration — that appears to be
the very formula of the whole universe.

'We see it exemplified in everything we study. The oak
comes from the acorn. The giant express engine of today
comes from the Rocket. The highest achievements of contemporary art are in a continuous line of descent from the rude
scratchings with which prehistoric man adorned the wall of
his cave.

'What are the ethics and philosophy of civilized man but
a miraculous elaboration of the most primitive instincts and
savage taboos? Each one of us has grown, through slow pre-
natal stages in which we were at first more like fish than mam-
mals, from a particle of matter too small to be seen. Man
himself springs from beasts: the organic from the inorganic.
Development is the key word. The march of all things is from
lower to higher.'

None of this, of course, was new to me or to anyone else
in the audience. But it was put very well (much better than
it appears in my reproduction) and the whole voice and figure
of the lecturer were impressive. At least they must have
impressed me, for otherwise I cannot account for the curious
dream I had that night.

I dreamed that I was still at the lecture, and the voice
from the platform was still going on. But it was saying all

the wrong things. At least it may have been saying the right things up to the very moment at which I began attending; but it certainly began going wrong after that. What I remembered on waking went like this: '. . . appears to be the very formula of the whole universe. We see it exemplified in everything we study. The acorn comes from a full-grown oak. The first crude engine, the Rocket, comes, not from a still cruder engine, but from something much more perfect than itself and much more complex, the mind of a man, and a man of genius. The first prehistoric drawings come, not from earlier scratchings, but from the hand and brain of human beings whose hand and brain cannot be shown to have been in any way inferior to our own; and indeed it is obvious that the man who first conceived the idea of making a picture must have been a greater genius than any of the artists who have succeeded him. The embryo with which the life of each one of us began did not originate from something even more embryonic; it originated from two fully-developed human beings, our parents. Descent, downward movement, is the key word. The march of all things is from higher to lower. The rude and imperfect thing always springs from something perfect and developed.'

I did not think much of this while I was shaving, but it so happened that I had no 10 o'clock pupil that morning, and when I had finished answering my letters I sat down and reflected on my dream.

It appeared to me that the Dream Lecturer had a good deal to be said for him. It is true that we do see all round us things growing up to perfection from small and rude beginnings; but then it is equally true that the small and rude beginnings themselves always come from some full-grown and developed thing. All adults were once babies, true: but then all babies were begotten and born by adults. Corn does come from seed: but then seed comes from corn. I could even give the Dream Lecturer an example he had missed. All civilizations grow from small beginnings; but when you look into it you always find that those small beginnings themselves have been 'dropped' (as an oak drops an acorn) by some other and mature civilization. The weapons and even the cookery of old Germanic barbarism are, so to speak, driftwood from the wrecked ship of Roman civilization. The starting point of Greek culture is the remains of older Minoan cultures, supplemented by oddments from civilized Egypt and Phoenicia.

But in that case, thought I, what about the first civilization of all? As soon as I asked this question I realised that the Dream Lecturer had been choosing his examples rather cautiously. He had talked only about things we can see going on around us. He had kept off the subject of absolute beginnings. He had quite correctly pointed out that in the present, and in the *historical* past, we see imperfect life coming from perfect just as much as *vice versa*. But he hadn't even attempted to answer the Real Lecturer about the beginnings of all life. The Real Lecturer's view was that when you got back far enough — back into those parts of the past which we know less about — you would find an absolute beginning, and it would be something small and imperfect.

That was a point in favour of the Real Lecturer. He at least had a theory about the absolute beginning, whereas the Dream Lecturer had slurred it over. But hadn't the Real Lecturer done a little slurring too? He had not given us a hint that his theory of the ultimate origins involved us in believing that Nature's habits have, since those days, altered completely. Her present habits show us an endless cycle — the bird coming from the egg and the egg from the bird. But he asked us to believe that the whole thing started with an egg which had been preceded by no bird. Perhaps it did. But the whole *prima facie* plausibility of his view — the ease with which the audience accepted it as something natural and obvious — depended on his slurring over the immense difference between this and the processes we actually observe. He put it over by drawing our attention to the fact that eggs develop into birds and making us forget that birds lay eggs; indeed, we have been trained to do this all our lives: trained to look at the universe with one eye shut. 'Developmentalism' is made to look plausible by a kind of trick.

For the first time in my life I began to look at the question with both eyes open. In the world I know, the perfect produces the imperfect, which again becomes perfect — egg leads to bird and bird to egg — in endless succession. If there ever was a life which sprang of its own accord out of a purely inorganic universe, or a civilization which raised itself by its own shoulder-straps out of pure savagery, then this event

210

was totally unlike the beginnings of every subsequent life and every subsequent civilization. The thing may have happened; but all its plausibility is gone. On any view, the first beginning must have been outside the ordinary processes of nature. An egg which came from no bird is no more 'natural' than a bird which had existed from all eternity. And since the egg-bird-egg sequence leads us to no plausible beginning, is it not reasonable to look for the real origin somewhere outside sequence altogether? You have to go outside the sequence of engines, into the world of men, to find the real originator of the Rocket. Is it not equally reasonable to look outside Nature for the real Originator of the natural order?

6

MEDITATION IN A TOOLSHED

I WAS STANDING TODAY IN THE DARK TOOLSHED. THE SUN was shining outside and through the crack at the top of the door there came a sunbeam. From where I stood that beam of light, with the specks of dust floating in it, was the most striking thing in the place. Everything else was almost pitch-black. I was seeing the beam, not seeing things by it.

Then I moved, so that the beam fell on my eyes. Instantly the whole previous picture vanished. I saw no toolshed, and (above all) no beam. Instead I saw, framed in the irregular cranny at the top of the door, green leaves moving on the branches of a tree outside and beyond that, 90 odd million miles away, the sun. Looking along the beam, and looking at the beam are very different experiences.

But this is only a very simple example of the difference between looking at and looking along. A young man meets a girl. The whole world looks different when he sees her. Her voice reminds him of something he has been trying to remember all his life, and ten minutes casual chat with her is more precious than all the favours that all other women in the world could grant. He is, as they say, 'in love'. Now comes a scientist and describes this young man's experience from the outside. For him it is all an affair of the young man's genes and a recognised biological stimulus. That is the difference between looking *along* the sexual impulse and looking *at* it.

When you have got into the habit of making this distinction you will find examples of it all day long. The mathematician sits thinking, and to him it seems that he is contemplating timeless and spaceless truths about quantity. But the cerebral physiologist, if he could look inside the mathematician's head, would find nothing timeless and spaceless there — only tiny movements in the grey matter. The savage dances in ecstasy at midnight before Nyonga and feels with every muscle that his dance is helping to bring the new green crops and the spring rain and the babies. The anthropologist, observing that savage, records that he is performing a fertility ritual of the type so-and-so. The girl cries over her broken doll and feels that she has lost a real friend; the psychologist says that her nascent maternal instinct has been temporarily lavished on a bit of shaped and coloured wax.

As soon as you have grasped this simple distinction, it raises a question. You get one experience of a thing when you look along it and another when you look at it. Which is the 'true' or 'valid' experience? Which tells you most about the thing? And you can hardly ask that question without noticing that for the last fifty years or so everyone has been taking the answer for granted. It has been assumed without discussion that if you want the true account of religion you must go, not to religious people, but to anthropologists; that if you want the true account of sexual love you must go, not to lovers, but to psychologists; that if you want to understand some 'ideology' (such as medieval chivalry or the nineteenth-century idea of a 'gentleman'), you must listen not to those who lived inside it, but to sociologists.

The people who look *at* things have had it all their own way; the people who look *along* things have simply been brow-beaten. It has even come to be taken for granted that the external account of a thing somehow refutes or 'debunks' the account given from inside. 'All these moral ideals which look so transcendental and beautiful from inside', says the wiseacre, 'are really only a mass of biological instincts and inherited taboos.' And no one plays the game the other way round by replying, 'If you will only step inside, the things that look to you like instincts and taboos will suddenly reveal their real and transcendental nature.'

That, in fact, is the whole basis of the specifically 'modern' type of thought. And is it not, you will ask, a very sensible basis? For, after all, we are often deceived by things from the inside. For example, the girl who looks so wonderful while we're in love, may really be a very plain, stupid, and disagreeable person. The savage's dance to Nyonga does not really cause the crops to grow. Having been so often deceived by looking along, are we not well advised to trust only to looking at? — in fact to discount all these inside experiences?

Well, no. There are two fatal objections to discounting them *all*. And the first is this. You discount them in order to think more accurately. But you can't think at all — and therefore, of course, can't think accurately — if you have nothing to think *about*. A physiologist, for example, can study pain and find out that it 'is' (whatever *is* means) such and such neural events. But the word *pain* would have no meaning for him unless he had 'been inside' by actually suffering. If he had never looked *along* pain he simply wouldn't know what he was looking *at*. The very subject for his inquiries from outside exists for him only because he has, at least once, been inside.

This case is not likely to occur, because every man has felt pain. But it is perfectly easy to go on all your life giving explanations of religion, love, morality, honour, and the like, without having been inside any of them. And if you do that, you are simply playing with counters. You go on explaining a thing without knowing what it is. That is why a great deal of contemporary thought is, strictly speaking, thought about nothing — all the apparatus of thought busily working in a vacuum.

The other objection is this: let us go back to the toolshed. I might have discounted what I saw when looking along the beam (i.e., the leaves moving and the sun) on the ground that it was 'really only a strip of dusty light in a dark shed'. That is, I might have set up as 'true' my 'side vision' of the beam. But then that side vision is itself an instance of the activity we call seeing. And this new instance could also be looked at from outside. I could allow a scientist to tell me that what seemed to be a beam of light in a shed was 'really only an agitation of my own optic nerves'. And that would be just as good (or as bad) a bit of debunking as the previous one. The picture of the beam in the toolshed would now have to be discounted just as the previous picture of the trees and the sun had been discounted. And then, where are you?

214

In other words, you can step outside one experience only by stepping inside another. Therefore, if all inside experiences are misleading, we are always misled. The cerebral physiologist may say, if he chooses, that the mathematician's thought is 'only' tiny physical movements of the grey matter. But then what about the cerebral physiologist's own thought at that very moment? A second physiologist, looking at it, could pronounce it also to be only tiny physical movements in the first physiologist's skull. Where is the rot to end?

The answer is that we must never allow the rot to begin. We must, on pain of idiocy, deny from the very outset the idea that looking *at* is, by its own nature, intrinsically truer or better than looking *along*. One must look both *along* and *at* everything. In particular cases we shall find reason for regarding the one or the other vision as inferior. Thus the inside vision of rational thinking must be truer than the outside vision which sees only movements of the grey matter; for if the outside vision were the correct one all thought (including this thought itself) would be valueless, and this is self-contradictory. You cannot have a proof that no proofs matter. On the other hand, the inside vision of the savage's dance to Nyonga may be found deceptive because we find reason to believe that crops and babies are not really affected by it. In fact, we must take each case on its merits. But we must start with no prejudice for or against either kind of looking. We do not know in advance whether the lover or the psychologist is giving the more correct account of love, or whether both accounts are equally correct in different ways, or whether both are equally wrong. We just have to find out. But the period of brow-beating has got to end.

7

SCRAPS

1

Y ES,' MY FRIEND SAID. 'I DON'T SEE WHY THERE SHOULDN'T
be books in Heaven. But you will find that your library in
Heaven contains only some of the books you had on earth.'
'Which?' I asked. 'The ones you gave away or lent.' 'I hope
the lent ones won't still have all the borrowers' dirty thumb
marks,' said I. 'Oh yes they will,' said he. 'But just as the
wounds of the martyrs will have turned into beauties, so you
will find that the thumb-marks have turned into beautiful
illuminated capitals or exquisite marginal woodcuts.'

2

'The angels', he said, 'have no senses; their experience is
purely intellectual and spiritual. That is why we know something about God which they don't. There are particular aspects
of His love and joy which can be communicated to a created
being only by sensuous experience. Something of God which
the Seraphim can never quite understand flows into us from
the blue of the sky, the taste of honey, the delicious embrace
of water whether cold or hot, and even from sleep itself.'

3

'You are always dragging me down,' said I to my Body.
'Dragging *you* down!' replied my Body. 'Well I like that! Who
taught me to like tobacco and alcohol? You, of course, with
your idiotic adolescent idea of being "grown-up". My palate
loathed both at first: but you would have your way. Who

put an end to all those angry and revengeful thoughts last night? Me, of course, by insisting on going to sleep. Who does his best to keep you from talking too much and eating too much by giving you dry throats and headaches and indigestion? Eh?' 'And what about sex?' said I. 'Yes, what about it?' retorted the Body. 'If you and your wretched imagination would leave me alone I'd give you no trouble. That's Soul all over; you give me orders and then blame me for carrying them out.'

4

'Praying for particular things', said I, 'always seems to me like advising God how to run the world. Wouldn't it be wiser to assume that He knows best?' 'On the same principle', said he, 'I suppose you never ask a man next to you to pass the salt, because God knows best whether you ought to have salt or not. And I suppose you never take an umbrella, because God knows best whether you ought to be wet or dry.' 'That's quite different,' I protested. 'I don't see why,' said he. 'The odd thing is that He should let us influence the course of events at all. But since He lets us do it in one way I don't see why He shouldn't let us do it in the other.'

8

THE DECLINE OF RELIGION

From what I see of junior Oxford at present it would be quite easy to draw opposite conclusions about the religious predicament of what we call 'the rising generation', though in reality the undergraduate body includes men and women almost as much divided from one another in age, outlook, and experience as they are divided from the dons. Plenty of evidence can be produced to show that religion is in its last decline among them, or that a revival of interest in religion is one of their most noticeable characteristics. And in fact something that may be called 'a decline' and something that may be called 'a revival' are both going on. It will be perhaps more useful to attempt to understand both than to try our luck at 'spotting the winner'.

The 'decline of religion' so often lamented (or welcomed) is held to be shown by empty chapels. Now it is quite true that chapels which were full in 1900 are empty in 1946. But this change was not gradual. It occurred at the precise moment when chapel ceased to be compulsory. It was not in fact a decline; it was a precipice. The sixty men who had come because chapel was a little later than 'rollers'[1] (its only alternative) came no more; the five Christians remained. The with-

---

[1] After there came to be a number of non-Anglican students in the Oxford colleges, those students who did not wish to attend the morning chapel service were required to report to the Dean five or ten minutes before the service and have their names put on his roll-call. Thus the 'rollers', who did not go to chapel, had to be up before those who did go. Neither chapel nor roll-call is compulsory now.

218

drawal of compulsion did not create a new religious situation, but only revealed the situation which had long existed. And this is typical of the 'decline in religion' all over England.

In every class and every part of the country the visible practice of Christianity has grown very much less in the last fifty years. This is often taken to show that the nation as a whole has passed from a Christian to a secular outlook. But if we judge the nineteenth century from the books it wrote, the outlook of our grandfathers (with a very few exceptions) was quite as secular as our own. The novels of Meredith, Trollope, and Thackeray are not written either by or for men who see this world as the vestibule of eternity, who regard pride as the greatest of the sins, who desire to be poor in spirit, and look for a supernatural salvation. Even more significant is the absence from Dickens' *Christmas Carol* of any interest in the Incarnation. Mary, the Magi, and the Angels are replaced by 'spirits' of his own invention, and the animals present are not the ox and ass in the stable but the goose and turkey in the poulterer's shop. Most striking of all is the thirty-third chapter of *The Antiquary,* where Lord Glenallan forgives old Elspeth for her intolerable wrong. Glenallan has been painted by Scott as a life-long penitent and ascetic, a man whose every thought has been for years fixed on the supernatural. But when he has to forgive, no motive of a Christian kind is brought into play: the battle is won by 'the generosity of his nature'. It does not occur to Scott that his facts, his solitudes, his beads and his confessor, however useful as romantic 'properties', could be effectively connected with a serious action which concerns the plot of the book.

I am anxious here not to be misunderstood. I do not mean that Scott was not a brave, generous, honourable man and a glorious writer. I mean that in his work, as in that of most of his contemporaries, only secular and natural values are taken seriously. Plato and Virgil are, in that sense, nearer to Christianity than they.

Thus the 'decline of religion' becomes a very ambiguous phenomenon. One way of putting the truth would be that the religion which has declined was not Christianity. It was a vague Theism with a strong and virile ethical code, which, far from standing over against the 'World', was absorbed into the whole fabric of English institutions and sentiment and therefore demanded church-going as (at best) a part of loyalty and good manners as (at worst) a proof of respectability. Hence a social pressure, like the withdrawal of the compulsion, did not create a new situation. The new freedom first allowed accurate observations to be made. When no man goes to church except because he seeks Christ the number of actual believers can at last be discovered. It should be added that this new freedom was partly caused by the very conditions which it revealed. If the various anti-clerical and anti-theistic forces at work in the nineteenth century had had to attack a solid phalanx of radical Christians the story might have been different. But mere 'religion' — 'morality tinged with emotion', 'what a man does with his solitude', 'the religion of all good men' — has little power of resistance. It is not good at saying No.

The decline of 'religion', thus understood, seems to me in some ways a blessing. At the very worst it makes the issue clear. To the modern undergraduate Christianity is, at least, one of the intellectual options. It is, so to speak, on the agenda: it can be discussed, and a conversion may follow. I can remember times when this was much more difficult. 'Religion' (as distinct from Christianity) was too vague to be discussed ('too sacred to be lightly mentioned') and so mixed up with sentiment and good form as to be one of the embarrassing subjects. If it had to be spoken of, it was spoken of in a hushed, medical voice. Something of the shame of the Cross is, and ought to be, irremovable. But the merely social and sentimental embarrassment is gone. The fog of 'religion' has lifted; the positions and numbers of both armies can be observed; and real shooting is now possible.

The decline of 'religion' is no doubt a bad thing for the 'World'. By it all the things that made England a fairly happy country are, I suppose, endangered: the comparative purity of her public life, the comparative humanity of her police, and the possibility of some mutual respect and kindness between political opponents. But I am not clear that it makes conversions to Christianity rarer or more difficult: rather the reverse. It makes the choice more unescapable. When the Round Table is broken every man must follow either Galahad or Mordred: middle things are gone.

So much for the Decline of Religion; now for a Christian

Revival. Those who claim that there is such a Revival would point to the success (I mean success in the sense that it can be tested by sales) of several explicitly and even violently Christian writers, the apparent popularity of lectures on theological subjects, and the brisk atmosphere of not unfriendly discussion on them in which we live. They point, in fact, to what I have heard described as 'the high-brow Christian racket'. It is difficult to describe the phenomenon in quite neutral terms: but perhaps no one would deny that Christianity is now 'on the map' among the younger *intelligentsia* as it was not, say, in 1920. Only freshmen now talk as if the anti-Christian position were self-evident. The days of 'simple un-faith' are as dead as those of 'simple faith'.

At this those who are on the same side as myself are quite properly pleased. We have cause to give thanks: and the comments which I have to add proceed, I hope, not from a natural middle-aged desire to pour cold water into any soup within reach, but only from a desire to forestall, and therefore to disarm, possible disappointments.

In the first place, it must be admitted by anyone who accepts Christianity, that an increased interest in it, or even a growing measure of intellectual assent to it, is a very different thing from the conversion of England or even of a single soul. Conversion requires an alteration of the will, and an alteration which, in the last resort, does not occur without the intervention of the supernatural. I do not in the least agree with those who therefore conclude that the spread of an intellectual (and imaginative) climate favourable to Christianity is useless. You do not prove munition workers useless by showing that they cannot themselves win battles, however proper this reminder would be if they attempted to claim the honour due to fighting men. If the intellectual climate is such that, when a man comes to the crisis at which he must either accept or reject Christ, his reason and imagination are not on the wrong side, then his conflict will be fought out under favourable conditions. Those who help to produce and spread such a climate are therefore doing useful work: and yet no such great matter after all. Their share is a modest one; and it is always possible that nothing — nothing whatever — may come of it. Far higher than they stands that character whom, to the best of my knowledge, the present Christian movement has

221

not yet produced — the *Preacher* in the full sense, the Evangelist, the man on fire, the man who infects. The propagandist, the apologist, only represents John Baptist: the Preacher represents the Lord Himself. He will be sent — or else he will not. But unless he comes we mere Christian intellectuals will not effect very much. That does not mean we should down tools.

In the second place we must remember that a widespread and lively interest in a subject is precisely what we call a Fashion. And it is the nature of Fashions not to last. The present Christian movement may, or may not, have a long run ahead of it. But sooner or later it must lose the public ear; in a place like Oxford such changes are extraordinarily rapid. Bradley and the other idealists fell in a few terms, the Douglas scheme even more suddenly, the Vorticists overnight.[2] (Who now remembers Pogo? Who now reads *Childermass*?[3]) Whatever in our present success mere Fashion has given us, mere Fashion will presently withdraw. The real conversions will remain: but nothing else will. In that sense we may be on the brink of a real and permanent Christian revival: but it will work slowly and obscurely and in small groups. The present sunshine (if I may so call it) is certainly temporary. The grain must be got into the barns before the wet weather comes.

This mutability is the fate of all movements, fashions, intellectual climates and the like. But a Christian movement is also up against something sterner than the mere fickleness of taste. We have not yet had (at least in junior Oxford) any really bitter opposition. But if we have many more successes, this will certainly appear. The enemy has not yet thought it worth while to fling his whole weight against us. But he soon will. This happens in the history of every Christian movement, beginning with the Ministry of Christ Himself. At first it is welcome to all who have no special reason for opposing it: at this stage he who is not against it is for it. What men notice

2 F. H. Bradley (1846-1924) was a Fellow of Merton College, Oxford, and the author of *Appearance and Reality* (London, 1893). Major C. H. Douglas, a socio-economist, wrote, among other works, *Social Credit* (London, 1933). The Vorticists were a school of artists of the 1920s.

3 No one, practically. As far as I can discover, Pogo, or the Pogo-stick, which was invented in 1922, is a stilt with a spring on which the player jumps about. *Childermass* is by P. Wyndham Lewis (London, 1928).

is its difference from those aspects of the World which they already dislike. But later on, as the real meaning of the Christian claim becomes apparent, its demand for total surrender, the sheer chasm between Nature and Supernature, men are increasingly 'offended'. Dislike, terror, and finally hatred succeed: none who will not give it what it asks (and it asks all) can endure it: all who are not with it are against it. That is why we must cherish no picture of the present intellectual movement simply growing and spreading and finally reclaiming millions by sweet reasonableness. Long before it became as important as that the real opposition would have begun, and to be on the Christian side would be costing a man (at the least) his career. But remember, in England the opposition will quite likely be *called* Christianity (or Christo-democracy, or British Christianity, or something of that kind).

I think — but how should I know? — that all is going reasonably well. But it is early days. Neither our armour nor our enemies' is yet engaged. Combatants always tend to imagine that the war is further on than it really is.

9
VIVISECTION

I T IS THE RAREST THING IN THE WORLD TO HEAR A RATIONAL discussion of vivisection. Those who disapprove of it are commonly accused of 'sentimentality', and very often their arguments justify the accusation. They paint pictures of pretty little dogs on dissecting tables. But the other side lie open to exactly the same charge. They also often defend the practice by drawing pictures of suffering women and children whose pain can be relieved (we are assured) only by the fruits of vivisection. The one appeal, quite as clearly as the other, is addressed to emotion, to the particular emotion we call pity. And neither appeal proves anything. If the thing is right — and if right at all, it is a duty — then pity for the animal is one of the temptations we must resist in order to perform that duty. If the thing is wrong, then pity for human suffering is precisely the temptation which will most probably lure us into doing that wrong thing. But the real question — whether it is right or wrong — remains meanwhile just where it was.

A rational discussion of this subject begins by inquiring whether pain is, or is not, an evil. If it is not, then the case against vivisection falls. But then so does the case for vivisection. If it is not defended on the ground that it reduces human suffering, on what ground can it be defended? And if pain is not an evil, why should human suffering be reduced? We must therefore assume as a basis for the whole discussion that pain is an evil, otherwise there is nothing to be discussed.

Now if pain is an evil then the infliction of pain, considered in itself, must clearly be an evil act. But there are such things as necessary evils. Some acts which would be bad, simply in themselves, may be excusable and even laudable when they are necessary means to a greater good. In saying that the infliction of pain, simply in itself, is bad, we are not saying that pain ought never to be inflicted. Most of us think that it can rightly be inflicted for a good purpose — as in dentistry or just and reformatory punishment. The point is that it always requires justification. On the man whom we find inflicting pain rests the burden of showing why an act which in itself would be simply bad is, in those particular circumstances, good. If we find a man giving pleasure it is for us to prove (if we criticise him) that his action is wrong. But if we find a man inflicting pain it is for him to prove that his action is right. If he cannot, he is a wicked man.

Now vivisection can only be defended by showing it to be right that one species should suffer in order that another species should be happier. And here we come to the parting of the ways. The Christian defender and the ordinary 'scientific' (i.e. naturalistic) defender of vivisection, have to take quite different lines.

The Christian defender, especially in the Latin countries, is very apt to say that we are entitled to do anything we please to animals because they 'have no souls'. But what does this mean? If it means that animals have no consciousness, then how is this known? They certainly behave as if they had, or at least the higher animals do. I myself am inclined to think that far fewer animals than is supposed have what we should recognise as consciousness. But that is only an opinion. Unless we know on other grounds that vivisection is right we must not take the moral risk of tormenting them on a mere opinion. On the other hand, the statement that they 'have no souls' may mean that they have no moral responsibilities and are not immortal. But the absence of 'soul' in that sense makes the infliction of pain upon them not easier but harder to justify. For it means that animals cannot deserve pain, nor profit morally by the discipline of pain, nor be recompensed by happiness in another life for suffering in this. Thus all the factors which render pain more tolerable or make it less totally evil in the case of human beings will be lacking in

225

the beasts. 'Soullessness', in so far as it is relevant to the question at all, is an argument against vivisection.

The only rational line for the Christian vivisectionist to take is to say that the superiority of man over beast is a real objective fact, guaranteed by Revelation, and that the propriety of sacrificing beast to man is a logical consequence. We are 'worth more than many sparrows',[1] and in saying this we are not merely expressing a natural preference for our own species simply because it is our own but conforming to a hierarchical order created by God and really present in the universe whether any one acknowledges it or not. The position may not be satisfactory. We may fail to see how a benevolent Deity could wish us to draw such conclusions from the hierarchical order He has created. We may find it difficult to formulate a human right of tormenting beasts in terms which would not equally imply an angelic right of tormenting men. And we may feel that though objective superiority is rightly claimed for man, yet that very superiority ought partly to *consist in* not behaving like a vivisector: that we ought to prove ourselves better than the beasts precisely by the fact of acknowledging duties to them which they do not acknowledge to us. But on all these questions different opinions can be honestly held. If on grounds of our real, divinely ordained, superiority a Christian pathologist thinks it right to vivisect, and does so with scrupulous care to avoid the least dram or scruple of unnecessary pain, in a trembling awe at the responsibility which he assumes, and with a vivid sense of the high mode in which human life must be lived if it is to justify the sacrifices made for it, then (whether we agree with him or not) we can respect his point of view.

But of course the vast majority of vivisectors have no such theological background. They are most of them naturalistic and Darwinian. Now here, surely, we come up against a very alarming fact. The very same people who will most contemptuously brush aside any consideration of animal suffering if it stands in the way of 'research' will also, on another context, most vehemently deny that there is any radical difference between man and the other animals. On the naturalistic view the beasts are at bottom just the same *sort* of thing as ourselves. Man is simply the cleverest of the anthropoids. All the

[1] Matthew x. 31.

grounds on which a Christian might defend vivisection are thus cut from under our feet. We sacrifice other species to our own not because our own has any objective metaphysical privilege over others, but simply because it is ours. It may be very natural to have this loyalty to our own species, but let us hear no more from the naturalists about the 'sentimentality' of anti-vivisectionists. If loyalty to our own species, preference for man simply because we are men, is not a sentiment, then what is? It may be a good sentiment or a bad one. But a sentiment it certainly is. Try to base it on logic and see what happens!

But the most sinister thing about modern vivisection is this. If a mere sentiment justifies cruelty, why stop at a sentiment for the whole human race? There is also a sentiment for the white man against the black, for a *Herrenvolk* against the non-Aryans, for 'civilized' or 'progressive' peoples against 'savage' or 'backward' peoples. Finally, for our own country, party, or class against others. Once the old Christian idea of a total difference in kind between man and beast has been abandoned, then no argument for experiments on animals can be found which is not also an argument for experiments on inferior men. If we cut up beasts simply because they cannot prevent us and because we are backing our own side in the struggle for existence, it is only logical to cut up imbeciles, criminals, enemies, or capitalists for the same reasons. Indeed, experiments on men have already begun. We all hear that Nazi scientists have done them. We all suspect that our own scientists may begin to do so, in secret, at any moment.

The alarming thing is that the vivisectors have won the first round. In the nineteenth and eighteenth century a man was not stamped as a 'crank' for protesting against vivisection. Lewis Carroll protested, if I remember his famous letter correctly, on the very same ground which I have just used.[2] Dr Johnson — a man whose mind had as much *iron* in it as any man's — protested in a note on *Cymbeline* which is worth quoting in full. In Act I, scene v, the Queen explains to the Doctor that she wants poisons to experiment on 'such crea-

---

[2] 'Vivisection as a Sign of the Times', *The Works of Lewis Carroll,* ed. Roger Lancelyn Green (London, 1965), pp. 1089-92. See also 'Some Popular Fallacies about Vivisection', *ib.,* pp. 1092-1100.

tures as We count not worth the hanging, — but none human.'[3]
The Doctor replies:

> Your Highness
> Shall from this practice but make hard your heart.[4]

Johnson comments: 'The thought would probably have been more amplified, had our author lived to be shocked with such experiments as have been published in later times, by a race of men that have practised tortures without pity, and related them without shame, and are yet suffered to erect their heads among human beings.'[5]

The words are his, not mine, and in truth we hardly dare in these days to use such calmly stern language. The reason why we do not dare is that the other side has in fact won. And though cruelty even to beasts is an important matter, their victory is symptomatic of matters more important still. The victory of vivisection marks a great advance in the triumph of ruthless, non-moral utilitarianism over the old world of ethical law; a triumph in which we, as well as animals, are already the victims, and of which Dachau and Hiroshima mark the more recent achievements. In justifying cruelty to animals we put ourselves also on the animal level. We choose the jungle and must abide by our choice.

You will notice I have spent no time in discussing what actually goes on in the laboratories. We shall be told, of course, that there is surprisingly little cruelty. That is a question with which, at present, I have nothing to do. We must first decide what should be allowed: after that it is for the police to discover what is already being done.

[3] Shakespeare, *Cymbeline*, I, v, 19-20.
[4] *Ibid.*, 23.
[5] *Johnson on Shakespeare: Essays and Notes Selected and Set Forth with an Introduction* by Sir Walter Raleigh (London, 1908), p. 181.

10

MODERN TRANSLATIONS
OF THE BIBLE

IT IS POSSIBLE THAT THE READER WHO OPENS THIS VOLUME[1]
on the counter of a bookshop may ask himself why we need
a new translation of any part of the Bible, and, if of any,
why of the Epistles. 'Do we not already possess', it may be
said, 'in the Authorised Version the most beautiful rendering
which any language can boast?' Some people whom I have
met go even further and feel that a modern translation is not
only unnecessary but even offensive. They cannot bear to see
the time-honoured words altered; it seems to them irreverent.

There are several answers to such people. In the first place
the kind of objection which they feel to a new translation
is very like the objection which was once felt to any English
translation at all. Dozens of sincerely pious people in the sixteenth century shuddered at the idea of turning the time-honoured Latin of the Vulgate into our common and (as they
thought) 'barbarous' English. A sacred truth seemed to them
to have lost its sanctity when it was stripped of the polysyllabic
Latin, long heard at Mass and at Hours, and put into 'language
such as men do use' — language steeped in all the commonplace associations of the nursery, the inn, the stable, and the
street. The answer then was the same as the answer now.
The only kind of sanctity which Scripture can lose (or, at

[1] This essay was originally published as an Introduction to J. B. Phillips' *Letters to Young Churches: A Translation of the New Testament
Epistles* (London, 1947).

least, New Testament scripture) by being modernized is an accidental kind which it never had for its writers or its earliest readers. The New Testament in the original Greek is not a work of literary art: it is not written in a solemn, ecclesiastical language, it is written in the sort of Greek which was spoken over the Eastern Mediterranean after Greek had become an international language and therefore lost its real beauty and subtlety. In it we see Greek used by people who have no real feeling for Greek words because Greek words are not the words they spoke when they were children. It is a sort of 'basic' Greek; a language without roots in the soil, a utilitarian, commercial and administrative language. Does this shock us? It ought not to, except as the Incarnation itself ought to shock us. The same divine humility which decreed that God should become a baby at a peasant-woman's breast, and later an arrested field-preacher in the hands of the Roman police, decreed also that He should be preached in a vulgar, prosaic and un-literary language. If you can stomach the one, you can stomach the other. The Incarnation is in that sense an irreverent doc-trine: Christianity, in that sense, an incurably irreverent re-ligion. When we expect that it should have come before the World in all the beauty that we now feel in the Authorised Version we are as wide of the mark as the Jews were in expect-ing that the Messiah would come as a great earthly King. The real sanctity, the real beauty and sublimity of the New Testa-ment (as of Christ's life) are of a different sort: miles deeper or *further in*.

In the second place, the Authorised Version has ceased to be a good (that is, a clear) translation. It is no longer modern English: the meanings of words have changed. The same antique glamour which has made it (in the superficial sense) so 'beautiful', so 'sacred', so 'comforting', and so 'inspiring', has also made it in many places unintelligible. Thus where St Paul says 'I know nothing against myself,' it translates 'I know nothing by myself.'[2] That was a good translation (though even then rather old-fashioned) in the sixteenth century: to the modern reader it means either nothing, or something quite different from what St Paul said. The truth is that if we are to have translation at all we must have periodical re-trans-

[2] I Corinthians iv. 4.

lation. There is no such thing as translating a book into another language once and for all, for a language is a changing thing. If your son is to have clothes it is no good buying him a suit once and for all: he will grow out of it and have to be re-clothed.

And finally, though it may seem a sour paradox — we must sometimes get away from the Authorised Version, if for no other reason, simply *because* it is so beautiful and so solemn. Beauty exalts, but beauty also lulls. Early associations endear but they also confuse. Through that beautiful solemnity the transporting or horrifying realities of which the Book tells may come to us blunted and disarmed and we may only sigh with tranquil veneration when we ought to be burning with shame or struck dumb with terror or carried out of ourselves by ravishing hopes and adorations. Does the word 'scourged'[3] really come home to us like 'flogged'? Does 'mocked him'[4] sting like 'jeered at him'?

We ought therefore to welcome all new translations (when they are made by sound scholars) and most certainly those who are approaching the Bible for the first time will be wise not to begin with the Authorised Version — except perhaps for the historical books of the Old Testament where its archa-isms suit the saga-like material well enough. Among modern translations those of Dr Moffatt[5] and Monsignor Knox[6] seem to me particularly good. The present volume concentrates on the epistles and furnishes more help to the beginner: its scope is different. The preliminary abstracts to each letter will be found especially useful, and the reader who has not read the letters before might do well to begin by reading and reflecting on these abstracts at some length before he attempts to tackle the text. It would have saved me a great deal of labour if this book had come into my hands when I first seriously began to try to discover what Christianity was.

For a man who wants to make that discovery must face the epistles. And whether we like it or not, most of them

---

[3] John xix. 1.

[4] Matthew xxvii. 29; Mark xv. 20; Luke xxii. 63; xxiii. 11, 36.

[5] James Moffatt (1870-1944), whose translation of the New Testa-ment appeared in 1913, his translation of the Old Testament in 1924, and the whole being revised in 1935.

[6] Ronald A. Knox (1888-1957) published a translation of the New Testament in 1945, and a translation of the Old Testament in 1949.

are by St Paul. He is the Christian author whom no one can by-pass.

A most astonishing misconception has long dominated the modern mind on the subject of St Paul. It is to this effect: that Jesus preached a kindly and simple religion (found in the Gospels) and that St Paul afterwards corrupted it into a cruel and complicated religion (found in the Epistles). This is really quite untenable. All the most terrifying texts come from the mouth of Our Lord: all the texts on which we can base such warrant as we have for hoping that all men will be saved come from St Paul. If it could be proved that St Paul altered the teaching of his Master in any way, he altered it in exactly the opposite way to that which is popularly supposed. But there is no real evidence for a pre-Pauline doctrine different from St Paul's. The Epistles are, for the most part, the earliest Christian documents we possess. The Gospels come later. They are not 'the gospel', the statement of the Christian belief. They were written for those who had already been converted, who had already accepted 'the gospel'. They leave out many of the 'complications' (that is, the theology) because they are intended for readers who have already been instructed in it. In that sense the Epistles are more primitive and more central than the Gospels — though not, of course, than the great events which the Gospels recount. God's act (the Incarnation, the Crucifixion, and the Resurrection) comes first: the earliest theological analysis of it comes in the Epistles: then, when the generation who had known the Lord was dying out, the Gospels were composed to provide for believers a record of the great Act and of some of the Lord's sayings. The ordinary popular conception has put everything upside down. Nor is the cause far to seek. In the earlier history of every rebellion there is a stage at which you do not yet attack the King in person. You say, 'The King is all right. It is his Ministers who are wrong. They misrepresent him and corrupt all his plans — which, I'm sure, are good plans if only the Ministers would let them take effect.' And the first victory consists in beheading a few Ministers: only at a later stage do you go on and behead the King himself. In the same way, the nineteenth-century attack on St Paul was really only a stage in the revolt against Christ. Men were not ready in large numbers to attack Christ Himself. They made the normal first move — that of attacking one of His principal ministers. Everything they disliked in Christianity was therefore attributed to St Paul. It was unfortunate that their case could not impress anyone who had really read the Gospels and the Epistles with attention: but apparently few people had, and so the first victory was won. St Paul was impeached and banished and the world went on to the next step — the attack on the King Himself. But to those who wish to know what St Paul and his fellow-teachers really said the present volume will give very great help.

11

PRIESTESSES IN
THE CHURCH?

I SHOULD LIKE BALLS INFINITELY BETTER', SAID CAROLINE
Bingley, 'if they were carried on in a different manner . . . It
would surely be much more rational if conversation instead
of dancing made the order of the day.' 'Much more rational,
I dare say,' replied her brother, 'but it would not be near
so much like a Ball.'[1] We are told that the lady was silenced:
yet it could be maintained that Jane Austen has not allowed
Bingley to put forward the full strength of his position. He
ought to have replied with a *distinguo*. In one sense conversation is more rational for conversation may exercise the reason
alone, dancing does not. But there is nothing irrational in
exercising other powers than our reason. On certain occasions
and for certain purposes the real irrationality is with those
who will not do so. The man who would try to break a horse
or write a poem or beget a child by pure syllogizing would be
an irrational man; though at the same time syllogizing is in
itself a more rational activity than the activities demanded
by these achievements. It is rational not to reason, or not to
limit oneself to reason, in the wrong place; and the more
rational a man is the better he knows this.

These remarks are not intended as a contribution to the
criticism of *Pride and Prejudice*. They came into my head
when I heard that the Church of England[2] was being advised

[1] *Pride and Prejudice*, ch. xi.
[2] Called the Episcopal Church in the United States.

to declare women capable of Priests' Orders. I am, indeed, informed that such a proposal is very unlikely to be seriously considered by the authorities. To take such a revolutionary step at the present moment, to cut ourselves off from the Christian past and to widen the divisions between ourselves and other Churches by establishing an order of priestesses in our midst, would be an almost wanton degree of imprudence. And the Church of England herself would be torn in shreds by the operation. My concern with the proposal is of a more theoretical kind. The question involves something even deeper than a revolution in order.

I have every respect for those who wish women to be priestesses. I think they are sincere and pious and sensible people. Indeed, in a way they are too sensible. That is where my dissent from them resembles Bingley's dissent from his sister. I am tempted to say that the proposed arrangement would make us much more rational 'but not near so much like a Church'.

For at first sight all the rationality (in Caroline Bingley's sense) is on the side of the innovators. We are short of priests. We have discovered in one profession after another that women can do very well all sorts of things which were once supposed to be in the power of men alone. No one among those who dislike the proposal is maintaining that women are less capable than men of piety, zeal, learning and whatever else seems necessary for the pastoral office. What, then, except prejudice begotten by tradition, forbids us to draw on the huge reserves which could pour into the priesthood if women were here, as in so many other professions, put on the same footing as men? And against this flood of common sense, the opposers (many of them women) can produce at first nothing but an inarticulate distaste, a sense of discomfort which they themselves find it hard to analyse.

That this reaction does not spring from any contempt for women is, I think, plain from history. The Middle Ages carried their reverence for one Woman to a point at which the charge could be plausibly made that the Blessed Virgin became in their eyes almost 'a fourth Person of the Trinity'. But never, so far as I know, in all those ages was anything remotely resembling a sacerdotal office attributed to her. All salvation depends on the decision which she made in the

235

words *Ecce ancilla;*[3] she is united in nine months' inconceivable intimacy with the eternal Word; she stands at the foot of the cross.[4] But she is absent both from the Last Supper[5] and from the descent of the Spirit at Pentecost.[6] Such is the record of Scripture. Nor can you daff it aside by saying that local and temporary conditions condemned women to silence and private life. There were female preachers. One man had four daughters who all 'prophesied', i.e. preached.[7] There were prophetesses even in Old Testament times. Prophetesses, not priestesses.

At this point the common sensible reformer is apt to ask why, if women can preach, they cannot do all the rest of a priest's work. This question deepens the discomfort of my side. We begin to feel that what really divides us from our opponents is a difference between the meaning which they and we give to the word 'priest'. The more they speak (and speak truly) about the competence of women in administration, their tact and sympathy as advisers, their national talent for 'visiting', the more we feel that the central thing is being forgotten. To us a priest is primarily a representative, a double representative, who represents us to God and God to us. Our very eyes teach us this in church. Sometimes the priest turns his back on us and faces the East — he speaks to God for us: sometimes he faces us and speaks to us for God. We have no objection to a woman doing the first: the whole difficulty is about the second. But why? Why should a woman not in this sense represent God? Certainly not because she is necessarily, or even probably, less holy or less charitable or stupider than a man. In that sense she may be as 'God-like' as a man; and a given women much more so than a given man. The sense in which she cannot represent God will perhaps be plainer if we look at the thing the other way round.

Suppose the reformer stops saying that a good woman may

[3] After being told by the angel Gabriel that she has found favour with God and that she should bear the Christ Child, the Virgin exclaims 'Behold the handmaid of the Lord' (Luke i. 38). The *Magnificat* follows in verses 46-55.

[4] Matthew xxvii. 55-6; Mark xv. 40-1; Luke xxiii. 49; John xix. 25.

[5] Matthew xxvi. 26; Mark xiv. 22; Luke xxii. 19.

[6] Acts ii. 1 *et seq.*

[7] Acts xxi. 9.

be like God and begins saying that God is like a good woman. Suppose he says that we might just as well pray to 'Our Mother which art in heaven' as to 'Our Father'. Suppose he suggests that the Incarnation might just as well have taken a female as a male form, and the Second Person of the Trinity be as well called the Daughter as the Son. Suppose, finally, that the mystical marriage were reversed, that the Church were the Bridegroom and Christ the Bride. All this, as it seems to me, is involved in the claim that a woman can represent God as a priest does.

Now it is surely the case that if all these supposals were ever carried into effect we should be embarked on a different religion. Goddesses have, of course, been worshipped: many religions have had priestesses. But they are religions quite different in character from Christianity. Common sense, disregarding the discomfort, or even the horror, which the idea of turning all our theological language into the feminine gender arouses in most Christians, will ask 'Why not? Since God is in fact not a biological being and has no sex, what can it matter whether we say *He* or *She, Father* or *Mother, Son* or *Daughter*?'

But Christians think that God Himself has taught us how to speak of Him. To say that it does not matter is to say either that all the masculine imagery is not inspired, is merely human in origin, or else that, though inspired, it is quite arbitrary and unessential. And this is surely intolerable: or, if tolerable, it is an argument not in favour of Christian priestesses but against Christianity. It is also surely based on a shallow view of imagery. Without drawing upon religion, we know from our poetical experience that image and apprehension cleave closer together than common sense is here prepared to admit; that a child who has been taught to pray to a Mother in Heaven would have a religious life radically different from that of a Christian child. And as image and apprehension are in an organic unity, so, for a Christian, are human body and human soul.

The innovators are really implying that sex is something superficial, irrelevant to the spiritual life. To say that men and women are equally eligible for a certain profession is to say that for the purposes of that profession their sex is irrelevant. We are, within that context, treating both as neuters.

237

As the State grows more like a hive or an ant-hill it needs an increasing number of workers who can be treated as neuters. This may be inevitable for our secular life. But in our Christian life we must return to reality. There we are not homogeneous units, but different and complementary organs of a mystical body. Lady Nunburnholme has claimed that the equality of men and women is a Christian principle.[8] I do not remember the text in scripture nor the Fathers, nor Hooker, nor the Prayer Book which asserts it; but that is not here my point. The point is that unless 'equal' means 'interchangeable', equality makes nothing for the priesthood of women. And the kind of equality which implies that the equals are interchangeable (like counters or identical machines) is, among humans, a legal fiction. It may be a useful legal fiction. But in church we turn our back on fictions. One of the ends for which sex was created was to symbolize to us the hidden things of God. One of the functions of human marriage is to express the nature of the union between Christ and the Church. We have no authority to take the living and semitive figures which God has painted on the canvas of our nature and shift them about as if they were mere geometrical figures.

This is what common sense will call 'mystical'. Exactly. The Church claims to be the bearer of a revelation. If that claim is false then we want not to make priestesses but to abolish priests. If it is true, then we should expect to find in the Church an element which unbelievers will call irrational and which believers will call supra-rational. There ought to be something in it opaque to our reason though not contrary to it — as the facts of sex and sense on the natural level are opaque. And that is the real issue. The Church of England can remain a church only if she retains this opaque element. If we abandon that, if we retain only what can be justified by standards of prudence and convenience at the bar of enlightened common sense, then we exchange revelation for that old wraith Natural Religion.

It is painful, being a man, to have to assert the privilege, or the burden, which Christianity lays upon my own sex. I am crushingly aware how inadequate most of us are, in our actual and historical individualities, to fill the place prepared

[8] Lady Marjorie Nunburnholme, 'A Petition to the Lambeth Conference', *Time and Tide*, vol. XXIX, No. 28 (10 July 1948), p. 720.

for us. But it is an old saying in the army that you salute the uniform not the wearer. Only one wearing the masculine uniform can (provisionally, and till the *Parousia*)[9] represent the Lord to the Church: for we are all, corporately and individually, feminine to Him. We men may often make very bad priests. That is because we are insufficiently masculine. It is no cure to call in those who are not masculine at all. A given man may make a very bad husband; you cannot mend matters by trying to reverse the roles. He may make a bad male partner in a dance. The cure for that is that men should more diligently attend dancing classes; not that the ballroom should henceforward ignore distinctions of sex and treat all dancers as neuter. That would, of course, be eminently sensible, civilized, and enlightened, but, once more, 'not near so much like a Ball'.

And this parallel between the Church and the Ball is not so fanciful as some would think. The Church ought to be more like a Ball than it is like a factory or a political party. Or, to speak more strictly, they are at the circumference and the Church at the Centre and the Ball comes in between. The factory and the political party are artificial creations — 'a breath can make them as a breath has made'. In them we are not dealing with human beings in their concrete entirety — only with 'hands' or voters. I am not of course using 'artificial' in any derogatory sense. Such artifices are necessary: but because they are our artifices we are free to shuffle, scrap and experiment as we please. But the Ball exists to stylize something which is natural and which concerns human beings in their entirety — namely, courtship. We cannot shuffle or tamper so much. With the Church, we are farther in: for there we are dealing with male and female not merely as facts of nature but as the live and awful shadows of realities utterly beyond our control and largely beyond our direct knowledge. Or rather, we are not dealing with them but (as we shall soon learn if we meddle) they are dealing with us.

[9] The future return of Christ in glory to judge the living and the dead.

12

GOD IN THE DOCK

I HAVE BEEN ASKED TO WRITE ABOUT THE DIFFICULTIES which a man must face in trying to present the Christian Faith to modern unbelievers. That is too wide a subject for my capacity or even for the scope of an article. The difficulties vary as the audience varies. The audience may be of this or that nation, may be children or adults, learned or ignorant. My own experience is of English audiences only, and almost exclusively of adults. It has, in fact, been mostly of men (and women) serving in the R.A.F.[1] This has meant that while very few of them have been learned in the academic sense of that word, a large number of them have had a smattering of elementary practical science, have been mechanics, electricians or wireless operators; for the rank and file of the R.A.F. belong to what may almost be called 'the Intelligentsia of the Proletariat'. I have also talked to students at the Universities. These strict limitations in my experience must be kept in mind by the readers. How rash it would be to generalise from such an experience I myself discovered on the single occasion when I spoke to soldiers. It became at once clear to me that the level of intelligence in our army is very much lower than in the R.A.F. and that quite a different approach was required.

The first thing I learned from addressing the R.A.F. was that I had been mistaken in thinking materialism to be our only considerable adversary. Among the English 'Intelligentsia of the Proletariat', materialism is only one among many non-

[1] Royal Air Force.

Christian creeds — Theosophy, Spiritualism, British Israelitism, etc. England has, of course, always been the home of 'cranks'; I see no sign that they are diminishing. Consistent Marxism I very seldom met. Whether this is because it is very rare, or because men speaking in the presence of their officers concealed it, or because Marxists did not attend the meetings at which I spoke, I have no means of knowing. Even where Christianity was professed, it was often much tainted with Pantheistic elements. Strict and well-informed Christian statements, when they occurred at all, usually came from Roman Catholics or from members of extreme Protestant sects (e.g. Baptists). My student audiences shared, in a less degree, the theological vagueness I found in the R.A.F., but among them strict and well-informed statements came from Anglo-Catholics and Roman Catholics; seldom, if ever, from Dissenters. The various non-Christian religions mentioned above hardly appeared.

The next thing I learned from the R.A.F. was that the English Proletariat is sceptical about History to a degree which academically educated persons can hardly imagine. This, indeed, seems to me to be far the widest cleavage between the learned and unlearned. The educated man habitually, almost without noticing it, sees the present as something that grows out of a long perspective of centuries. In the minds of my R.A.F. hearers this perspective simply did not exist. It seemed to me that they did not really believe that we have any reliable knowledge of historic man. But this was often curiously combined with a conviction that we knew a great deal about Pre-Historic Man: doubtless because Pre-Historic Man is labelled 'Science' (which is reliable) whereas Napoleon or Julius Caesar is labelled as 'History' (which is not). Thus a pseudo-scientific picture of the 'Cave-man' and a picture of 'the Present' filled almost the whole of their imaginations; between these, there lay only a shadowy and unimportant region in which the phantasmal shapes of Roman soldiers, stage-coaches, pirates, knights-in-armour, highwaymen, etc., moved in a mist. I had supposed that if my hearers disbelieved the Gospels, they would do so because the Gospels recorded miracles. But my impression is that they disbelieved them simply because they dealt with events that happened a long time ago: that they would be almost as incredulous of

241

the Battle of Actium as of the Resurrection — and for the same reason. Sometimes this scepticism was defended by the argument that all books before the invention of printing must have been copied and re-copied till the text was changed beyond recognition. And here came another surprise. When their historical scepticism took that rational form, it was sometimes easily allayed by the mere statement that there existed a 'science called textual criticism' which gave us a reasonable assurance that some ancient texts were accurate. This ready acceptance of the authority of specialists is significant, not only for its ingenuousness but also because it underlines a fact of which my experiences have on the whole convinced me; i.e. that very little of the opposition we meet is inspired by malice or suspicion. It is based on genuine doubt, and often on doubt that is reasonable in the state of the doubter's knowledge.

My third discovery is of a difficulty which I suspect to be more acute in England than elsewhere. I mean the difficulty occasioned by language. In all societies, no doubt, the speech of the vulgar differs from that of the learned. The English language with its double vocabulary (Latin and native), English manners (with their boundless indulgence to slang, even in polite circles) and English culture which allows nothing like the French Academy, make the gap unusually wide. There are almost two languages in this country. The man who wishes to speak to the uneducated in English must learn their language. It is not enough that he should abstain from using what he regards as 'hard words'. He must discover empirically what words exist in the language of his audience and what they mean in that language: e.g. that *potential* means not 'possible' but 'power', that *creature* means not creature but 'animal', that *primitive* means 'rude' or 'clumsy', that *rude* means (often) 'scabrous', 'obscene', that the *Immaculate Conception* (except in the mouths of Roman Catholics) means 'the Virgin Birth'. A *Being* means 'a personal being': a man who said to me 'I believe in the Holy Ghost, but I don't think it is a being', meant: 'I believe there is such a Being, but that it is not personal.' On the other hand, *personal* sometimes means 'corporeal'. When an uneducated Englishman says that he believes 'in God, but not in a personal God', he may mean simply and solely that he is not an Anthropomorphist in the strict and original sense of that word. *Abstract* seems to have two meanings: (a) 'immaterial', (b) 'vague', obscure and unpractical. Thus Arithmetic is not, in their language, an 'abstract' science. *Practical* means often 'economic' or 'utilitarian'. *Morality* nearly always means 'chastity': thus in their language the sentence 'I do not say that this woman is immoral but I do say that she is a thief,' would not be nonsense, but would mean: 'She is chaste but dishonest.' *Christian* has an eulogistic rather than a descriptive sense: e.g. 'Christian standards' means simply 'high moral standards'. The proposition 'So and so is not a Christian' would only be taken to be a criticism of his behaviour, never to be merely a statement of his beliefs. It is also important to notice that what would seem to the learned to be the harder of two words may in fact, to the uneducated, be the easier. Thus it was recently proposed to emend a prayer used in the Church of England that magistrates 'may truly and indifferently administer justice' to 'may truly and impartially administer justice'. A country priest told me that his sexton understood and could accurately explain the meaning of 'indifferently' but had no idea of what 'impartially' meant.

The popular English language, then, simply has to be learned by him who would preach to the English: just as a missionary learns Bantu before preaching to the Bantus. This is the more necessary because once the lecture or discussion has begun, digressions on the meaning of words tend to bore uneducated audiences and even to awaken distrust. There is no subject in which they are less interested than Philology. Our problem is often simply one of translation. Every examination for ordinands ought to include a passage from some standard theological work for translation into the vernacular. The work is laborious but it is immediately rewarded. By trying to translate our doctrines into vulgar speech we discover how much we understand them ourselves. Our failure to translate may sometimes be due to our ignorance of the vernacular; much more often it exposes the fact that we do not exactly know what we mean.

Apart from this linguistic difficulty, the greatest barrier I have met is the almost total absence from the minds of my audience of any sense of sin. This has struck me more forcibly when I spoke to the R.A.F. than when I spoke to students: whether (as I believe) the Proletariat is more self-righteous than other classes, or whether educated people are cleverer at concealing their pride, this creates for us a new situation. The early Christian preachers could assume in their hearers, whether Jews, *Metuentes* or Pagans, a sense of guilt. (That this was common among Pagans is shown by the fact that both Epicureanism and the Mystery Religions both claimed, though in different ways, to assuage it.) Thus the Christian message was in those days unmistakably the *Evangelium,* the Good News. It promised healing to those who knew they were sick. We have to convince our hearers of the unwelcome diagnosis before we can expect them to welcome the news of the remedy.

The ancient man approached God (or even the gods) as the accused person approaches his judge. For the modern man the roles are reversed. He is the judge: God is in the dock. He is quite a kindly judge: if God should have a reasonable defence for being the god who permits war, poverty and disease, he is ready to listen to it. The trial may even end in God's acquittal. But the important thing is that Man is on the Bench and God in the Dock.

It is generally useless to try to combat this attitude, as older preachers did, by dwelling on sins like drunkenness and unchastity. The modern Proletariat is not drunken. As for fornication, contraceptives have made a profound difference. As long as this sin might socially ruin a girl by making her the mother of a bastard, most men recognised the sin against charity which it involved, and their consciences were often troubled by it. Now that it need have no such consequences, it is not, I think, generally felt to be a sin at all. My own experience suggests that if we can awake the conscience of our hearers at all, we must do so in quite different directions. We must talk of conceit, spite, jealousy, cowardice, meanness, etc. But I am very far from believing that I have found the solution of this problem.

Finally, I must add that my own work has suffered very much from the incurable intellectualism of my approach. The simple, emotional appeal ('Come to Jesus') is still often successful. But those who, like myself, lack the gift for making it, had better not attempt it.

13

BEHIND THE SCENES

WHEN I WAS TAKEN TO THE THEATRE AS A SMALL BOY what interested me most of all was the stage scenery. The interest was not an aesthetic one. No doubt the gardens, balconies and palaces of the Edwardian 'sets' looked prettier to me than they would now, but that had nothing to do with it. Ugly scenery would have served my turn just as well. Still less did I mistake these canvas images for realities. On the contrary, I believed (and wished) all things on the stage to be more artificial than they actually were.

When an actor came on in ordinary modern clothes I never believed he was wearing a real suit with veritable waistcoat and trousers put on in the ordinary way. I thought he was wearing — and I somehow felt he ought to be wearing — some kind of theatrical overalls which were slipped on all in one piece and fastened invisibly up the back. The stage suit ought not to be a suit; it ought to be something quite different which nevertheless (that's where the pleasure comes) looked like a suit from the stalls. Perhaps this is why I continued, even after I was grown up, to believe in the Cold Tea theory; until a real actor pointed out that a man who played a leading part in a London theatre could afford to, and would certainly rather, provide real whisky (if need were) at his own charges than drink a tumbler of cold tea every evening shortly after his dinner.

No. I knew very well that the scenery was painted canvas; that the stage rooms and stage trees, seen from behind, would not look like rooms or trees at all. That was where the interest lay. That was the fascination of our toy theatre at home, where we made our own scenery. You cut out your piece of cardboard in the shape of a tower and you painted it, and then you gummed an ordinary nursery block on to the back to make it stand upright. The rapture was to dart to and fro. You went in front and there was your tower. You went behind and there — raw, brown cardboard and a block.

In the real theatre you couldn't go 'behind', but you knew it would be the same. The moment the actor vanished into the wings he entered a different world. One knew it was not a world of any particular beauty or wonder; somebody must have told me — at any rate I believed — it would be a rather dingy world of bare floors and whitewashed walls. The charm lay in the idea of being able thus to pass in and out of a world by taking three strides.

One wanted to be an actor not (at that age) for the sake of fame or applause, but simply that one might have this privilege of transition. To come from dressing rooms and bare walls and utilitarian corridors — and to come suddenly — into Aladdin's cave or the Darlings' nursery or whatever it was — to become what you weren't and be where you weren't — this seemed most enviable.

It was best of all when the door at the back of the stage room opened to show a little piece of passage — unreal passage, of course, its panels only canvas, intended to suggest (which one knew to be false) that the sham room on the stage was part of a whole house. 'You can see just a little *peep* of the passage in Looking Glass House . . . and it's very like our passage as far as you can see, only you know it may be quite different on beyond.' Thus Alice to the Kitten.[1] But the stage passage did not leave one to conjecture. One *knew* it was quite different 'on beyond', that it ceased to be a passage at all.

I envied the children in stage boxes. If one sat so far to the side as that, then by craning one's neck one might squint along the sham passage and actually see the point at which it ceased to exist: the joint between the real and the apparent.

Years afterwards I was 'behind'. The stage was set for an Elizabethan play. The back-cloth represented a palace front, with a practicable balcony on it. I stood (from one point

[1] 'Lewis Carroll', *Through the Looking-Glass and What Alice Found There,* ch. 1.

of view) on that palace balcony; that is (from the other point of view) I stood on a plank supported by trestles looking out through a square hole in a sheet of canvas. It was a most satisfactory moment.

Now what, I wonder, is behind all this? And what, if anything, comes of it? I have no objection to the inclusion of Freudian explanations provided they are not allowed to exclude all others. It may, as I suppose someone will think, be mixed up with infantile curiosities about the female body. It doesn't feel at all like that. 'Of course not', they'll reply. 'You mustn't expect it to; no more than — let's see what would be a good parallel — why, no more than the stage rooms and forests look (from the front) like a collection of oddly shaped lath-and-canvas objects grouped in front of the dusty, draughty, whitewashed place "behind".'

The parallel is fairly exact. The complex, worming its way along in the unimaginable Unconscious, and then suddenly transforming itself (and gaining admission only by that transformation) as it steps into the only 'mind' I can ever directly know, is really very like the actor, with his own unhistrionic expression, walking along that bare, draughty 'off-stage' and then suddenly appearing as Mr Darling in the nursery or Aladdin in the cave.

But oddly enough we could fit the Freudian theory into the pleasure I started with quite as easily as we fit it into the Freudian theory. Is not our pleasure (even I take some) in Depth Psychology itself one instance of this pleasure in the contrast between 'behind the scenes' and 'on stage'? I begin to wonder whether that theatrical antithesis moves us because it is a ready-made symbol of something universal.

All sorts of things are, in fact, doing just what the actor does when he comes through the wings. Photons or waves (or whatever it is) come towards us from the sun through space. They are, in a scientific sense, 'light'. But as they enter the air they become 'light' in a different sense: what ordinary people call *sunlight* or *day,* the bubble of blue or grey or greenish luminosity in which we walk about and see. Day is thus a kind of stage set.

Other waves (this time, of air) reach my eardrum and travel up a nerve and tickle my brain. All this is behind the scenes; as soundless as the whitewashed passages are undramatic. Then somehow (I've never seen it explained) they step on to the stage (no one can tell me *where* this stage is) and become, say, a friend's voice or the *Ninth Symphony*. Or, of course, my neighbour's wireless — the actor may come on stage to play a drivelling part in a bad play. But there is always the transformation.

Biological needs, producing, or stimulated by, temporary physiological states, climb into a young man's brain, pass on to the mysterious stage and appear as 'Love' — it may be (since all sorts of plays are performed there) the love celebrated by Dante, or it may be the love of a Guido[2] or a Mr Guppy.[3]

We can call this the contrast of Reality and Appearance. But perhaps the fact of having first met it in the theatre will protect us from the threat of derogation which lurks in the word Appearance. For in the theatre of course the play, the 'appearance', is the thing. All the backstage 'realities' exist only for its sake and are valuable only in so far as they promote it. A good, neutral parable is Schopenhauer's story of the two Japanese who attend an English theatre. One devoted himself to trying to understand the play although he did not know a word of the language. The other devoted himself to trying to understand how the scenery, lighting and other machinery worked, though he had never been behind the scenes in a theatre. 'Here', said Schopenhauer, 'you have the philosopher and the scientist.'[4] But for 'philosopher' he might also have written 'poet', 'lover', 'worshipper', 'citizen', 'moral agent' or 'plain man'.

But notice that in two ways Schopenhauer's parable breaks down. The first Japanese could have taken steps to learn Eng-

---

[2] One of the principal characters in Robert Browning's *The Ring and the Book*.

[3] A character in Charles Dickens' *Bleak House*.

[4] Lewis was probably recalling from memory the parable in Arthur Schopenhauer's *Studies in Pessimism* which runs: 'Two Chinamen travelling in Europe went to the theatre for the first time. One of them did nothing but study the machinery, and he succeeded in finding out how it was worked. The other tried to get at the meaning of the piece in spite of his ignorance of the language. Here you have the Astronomer and the Philosopher.' The parable is found in Schopenhauer's *Essays from the Parerga and Paralipomena*, trans. T. Bailey Saunders (London, 1951), pp. 80-1.

lish; but have we ever been given any grammar or dictionary, can we find the teacher, of the language in which this universal drama is being performed? Some (I among them) would say Yes; others would say No; the debate continues. And the second Japanese could have taken steps — could have pulled wires and got introductions — to win admission behind the scenes and see the off-stage things for himself. At the very least he knew there were such things.

We lack both these advantages. Nobody ever can go 'behind'. No one can, in any ordinary sense, meet or experience a photon, a sound wave or the unconscious. (That may be one reason why 'going behind' in the theatre is exciting; we are doing what, in most cases, is impossible.) We are not even, in the last resort, absolutely sure that such things exist. They are constructs, things assumed to account for our experience, but never to be experienced themselves. They may be assumed with great probability; but they are, after all, hypothetical.

Even the off-stage existence of the actors is hypothetical. Perhaps they do not exist before they enter the scene. And, if they do, then, since we cannot go behind, they may, in their off-stage life and character, be very unlike what we suppose and very unlike one another.

14

REVIVAL OR DECAY?

Bᴜᴛ ᴡᴏᴜʟᴅ ʏᴏᴜ ᴅᴇɴʏ', ꜱᴀɪᴅ ᴛʜᴇ Hᴇᴀᴅᴍᴀꜱᴛᴇʀ, 'ᴛʜᴀᴛ there is, here in the West, a great, even growing, interest in religion?'

It is not the sort of question I find easy to answer. *Great* and *growing* would seem more to involve statistics, and I had no statistics. I supposed there was a fairly widespread interest. But I didn't feel sure the Headmaster was interpreting it correctly. In the days when most people had a religion, what he meant by 'an interest in religion' could hardly have existed. For of course religious people — that is, people when they are being religious — are not 'interested in religion'. Men who have gods worship those gods; it is the spectators who describe this as 'religion'. The Maenads thought about Dionysus, not about religion. *Mutatis mutandis* this goes for Christians too. The moment a man seriously accepts a deity his interest in 'religion' is at an end. He's got something else to think about. The ease with which we can now get an audience for a discussion of religion does not prove that more people are becoming religious. What it really proves is the existence of a large 'floating vote'. Every conversion will reduce this potential audience.

Once the climate of opinion allows such a floating vote to form I see no reason why it should speedily diminish. Indecision, often very honest, is very natural. It would be foolish, however, not to realise that it is also no hardship. Floating is a very agreeable operation; a decision either way costs something. Real Christianity and consistent Atheism

250

both make demands on a man. But to admit, on occasion, and as possibilities, all the comforts of the one without its discipline — to enjoy all the liberty of the other without its philosophical and emotional abstinences — well, this may be honest, but there's no good pretending it is uncomfortable.

'And would you, further, deny', said the Headmaster, 'that Christianity commands more respect in the most highly educated circles than it has done for centuries? The Intelligentsia are coming over. Look at men like Maritain, like Bergson, like — '

But I didn't feel at all happy about this. Of course the converted Intellectual is a characteristic figure of our times. But this phenomenon would be more hopeful if it had not occurred at a moment when the Intelligentsia (scientists apart) are losing all touch with, and all influence over, nearly the whole human race. Our most esteemed poets and critics are read by our most esteemed critics and poets (who don't usually like them much) and nobody else takes any notice. An increasing number of highly literate people simply ignore what the 'Highbrows' are doing. It says nothing to them. The Highbrows in return ignore or insult them. Conversions from the Intelligentsia are not therefore likely to be very widely influential. They may even raise a horrid suspicion that Christianity itself has become a part of the general 'Highbrow racket', has been adopted, like Surrealism and the pictures painted by chimpanzees, as one more method of 'shocking the bourgeois'. This would be dreadfully uncharitable, no doubt; but then the Intelligentsia have said a great many uncharitable things about the others.

'Then again', boomed the Headmaster, 'even where there is, or is as yet, no explicit religion, do we not see a vast rallying to the defence of those standards which, whether recognised or not, make part of our spiritual heritage? The Western — may I not say the Christian — values . . .'

We all winced. And to me in particular there came back the memory of a corrugated iron hut used as an R.A.F. chapel — a few kneeling airmen — and a young chaplain uttering the prayer, 'Teach us, O Lord, to love *the things Thou standest for.*' He was perfectly sincere, and I willingly believe that the *things* in question included something more and better than 'the Western values', whatever those may be.

251

And yet . . . his words seemed to me to imply a point of view incompatible with Christianity or indeed with any serious Theism whatever. God is not, for it, the goal or end. He is (and how fortunate!) enlightened; has, or 'stands for', the right ideals. He is valued for that reason. He ranks, admittedly, as a leader. But of course a leader leads to something beyond himself. That something else is the real goal. This is miles away from 'Thou hast made us for Thyself and our heart has no rest till it comes to Thee.' The Maenads were more religious.

'And the substitutes for religion are being discredited,' continued the Headmaster. 'Science has become more a bogy than a god. The Marxist heaven on earth — '

And only the other day a lady told me that a girl to whom she had mentioned death replied 'Oh, but by the time I'm *that* age Science will have done something about it.' And then I remembered how often, in disputing before simple audiences, I had found the assured belief that whatever was wrong with man would in the long run (and not so very long a run either) be put right by 'Education'. And that led me to think of all the 'approaches' to 'religion' I actually meet. An anonymous postcard tells me that I ought to be flogged at the cart's tail for professing to believe in the Virgin Birth. A distinguished literary atheist to whom I am introduced mutters, looks away, and walks swiftly to the far end of the room. An unknown American writes to ask me whether Elijah's fiery chariot was really a Flying Saucer. I encounter Theosophists, British Israelites, Spiritualists, Pantheists. Why do people like the Headmaster always talk about 'religion'? Why not religions? We seethe with religions. Christianity, I am pleased to note, is one of them. I get letters from saints, who have no notion they are any such thing, showing in every line radiant faith, joy, humility, and even humour, in appalling suffering. I get others from converts who want to apologise for some small incivility they committed against me in print years ago.

These bits and pieces are all 'the West' I really know at first hand. They escape the Headmaster's treatment. He speaks from books and articles. The real sanctities, hatreds, and lunacies which surround us are hardly represented there. Still less, the great negative factor. It is something more than ignorance as he would understand the word. Most people's thinking lacks

252

a dimension which he takes for granted. Two instances may make the distinction clear. Once, after I had said something on the air about Natural Law, an old Colonel (obviously *anima candida*)[1] wrote to say that this had interested him very much and could I just tell him of 'some handy little *brochure* which dealt with the subject fully'. That is ignorance, striking only in degree. Here is the other. A vet, a workman, and I were wearily stumbling about on a Home Guard patrol in the small hours. The vet and I got talking about the causes of wars and arrived at the conclusion that we must expect them to recur. 'But — but — but — ' gasped the workman. There was a moment's silence, and he broke out, 'But then what's the good of the ruddy world going on?' I got a very clear impression of what was happening. For the first time in his life a really ultimate question was before him. The sort of thing we have been considering all our lives — the meaning of existence — had just broken upon him. It was a wholly new dimension.

Is there a homogeneous 'West'? I doubt it. Everything that can go on is going on all round us. Religions buzz about us like bees. A serious sex worship — quite different from the cheery lechery endemic in our species — is one of them. Traces of embryonic religions occur in science-fiction. Meanwhile, as always, the Christian way too is followed. But nowadays, when it is not followed, it need not be feigned. That fact covers a good deal of what is called the decay of religion. Apart from that, is the present so very different from other ages or 'the West' from anywhere else?

[1] 'a candid, frank soul.'

15

BEFORE WE CAN
COMMUNICATE

I HAVE BEEN ASKED TO WRITE ABOUT 'THE PROBLEM OF COM-
munication'; by which my inquirer meant 'communication under modern conditions between Christians and the outer
world'. And, as usually happens to me when I am questioned,
I feel a little embarrassed by the simplicity and unexciting-
ness of the answer I want to give. I feel that what I have to
say is on a cruder and lower level than was hoped for.

My ideas about 'communication' are purely empirical, and
two anecdotes (both strictly true) will illustrate the sort of
experience on which they are based.

1. The old Prayer Book prayed that the magistrates might
'truly and indifferently administer justice'. Then the revisers
thought they would make this easier by altering *indifferently*
to *impartially*. A country clergyman of my acquaintance asked
his sexton what he thought *indifferently* meant, and got the correct answer, 'It means making no difference between one chap
and another.' 'And what', continued the parson, 'do you think
impartially means?' 'Ah', said the sexton after a pause, 'I
wouldn't know *that*.'

Everyone sees what the revisers had in mind. They were
afraid that the 'man in the pew' would take *indifferently* to
mean, as it often does, 'carelessly', without concern. They
knew that this error would not be made by highly-educated
people, but they thought it would be made by everyone else.
The sexton's reply, however, reveals that it will not be made

254

by the least educated class of all. It will be made only by those who are educationally in the middle; those whose language is fashionable (our elders would have said 'polite') without being scholarly. The highest and lowest classes are both equally safe from it; and *impartially,* which guards the 'middle' churchgoers from misunderstanding, is meaningless to the simple.

2. During the war I got into a discussion with a working man about the Devil. He said he believed in a Devil, but 'not a personal Devil'. As the discussion proceeded it grew more and more perplexing to both parties. It became clear that we were somehow at cross-purposes. Then, suddenly and almost by accident, I discovered what was wrong. It became obvious that he had, all along, been meaning by the word *personal* nothing more or less or other than *corporeal.* He was a very intelligent man, and, once this discovery had been made, there was no difficulty. Apparently we had not really disagreed about anything: the difference between us was merely one of vocabulary. It set me wondering how many of the thousands of people who say they 'believe in God but not in a personal God' are really trying to tell us no more than that they are not, in the strict sense, *anthropomorphists* and are, in fact, asserting, on this point, their perfect orthodoxy.

Where the revisers of the Prayer Book and I both went wrong was this. We both had *a priori* notions of what simple people mean by words. I assumed that the workman's usage was the same as my own. The revisers, more subtly but not more correctly, assumed that all would know the sense of *indifferently* which they were guarding against when they amended it. But apparently we must not decide *a priori* what other people mean by English words any more than what Frenchmen mean by French words. We must be wholly empirical. We must listen, and note, and memorise. And of course we must set aside every trace of snobbery or pedantry about 'right' or 'wrong' usages.

Now this is, I feel, very hum-drum and work-a-day. When one wants to discuss the problem of communication on a grand, philosophical level, when one wants to talk about conflicts of *Weltanschauung* and the predicament of modern, or urban, or crisis consciousness, it is chilling to be told that the first step is simply linguistic in the crudest sense. But it is.

What we want to see in every ordination exam is a compulsory paper on (simply) translation; a passage from some theological work to be turned into plain vernacular English. Just turned; not adorned, nor diluted, nor made 'matey'. The exercise is very like doing Latin prose. Instead of saying, 'How would Cicero have said that?', you have to ask yourself, 'How would my scout or bedmaker have said that?'

You will at once find that this labour has two useful by-products.

1. In the very process of eliminating from your matter all that is technical, learned, or allusive, you will discover, perhaps for the first time, the true value of learned language: namely, brevity. It can say in ten words what popular speech can hardly get into a hundred. Your popularisation of the passage set will have to be very much longer than the original. And this we must just put up with.

2. You will also discover — at least I, a copious 'translator', think I have discovered — just how much you yourself have, up to that moment, been understanding the language which you are now trying to translate. Again and again I have been most usefully humiliated in this way. One holds, or thinks one holds, a particular view, say, of the Atonement or Orders or Inspiration. And you can go on for years discussing and defending it to others *of your own sort*. New refinements can be introduced to meet its critics; brilliant metaphors can seem to illuminate its obscurities; comparisons with other views, 'placings' of it, are somehow felt to establish its position in a sort of aristocracy of ideas. For the others are all talking the same language and all move in the same world of discourse. All seems well. Then turn and try to expound this same view to an intelligent mechanic or a sincerely inquisitive, but superficially quite irreverent, schoolboy. Some question of shattering crudity (it would never be asked in learned circles) will be shot at you. You are like a skilled swordsman transfixed by an opponent who wins just because he knows none of the first principles. The crude question turns out to be fatal. You have never, it now appears, really understood what you have so long maintained. You haven't really thought it out; not to the end; not to 'the absolute ruddy end'.

You must either give it up, or else begin it all over again. If, given patience and ordinary skill, you cannot explain a thing to any sensible person whatever (provided he will listen), then you don't really understand it yourself. Here too it is very like doing Latin prose; the bits you can't get into Latin are usually the bits you haven't really grasped in the English.

What we need to be particularly on our guard against are precisely the vogue-words, the incantatory words, of our own circle. For your generation they are, perhaps, *engagement, commitment, over against, under judgment, existential, crisis,* and *confrontation.* These are, of all expressions, the least likely to be intelligible to anyone divided from you by a school of thought, by a decade, by a social class. They are like a family language, or a school slang. And our private language may delude ourselves as well as mystifying outsiders. Enchanted words seem so full of meaning, so illuminating. But we may be deceived. What we derive from them may sometimes be not so much a clear conception as a heart-warming sense of being at home and among our own sort. 'We understand one another' often means 'We are in sympathy.' Sympathy is a good thing. It may even be in some ways a better thing than intellectual understanding. But not the same thing.

16

CROSS-EXAMINATION

[The following is an interview with C. S. Lewis, held on the 7th May 1963 in Lewis's rooms in Magdalene College, Cambridge. The interviewer is Mr Sherwood E. Wirt of the Billy Graham Evangelistic Association Ltd.]

Mr Wirt:

Professor Lewis, if you had a young friend with some interest in writing on Christian subjects, how would you advise him to prepare himself?

Lewis:

I would say if a man is going to write on chemistry, he learns chemistry. The same is true of Christianity. But to speak of the craft itself, I would not know how to advise a man how to write. It is a matter of talent and interest. I believe he must be strongly moved if he is to become a writer. Writing is like a 'lust', or like 'scratching when you itch'. Writing comes as a result of a very strong impulse, and when it does come, I for one must get it out.

Mr Wirt:

Can you suggest an approach that would spark the creation of a body of Christian literature strong enough to influence our generation?

Lewis:

There is no formula in these matters. I have no recipe, no tablets. Writers are trained in so many individual ways that it is not for us to prescribe. Scripture itself is not systematic; the New Testament shows the greatest variety. God has shown us that he can use any instrument. Balaam's ass, you remember, preached a very effective sermon in the midst of his 'hee-haws'.[1]

Mr Wirt:

A light touch has been characteristic of your writings, even when you are dealing with heavy theological themes. Would you say there is a key to the cultivation of such an attitude?

Lewis:

I believe this is a matter of temperament. However, I was helped in achieving this attitude by my studies of the literary men of the Middle Ages, and by the writings of G. K. Chesterton. Chesterton, for example, was not afraid to combine serious Christian themes with buffoonery. In the same way, the miracle plays of the Middle Ages would deal with a sacred subject such as the nativity of Christ, yet would combine it with a farce.

Mr Wirt:

Should Christian writers, then, in your opinion, attempt to be funny?

Lewis:

No. I think that forced jocularities on spiritual subjects are an abomination, and the attempts of some religious writers to be humorous are simply appalling. Some people write heavily, some write lightly. I prefer the light approach because I believe there is a great deal of false reverence about. There is too much solemnity and intensity in dealing with sacred matters; too much speaking in holy tones.

Mr Wirt:

But is not solemnity proper and conducive to a sacred atmosphere?

Lewis:

Yes and no. There is a difference between a private devotional life and a corporate one. Solemnity is proper in church, but things that are proper in church are not necessarily proper outside, and vice versa. For example, I can say a prayer while washing my teeth, but that does not mean I should wash my teeth in church.

[1] Numbers xxii. 1-35.

Mr Wirt:

What is your opinion of the kind of writing being done within the Christian church today?

Lewis:

A great deal of what is being published by writers in the religious tradition is a scandal and is actually turning people away from the church. The liberal writers who are continually accommodating and whittling down the truth of the Gospel are responsible. I cannot understand how a man can appear in print claiming to disbelieve everything that he presupposes when he puts on the surplice. I feel it is a form of prostitution.

Mr Wirt:

What do you think of the controversial new book, *Honest to God,* by John Robinson, the Bishop of Woolwich?

Lewis:

I prefer being honest to being 'honest to God'.

Mr Wirt:

What Christian writers have helped you?

Lewis:

The contemporary book that has helped me the most is Chesterton's *The Everlasting Man.* Others are Edwyn Bevan's book, *Symbolism and Belief,* and Rudolf Otto's *The Idea of the Holy,* and the plays of Dorothy Sayers.[2]

Mr Wirt:

I believe it was Chesterton who was asked why he became a member of the church, and he replied, 'To get rid of my sins.'

Lewis:

It is not enough to want to get rid of one's sins. We also need to believe in the One who saves us from our sins. Not only do we need to recognize that we are sinners; we need to believe in a Saviour who takes away sin. Matthew Arnold once wrote, 'Nor does the being hungry prove that we have bread.' Because we are sinners, it does not follow that we are saved.

[2] Such as *The Man Born to be King* (London, 1943; reprinted Grand Rapids, 1970).

Mr Wirt:

In your book *Surprised by Joy* you remark that you were brought into the Faith kicking and struggling and resentful, with eyes darting in every direction looking for an escape.[3] You suggest that you were compelled, as it were, to become a Christian. Do you feel that you made a decision at the time of your conversion?

Lewis:

I would not put it that way. What I wrote in *Surprised by Joy* was that 'before God closed in on me, I was in fact offered what now appears a moment of wholly free choice.'[4] But I feel my decision was not so important. I was the object rather than the subject in this affair. I was decided upon. I was glad afterwards at the way it came out, but at the moment what I heard was God saying, 'Put down your gun and we'll talk.'

Mr Wirt:

That sounds to me as if you came to a very definite point of decision.

Lewis:

Well, I would say that the most deeply compelled action is also the freest action. By that I mean, no part of you is outside the action. It is a paradox. I expressed it in *Surprised by Joy* by saying that I chose, yet it really did not seem possible to do the opposite.[5]

Mr Wirt:

You wrote 20 years ago that 'A man who was merely a man and said the sort of things Jesus said would not be a great moral teacher. He would either be a lunatic — on a level with the man who says he is a poached egg — or else he would be the Devil of Hell. You must make your choice. Either this man was, and is, the Son of God: or else a madman or something worse. You can shut Him up for a fool, you can spit at Him and kill Him as a demon; or you can fall at His feet and call Him Lord and God. But let us not come with any patronizing nonsense about His being a great human teacher.

[3] (London, 1955), ch. xiv, p. 215.
[4] *Ibid.*, p. 211.
[5] *Ibid.*

He has not left that open to us. He did not intend to.'[6] Would you say your view of this matter has changed since then?

Lewis:

I would say there is no substantial change.

Mr Wirt:

Would you say that the aim of Christian writing, including your own writing, is to bring about an encounter of the reader with Jesus Christ?

Lewis:

That is not my language, yet it is the purpose I have in view. For example, I have just finished a book on prayer, an imaginary correspondence with someone who raises questions about difficulties in prayer.[7]

Mr Wirt:

How can we foster the encounter of people with Jesus Christ?

Lewis:

You can't lay down any pattern for God. There are many different ways of bringing people into His Kingdom, even some ways that I specially dislike! I have therefore learned to be cautious in my judgment.

But we can block it in many ways. As Christians we are tempted to make unnecessary concessions to those outside the Faith. We give in too much. Now, I don't mean that we should run the risk of making a nuisance of ourselves by witnessing at improper times, but there comes a time when we must show that we disagree. We must show our Christian colours, if we are to be true to Jesus Christ. We cannot remain silent or concede everything away.

There is a character in one of my children's stories named Aslan, who says, 'I never tell anyone any story except his own.'[8] I cannot speak for the way God deals with others; I only know how He deals with me personally. Of course, we are to pray for spiritual awakening, and in various ways we

[6] *Mere Christianity* (London, 1952), ch. iii, p. 42.

[7] He is speaking of his *Letters to Malcolm: Chiefly on Prayer* (London, 1964).

[8] Except for slight variations in the wording, Aslan says this to two children who ask Him about other people's lives in *The Horse and His Boy* (London, 1954), ch. xi, p. 147 and ch. xiv, p. 180.

262

can do something toward it. But we must remember that neither Paul nor Apollos gives the increase.[9] As Charles Williams once said, 'The altar must often be built in one place so that the fire may come down in another place.'[10]

Mr Wirt:

Professor Lewis, your writings have an unusual quality not often found in discussions of Christian themes. You write as though you enjoyed it.

Lewis:

If I didn't enjoy writing I wouldn't continue to do it. Of all my books, there was only one I did not take pleasure in writing.

Mr Wirt:
Which one?

Lewis:

The Screwtape Letters. They were dry and gritty going. At the time, I was thinking of objections to the Christian life, and decided to put them into the form, 'That's what the devil would say.' But making goods 'bad' and bads 'good' gets to be fatiguing.

Mr Wirt:

How would you suggest a young Christian writer go about developing a style?

Lewis:

The way for a person to develop a style is (a) to know exactly what he wants to say, and (b) to be sure he is saying exactly that. The reader, we must remember, does not start by knowing what we mean. If our words are ambiguous, our meaning will escape him. I sometimes think that writing is like driving sheep down a road. If there is any gate open to the left or the right the readers will most certainly go into it.

[9] I Corinthians iii. 6.
[10] 'Usually the way must be made ready for heaven, and then it will come by some other; the sacrifice must be made ready, and the fire will strike on another altar.' Charles Williams, *He Came Down from Heaven* (London, 1938), ch. ii, p. 25.

Mr Wirt:

Do you believe that the Holy Spirit can speak to the world through Christian writers today?

Lewis:

I prefer to make no judgment concerning a writer's direct 'illumination' by the Holy Spirit. I have no way of knowing whether what is written is from heaven or not. I do believe that God is the Father of lights — natural lights as well as spiritual lights (James i. 17). That is, God is not interested only in Christian writers as such. He is concerned with all kinds of writing. In the same way a sacred calling is not limited to ecclesiastical functions. The man who is weeding a field of turnips is also serving God.

Mr Wirt:

An American writer, Mr Dewey Beegle, has stated that in his opinion the Isaac Watts hymn, 'When I Survey the Wondrous Cross', is more inspired by God than is the 'Song of Solomon' in the Old Testament. What would be your view?

Lewis:

The great saints and mystics of the church have felt just the opposite about it. They have found tremendous spiritual truth in the 'Song of Solomon'. There is a difference of levels here. The question of the canon is involved. Also we must remember that what is meat for a grown person might be unsuited to the palate of a child.

Mr Wirt:

How would you evaluate modern literary trends as exemplified by such writers as Ernest Hemingway, Samuel Beckett and Jean-Paul Sartre?

Lewis:

I have read very little in this field. I am not a contemporary scholar. I am not even a scholar of the past, but I am a lover of the past.

Mr Wirt:

Do you believe that the use of filth and obscenity is necessary in order to establish a realistic atmosphere in contemporary literature?

264

Lewis:

I do not. I treat this development as a symptom, a sign of a culture that has lost its faith. Moral collapse follows upon spiritual collapse. I look upon the immediate future with great apprehension.

Mr Wirt:

Do you feel, then, that modern culture is being de-Christianized?

Lewis:

I cannot speak to the political aspects of the question, but I have some definite views about the de-Christianizing of the church. I believe that there are many accommodating preachers, and too many practitioners in the church who are not believers. Jesus Christ did not say 'Go into all the world and tell the world that it is quite right.' The Gospel is something completely different. In fact, it is directly opposed to the world.

The case against Christianity that is made out in the world is quite strong. Every war, every shipwreck, every cancer case, every calamity, contributes to making a *prima facie* case against Christianity. It is not easy to be a believer in the face of this surface evidence. It calls for a strong faith in Jesus Christ.

Mr Wirt:

Do you approve of men such as Bryan Green and Billy Graham asking people to come to a point of decision regarding the Christian life?

Lewis:

I had the pleasure of meeting Billy Graham once. We had dinner together during his visit to Cambridge University in 1955, while he was conducting a mission to students. I thought he was a very modest and a very sensible man, and I liked him very much indeed.

In a civilization like ours, I feel that everyone has to come to terms with the claims of Jesus Christ upon his life, or else be guilty of inattention or of evading the question. In the Soviet Union it is different. Many people living in Russia today have never had to consider the claims of Christ because they have never heard of those claims.

In the same way, we who live in English-speaking countries

265

have never really been forced to consider the claims, let us say, of Hinduism. But in our Western civilization we are obligated both morally and intellectually to come to grips with Jesus Christ; if we refuse to do so we are guilty of being bad philosophers and bad thinkers.

Mr Wirt:

What is your view of the daily discipline of the Christian life — the need for taking time to be alone with God?

Lewis:

We have our New Testament regimental orders upon the subject. I would take it for granted that everyone who becomes a Christian would undertake this practice. It is enjoined upon us by Our Lord; and since they are His commands, I believe in following them. It is always just possible that Jesus Christ meant what He said when He told us to seek the secret place and to close the door.[11]

Mr Wirt:

What do you think is going to happen in the next few years of history, Mr Lewis?

Lewis:

I have no way of knowing. My primary field is the past. I travel with my back to the engine, and that makes it difficult when you try to steer. The world might stop in ten minutes; meanwhile, we are to go on doing our duty. The great thing is to be found at one's post as a child of God, living each day as though it were our last, but planning as though our world might last a hundred years.

We have, of course, the assurance of the New Testament regarding events to come.[12] I find it difficult to keep from laughing when I find people worrying about future destruction of some kind or other. Didn't they know they were going to die anyway? Apparently not. My wife once asked a young woman friend whether she had ever thought of death, and she replied, 'By the time I reach that age science will have done something about it!'

[11] Matthew vi. 5-6.
[12] Matthew xxiv. 4-44; Mark xiii. 5-27; Luke xxi. 8-33.

266

Mr Wirt:

Do you think there will be wide-spread travel in space?

Lewis:

I look forward with horror to contact with the other inhabited planets, if there are such. We would only transport to them all of our sin and our acquisitiveness, and establish a new colonialism. I can't bear to think of it. But if we on earth were to get right with God, of course, all would be changed. Once we find ourselves spiritually awakened, we can go to outer space and take the good things with us. That is quite a different matter.

PART III

1

'BULVERISM'

OR, THE FOUNDATION OF 20TH CENTURY THOUGHT

I T IS A DISASTROUS DISCOVERY, AS EMERSON SAYS SOMEWHERE, that we exist. I mean, it is disastrous when instead of merely attending to a rose we are forced to think of ourselves looking at the rose, with a certain type of mind and a certain type of eyes. It is disastrous because, if you are not very careful, the colour of the rose gets attributed to our optic nerves and its scent to our noses, and in the end there is no rose left. The professional philosophers have been bothered about this universal black-out for over two hundred years, and the world has not much listened to them. But the same disaster is now occurring on a level we can all understand.

We have recently 'discovered that we exist' in two new senses. The Freudians have discovered that we exist as bundles of complexes. The Marxians have discovered that we exist as members of some economic class. In the old days it was supposed that if a thing seemed obviously true to a hundred men, then it was probably true in fact. Nowadays the Freudian will tell you to go and analyze the hundred: you will find that they all think Elizabeth [I] a great queen because they all have a mother-complex. Their thoughts are psychologically tainted at the source. And the Marxist will tell you to go and examine the economic interests of the hundred; you will find that they all think freedom a good thing because they are all members of the bourgeoisie whose prosperity is increased by a policy of *laissez-faire*. Their thoughts are 'ideologically tainted' at the source.

Now this is obviously great fun; but it has not always been noticed that there is a bill to pay for it. There are two questions that people who say this kind of things ought to be asked. The first is, Are *all* thoughts thus tainted at the source, or only some? The second is, Does the taint invalidate the tainted thought — in the sense of making it untrue — or not?

If they say that *all thoughts* are thus tainted, then, of course, we must remind them that Freudianism and Marxism are as much systems of thought as Christian theology or philosophical idealism. The Freudian and the Marxian are in the same boat with all the rest of us, and cannot criticize us from outside. They have sawn off the branch they were sitting on. If, on the other hand, they say that the taint need not invalidate their thinking, then neither need it invalidate ours. In which case they have saved their own branch, but also saved ours along with it.

The only line they can really take is to say that some thoughts are tainted and others are not — which has the advantage (if Freudians and Marxians regard it as an advantage) of being what every sane man has always believed. But if that is so, we must then ask how you find out which are tainted and which are not. It is no earthly use saying that those are tainted which agree with the secret wishes of the thinker. *Some* of the things I should like to believe must in fact be true; it is impossible to arrange a universe which contradicts everyone's wishes, in every respect, at every moment. Suppose I think, after doing my accounts, that I have a large balance at the bank. And suppose you want to find out whether this belief of mine is 'wishful thinking'. You can never come to any conclusion by examining my psychological condition. Your only chance of finding out is to sit down and work through the sum yourself. When you have checked my figures, then, and then only, will you know whether I have that balance or not. If you find my arithmetic correct, then no amount of vapouring about my psychological condition can be anything but a waste of time. If you find my arithmetic wrong, then it may be relevant to explain psychologically how I came to be so bad at my arithmetic, and the doctrine of the concealed wish will become relevant — but only *after* you have yourself

done the sum and discovered me to be wrong on purely arithmetical grounds. It is the same with all thinking and all systems
of thought. If you try to find out which are tainted by speculating about the wishes of the thinkers, you are merely making
a fool of yourself. You must first find out on purely logical
grounds which of them do, in fact, break down as arguments.
Afterwards, if you like, go on and discover the psychological
causes of the error.

In other words, you must show *that* a man is wrong before
you start explaining *why* he is wrong. The modern method
is to assume without discussion *that* he is wrong and then
distract his attention from this (the only real issue) by busily
explaining how he became so silly. In the course of the last
fifteen years I have found this vice so common that I have
had to invent a name for it. I call it Bulverism. Some day I
am going to write the biography of its imaginary inventor,
Ezekiel Bulver, whose destiny was determined at the age of five
when he heard his mother say to his father — who had been
maintaining that two sides of a triangle were together greater
than the third — 'Oh you say that *because you are a man.*'
'At that moment', E. Bulver assures us, 'there flashed across
my opening mind the great truth that refutation is no necessary
part of argument. Assume that your opponent is wrong, and
then explain his error, and the world will be at your feet.
Attempt to prove that he is wrong or (worse still) try to find
out whether he is wrong or right, and the national dynamism
of our age will thrust you to the wall.' That is how Bulver
became one of the makers of the Twentieth Century.

I find the fruits of his discovery almost everywhere. Thus
I see my religion dismissed on the grounds that 'the comfortable parson had every reason for assuring the nineteenth century worker that poverty would be rewarded in another world'.
Well, no doubt he had. On the assumption that Christianity
is an error, I can see early enough that some people would
still have a motive for inculcating it. I see it so easily that I
can, of course, play the game the other way round, by saying
that 'the modern man has every reason for trying to convince
himself that there are no eternal sanctions behind the morality
he is rejecting'. For Bulverism is a truly democratic game in
the sense that all can play it all day long, and that it gives
no unfair privilege to the small and offensive minority who

reason. But of course it gets us not one inch nearer to deciding whether, as a matter of fact, the Christian religion is true or false. That question remains to be discussed on quite different grounds — a matter of philosophical and historical argument. However it were decided, the improper motives of some people, both for believing it and for disbelieving it, would remain just as they are.

I see Bulverism at work in every political argument. The capitalists must be bad economists because we know why they want capitalism, and equally the Communists must be bad economists because we know why they want Communism. Thus, the Bulverists on both sides. In reality, of course, either the doctrines of the capitalists are false, or the doctrines of the Communists, or both; but you can only find out the rights and wrongs by reasoning — never by being rude about your opponent's psychology.

Until Bulverism is crushed, reason can play no effective part in human affairs. Each side snatches it early as a weapon against the other; but between the two reason itself is discredited. And why should reason not be discredited? It would be easy, in answer, to point to the present state of the world, but the real answer is even more immediate. The forces discrediting reason, themselves depend on reasoning. You must reason even to Bulverize. You are trying to *prove* that all *proofs* are invalid. If you fail, you fail. If you succeed, then you fail even more — for the proof that all proofs are invalid must be invalid itself.

The alternative then is either sheer self-contradicting idiocy or else some tenacious belief in our power of reasoning, held in the teeth of all the evidence that Bulverists can bring for a 'taint' in this or that human reasoner. I am ready to admit, if you like, that this tenacious belief has something transcendental or mystical about it. What then? Would you rather be a lunatic than a mystic?

So we see there is justification for holding on to our belief in Reason. But can this be done without theism? Does 'I know' involve that God exists? Everything I know is an inference from sensation (except the present moment). All our knowledge of the universe beyond our immediate experiences depends on inferences from these experiences. If our inferences do not give a genuine insight into reality, then we can know

274

nothing. A theory cannot be accepted if it does not allow our thinking to be a genuine insight, nor if the fact of our knowledge is not explicable in terms of that theory.

But our thoughts can only be accepted as a genuine insight under certain conditions. All beliefs have causes but a distinction must be drawn between (1) ordinary causes and (2) a special kind of cause called 'a reason'. Causes are mindless events which can produce other results than belief. Reasons arise from axioms and inferences and affect only beliefs. Bulverism tries to show that the other man has causes and not reasons and that we have reasons and not causes. A belief which can be accounted for entirely in terms of causes is worthless. This principle must not be abandoned when we consider the beliefs which are the basis of others. Our knowledge depends on our certainty about axioms and inferences. If these are the result of causes, then there is no possibility of knowledge. Either we can know nothing *or* thought has reasons only, and no causes.

> [The remainder of this essay, which was originally read to the Socratic Club before publication in the *Socratic Digest,* continues in the form of notes taken down by the Secretary of the Club. This explains why it is not all in the first-person, as is the text-proper.]

One might argue, Mr Lewis continued, that reason had developed by natural selection, only those methods of thought which had proved useful surviving. But the theory depends on an inference from usefulness to truth, of which the validity would have to be *assumed*. All attempts to treat thought as a natural event involve the fallacy of excluding the thought of the man making the attempt.

It is admitted that the mind is affected by physical events; a wireless set is influenced by atmospherics, but it does not originate its deliverances — we'd take no notice of it if we thought it did. Natural events we can relate one to another until we can trace them finally to the space-time continuum. But thought has no father but thought. It is conditioned, yes, not caused. *My* knowledge *that* I have nerves is inferential.

The same argument applies to our values, which are affected by social factors, but if they are caused by them we cannot know that they are right. One can reject morality as an illusion,

275

but the man who does so often tacitly excepts his own ethical motive: for instance the duty of freeing morality from superstition and of spreading enlightenment.

Neither Will nor Reason is the product of Nature. Therefore either I am self-existent (a belief which no one can accept) *or* I am a colony of some Thought and Will that are self-existent. Such reason and goodness as we can attain must be derived from a self-existent Reason and Goodness outside ourselves, in fact, a Supernatural.

Mr Lewis went on to say that it was often objected that the existence of the Supernatural is too important to be discernible only by abstract argument, and thus only by the leisured few. But in all other ages the plain man has accepted the findings of the mystics and the philosophers for his initial belief in the existence of the Supernatural. Today the ordinary man is forced to carry that burden himself. Either mankind has made a ghastly mistake in rejecting authority, or the power or powers ruling his destiny are making a daring experiment, and all are to become sages. A society consisting solely of plain men must end in disaster. If we are to survive we must either believe the seers or scale those heights ourselves.

Evidently, then, something beyond Nature exists. Man is on the border line between the Natural and the Supernatural. Material events cannot produce spiritual activity, but the latter can be responsible for many of our actions on Nature. Will and Reason cannot depend on anything but themselves, but Nature can depend on Will and Reason, or, in other words, God created Nature.

The relation between Nature and Supernature, which is not a relation in space and time, becomes intelligible if the Supernatural made the Natural. We even have an idea of this making, since we know the power of imagination, though we can create nothing new, but can only rearrange our material provided through sense data. It is not inconceivable that the universe was created by an Imagination strong enough to impose phenomena on other minds.

It has been suggested, Mr Lewis concluded, that our ideas of making and causing are wholly derived from our experience of will. The conclusion usually drawn is that there is no making or causing, only 'projection'. But 'projection' is itself a form of causing, and it is more reasonable to suppose that Will is the only cause we know, and that therefore Will is the cause of Nature.

A discussion followed. Points arising:

All reasoning assumes the hypothesis that inference is valid. Correct inference is self-evident.

'Relevant' (re evidence) is a *rational* term.

The universe doesn't claim to be *true:* it's just *there.*

Knowledge by revelation is more like empirical than rational knowledge.

Question: What is the criterion of truth, if you distinguish between cause and reason?

Mr Lewis: A mountainous country might have several maps made of it, only one of which was a *true* one, i.e. corresponding with the actual contours. The map drawn by Reason claims to be that *true* one. I couldn't get at the universe unless I could trust my reason. If we couldn't trust inference we could know nothing but our own existence. Physical reality is an *inference* from sensations.

Question: How can an axiom claim self-evidence any more than an empirical judgment on evidence?

[The essay ends here, leaving this question unanswered.]

2

FIRST AND SECOND THINGS

When I read in *Time and Tide* on June 6 [1942] that the Germans have selected Hagen in preference to Siegfried as their national hero, I could have laughed out loud for pleasure. For I am a romantic person who has frankly revelled in my Nibelungs, and specially in Wagner's version of the story, ever since one golden summer in adolescence when I first heard the 'Ride of the Valkyries' on a gramophone and saw Arthur Rackham's illustrations to *The Ring*. Even now the very smell of those volumes can come over me with the poignancy of remembered calf-love. It was, therefore, a bitter moment when the Nazis took over my treasure and made it part of their ideology. But now all is well. They have proved unable to digest it. They can retain it only by standing the story on its head and making one of the minor villains the hero. Doubtless the logic of their position will presently drive them further, and Alberich will be announced as the true personification of the Nordic spirit. In the meantime, they have given me back what they stole.

The mention of the Nordic spirit reminds me that their attempted appropriation of *The Ring* is only one instance of their larger attempt to appropriate 'the Nordic' as a whole, and this larger attempt is equally ridiculous. What business have people who call might right to say they are worshippers of Odin? The whole point about Odin was that he had the right but not the might. The whole point about Norse religion was that it alone of all mythologies told men to serve gods who were admittedly fighting with their backs to the wall and

278

would certainly be defeated in the end. 'I am off to die with Odin' said the rover in Stevenson's fable,[1] thus proving that Stevenson understood something about the Nordic spirit which Germany has never been able to understand at all. The gods will fall. The wisdom of Odin, the humorous courage of Thor (Thor was something of a Yorkshireman) and the beauty of Balder will all be smashed eventually by the *realpolitik* of the stupid giants and misshapen trolls. But that does not in the least alter the allegiance of any free man. Hence, as we should expect, real Germanic poetry is all about heroic stands, and fighting against hopeless odds.

At this stage it occurred to me that I had stumbled on a rather remarkable paradox. How is it that the only people in Europe who have tried to revive their pre-Christian mythology as a living faith should also be the people that shows itself incapable of understanding that mythology in its very rudiments? The retrogression would, in any case, be deplorable — just as it would be deplorable if a full-grown man reverted to the *ethos* of his preparatory school. But you would expect him at least to get the no-sneaking rule right, and to be quite clear that new boys ought not to put their hands in their pockets. To sacrifice the greater good for the less and then not to get the lesser good after all — that is the surprising folly. To sell one's birthright for a mess of mythology and then to get the mythology all wrong — how did they do it? For it is quite clear that I (who would rather paint my face bright blue with woad than suggest that there is a real Odin) am actually getting out of Odin all the good and all the fun that Odin can supply, while the Nazi Odinists are getting none of it.

And yet, it seemed to me as I thought about it, this may not be such a paradox as it looks. Or, at least, it is a paradox which turns up so often that a man ought by now to be accustomed to it. Other instances began to come to mind. Until quite modern times — I think, until the time of the Romantics — nobody ever suggested that literature and the arts were an end in themselves. They 'belonged to the ornamental part of life', they provided 'innocent diversion'; or else they 'refined our manners' or 'incited us to virtue' or glorified the gods. The

[1] This is found in R. L. Stevenson's fable entitled 'Faith, Half-Faith, and No Faith', which was first published in *The Strange Case of Dr. Jekyll and Mr. Hyde with other Fables* (London, 1896).

great music had been written for Masses, the great pictures painted to fill up a space on the wall of a noble patron's dining-room or to kindle devotion in a church; the great tragedies were produced either by religious poets in honour of Dionysus or by commercial poets to entertain Londoners on half-holidays.

It was only in the nineteenth century that we became aware of the full dignity of art. We began to 'take it seriously' as the Nazis take mythology seriously. But the result seems to have been a dislocation of the aesthetic life in which little is left for us but high-minded works which fewer and fewer people want to read or hear or see, and 'popular' works of which both those who make them and those who enjoy them are half ashamed. Just like the Nazis, by valuing too highly a real, but subordinate good, we have come near to losing that good itself.

The longer I looked into it the more I came to suspect that I was perceiving a universal law. *On cause mieux quand on ne dit pas Causons.*[2] The woman who makes a dog the centre of her life loses, in the end, not only her human usefulness and dignity but even the proper pleasure of dog-keeping. The man who makes alcohol his chief good loses not only his job but his palate and all power of enjoying the earlier (and only pleasurable) levels of intoxication. It is a glorious thing to feel for a moment or two that the whole meaning of the universe is summed up in one woman — glorious so long as other duties and pleasures keep tearing you away from her. But clear the decks and so arrange your life (it is sometimes feasible) that you will have nothing to do but contemplate her, and what happens? Of course this law has been discovered before, but it will stand re-discovery. It may be stated as follows: every preference of a small good to a great, or a partial good to a total good, involves the loss of the small or partial good for which the sacrifice was made.

Apparently the world is made that way. If Esau really got the pottage in return for his birthright,[3] then Esau was a lucky exception. You can't get second things by putting them first; you can get second things only by putting first things first. From which it would follow that the question, What things are first? is of concern not only to philosophers but to everyone.

[2] 'One converses better when one does not say "Let us converse." '
[3] Genesis xxvii.

It is impossible, in this context, not to inquire what our own civilization has been putting first for the last thirty years. And the answer is plain. It has been putting itself first. To preserve civilization has been the great aim; the collapse of civilization, the great bugbear. Peace, a high standard of life, hygiene, transport, science and amusement — all these, which are what we usually mean by civilization, have been our ends. It will be replied that our concern for civilization is very natural and very necessary at a time when civilization is so imperilled. But how if the shoe is on the other foot? — how if civilization has been imperilled precisely by the fact that we have all made civilization our *summum bonum?* Perhaps it can't be preserved in that way. Perhaps civilization will never be safe until we care for something else more than we care for it.

The hypothesis has certain facts to support it. As far as peace (which is one ingredient in our idea of civilization) is concerned, I think many would now agree that a foreign policy dominated by desire for peace is one of the many roads that lead to war. And was civilization ever seriously endangered until civilization became the exclusive aim of human activity? There is much rash idealization of past ages about, and I do not wish to encourage more of it. Our ancestors were cruel, lecherous, greedy and stupid, like ourselves. But while they cared for other things more than for civilization — and they cared at different times for all sorts of things, for the will of God, for glory, for personal honour, for doctrinal purity, for justice — was civilization often in serious danger of disappearing?

At least the suggestion is worth a thought. To be sure, if it were true that civilization will never be safe till it is put second, that immediately raises the question, second to what? What is the first thing? The only reply I can offer here is that if we do not know, then the first and only truly practical thing is to set about finding out.

3

THE SERMON
AND THE LUNCH

AND SO', SAID THE PREACHER, 'THE HOME MUST BE THE foundation of our national life. It is there, all said and done, that character is formed. It is there that we appear as we really are. It is there we can fling aside the weary disguises of the outer world and be ourselves. It is there that we retreat from the noise and stress and temptation and dissipation of daily life to seek the sources of fresh strength and renewed purity . . .' And as he spoke I noticed that all confidence in him had departed from every member of that congregation who was under thirty. They had been listening well up to this point. Now the shufflings and coughings began. Pews creaked; muscles relaxed. The sermon, for all practical purposes, was over; the five minutes for which the preacher continued talking were a total waste of time — at least for most of us.

Whether I wasted them or not is for you to judge. I certainly did not hear any more of the sermon. I was thinking; and the starting-point of my thought was the question, 'How can he? How can *he* of all people?' For I knew the preacher's own home pretty well. In fact, I had been lunching there that very day, making a fifth to the Vicar and the Vicar's wife and the son (R.A.F.)[1] and the daughter (A.T.S.),[2] who happened both to be on leave. I could have avoided it, but the girl had whispered to me, 'For God's sake stay to lunch if

[1] Royal Air Force.
[2] Auxiliary Territorial Service.

they ask you. It's always a little less frightful when there's a visitor.'

Lunch at the vicarage nearly always follows the same pattern. It starts with a desperate attempt on the part of the young people to keep up a bright patter of trivial conversation: trivial not because they are trivially minded (you can have real conversation with them if you get them alone), but because it would never occur to either of them to say at home anything they were really thinking, unless it is forced out of them by anger. They are talking only to try to keep their parents quiet. They fail. The Vicar, ruthlessly interrupting, cuts in on a quite different subject. He is telling us how to re-educate Germany. He has never been there and seems to know nothing either of German history or the German language. 'But, father,' begins the son, and gets no further. His mother is now talking, though nobody knows exactly when she began. She is in the middle of a complicated story about how badly some neighbour has treated her. Though it goes on a long time, we never learn either how it began or how it ended: it is all middle. 'Mother, that's not quite fair,' says the daughter at last. 'Mrs Walker never said —' but her father's voice booms in again. He is telling his son about the organization of the R.A.F. So it goes on until either the Vicar or his wife says something so preposterous that the boy or the girl contradicts and insists on making the contradiction heard. The real minds of the young people have at last been called into action. They talk fiercely, quickly, contemptuously. They have facts and logic on their side. There is an answering flare up from the parents. The father storms; the mother is (oh, blessed domestic queen's move!) 'hurt'— plays pathos for all she is worth. The daughter becomes ironical. The father and son, elaborately ignoring each other, start talking to me. The lunch party is in ruins.

The memory of that lunch worries me during the last few minutes of the sermon. I am not worried by the fact that the Vicar's practice differs from his precept. That is, no doubt, regrettable, but it is nothing to the purpose. As Dr Johnson said, precept may be very sincere (and, let us add, very profitable) where practice is very imperfect,[3] and no one but a

[3] James Boswell, *Life of Johnson,* ed. George Birkbeck Hill (Oxford, 1934), vol. IV, p. 397 (2 December 1784).

fool would discount a doctor's warnings about alcoholic poisoning because the doctor himself drank too much. What worries me is the fact that the Vicar is not telling us at all that home life is difficult and has, like every form of life, its own proper temptations and corruptions. He keeps on talking as if 'home' were a panacea, a magical charm which of itself was bound to produce happiness and virtue. The trouble is not that he is insincere but that he is a fool. He is not talking from his own experience of family life at all: he is automatically reproducing a sentimental tradition — and it happens to be a false tradition. That is why the congregation have stopped listening to him.

If Christian teachers wish to recall Christian people to domesticity — and I, for one, believe that people must be recalled to it — the first necessity is to stop telling lies about home life and to substitute realistic teaching. Perhaps the fundamental principles would be something like this.

1. Since the Fall no organization or way of life whatever has a natural tendency to go right. In the Middle Ages some people thought that if only they entered a religious order they would find themselves automatically becoming holy and happy: the whole native literature of the period echoes with the exposure of that fatal error. In the nineteenth century some people thought that monogamous family life would automatically make them holy and happy; the savage anti-domestic literature of modern times — the Samuel Butlers, the Gosses, the Shaws — delivered the answer. In both cases the 'debunkers' may have been wrong about principles and may have forgotten the maxim *abusus non tollit usum*:[4] but in both cases they were pretty right about matter of fact. Both family life and monastic life were often detestable, and it should be noticed that the serious defenders of both are well aware of the dangers and free of the sentimental illusion. The author of the *Imitation of Christ* knows (no one better) how easily monastic life goes wrong. Charlotte M. Yonge makes it abundantly clear that domesticity is no passport to heaven on earth but an arduous vocation — a sea full of hidden rocks and perilous ice shores only to be navigated by one who uses a celestial chart. That is the first point on which

---

[4] 'The abuse does not abolish the use.'

we must be absolutely clear. The family, like the nation, can be offered to God, can be converted and redeemed, and will then become the channel of particular blessings and graces. But, like everything else that is human, it needs redemption. Unredeemed, it will produce only particular temptations, corruptions, and miseries. Charity begins at home: so does uncharity.

2. By the conversion or sanctification of family life we must be careful to mean something more than the preservation of 'love' in the sense of natural affection. Love (in that sense) is not enough. Affection, as distinct from charity, is not a cause of lasting happiness. Left to its natural bent affection becomes in the end greedy, naggingly solicitous, jealous, exacting, timorous. It suffers agony when its object is absent — but is not repaid by any long enjoyment when the object is present. Even at the Vicar's lunch table affection was partly the cause of the quarrel. That son would have borne patiently and humorously from any other old man the silliness which enraged him in his father. It is because he still (in some fashion) 'cares' that he is impatient. The Vicar's wife would not be quite that endless whimper of self-pity which she now is if she did not (in a sense) 'love' the family: the continued disappointment of her continued and ruthless demand for sympathy, for affection, for appreciation has helped to make her what she is. I do not think this aspect of affection is nearly enough noticed by most popular moralists. The greed to be loved is a fearful thing. Some of those who say (and almost with pride) that they live only for love come, at last, to live in incessant resentment.

3. We must realize the yawning pitfall in that very characteristic of home life which is so often glibly paraded as its principal attraction. 'It is there that we appear as we really are: it is there that we can fling aside the disguises and be ourselves.' These words, in the Vicar's mouth, were only too true and he showed at the lunch table what they meant. Outside his own house he behaves with ordinary courtesy. He would not have interrupted any other young man as he interrupted his son. He would not, in any other society, have talked confident nonsense about subjects of which he was totally ignorant: or, if he had, he would have accepted correction with good temper. In fact, he values home as the

place where he can 'be himself' in the sense of trampling on all the restraints which civilized humanity has found indispensable for tolerable social intercourse. And this, I think, is very common. What chiefly distinguishes domestic from public conversation is surely very often simply its downright rudeness. What distinguishes domestic behaviour is often its selfishness, slovenliness, incivility — even brutality. And it will often happen that those who praise home life most loudly are the worst offenders in this respect: they praise it — they are always glad to get home, hate the outer world, can't stand visitors, can't be bothered meeting people, etc. — because the freedoms in which they indulge themselves at home have ended by making them unfit for civilized society. If they practised elsewhere the only behaviour they now find 'natural' they would simply be knocked down.

4. How, then, *are* people to behave at home? If a man can't be comfortable and unguarded, can't take his ease and 'be himself' in his own house, where can he? That is, I confess, the trouble. The answer is an alarming one. There is *nowhere* this side of heaven where one can safely lay the reins on the horse's neck. It will never be lawful simply to 'be ourselves' until 'ourselves' have become sons of God. It is all there in the hymn — 'Christian, seek not yet repose.' This does not mean, of course, that there is no difference between home life and general society. It does mean that home life has its own rule of courtesy — a code more intimate, more subtle, more sensitive, and, therefore, in some ways more difficult, than that of the outer world.

5. Finally, must we not teach that if the home is to be a means of grace it must be a place of *rules?* There cannot be a common life without a *regula.* The alternative to rule is not freedom but the unconstitutional (and often unconscious) tyranny of the most selfish member.

In a word, must we not either cease to preach domesticity or else begin to preach it seriously? Must we not abandon sentimental eulogies and begin to give practical advice on the high, hard, lovely, and adventurous art of really creating the Christian family?

4

THE HUMANITARIAN
THEORY OF PUNISHMENT

IN ENGLAND WE HAVE LATELY HAD A CONTROVERSY ABOUT
Capital Punishment. I do not know whether a murderer is
more likely to repent and make a good end on the gallows
a few weeks after his trial or in the prison infirmary thirty
years later. I do not know whether the fear of death is an
indispensable deterrent. I need not, for the purpose of this
article, decide whether it is a morally permissible deterrent.
Those are questions which I propose to leave untouched. My
subject is not Capital Punishment in particular, but that theory
of punishment in general which the controversy showed to be
almost universal among my fellow-countrymen. It may be
called the Humanitarian theory. Those who hold it think that
it is mild and merciful. In this I believe that they are seriously
mistaken. I believe that the 'Humanity' which it claims is a
dangerous illusion and disguises the possibility of cruelty and
injustice without end. I urge a return to the traditional or
Retributive theory not solely, not even primarily, in the
interests of society, but in the interests of the criminal.

According to the Humanitarian theory, to punish a man
because he deserves it, and as much as he deserves, is mere
revenge, and, therefore, barbarous and immoral. It is maintained that the only legitimate motives for punishing are the
desire to deter others by example or to mend the criminal.
When this theory is combined, as frequently happens, with the
belief that all crime is more or less pathological, the idea of

mending tails off into that of healing or curing and punishment becomes therapeutic. Thus it appears at first sight that we have passed from the harsh and self-righteous notion of giving the wicked their deserts to the charitable and enlightened one of tending the psychologically sick. What could be more amiable? One little point which is taken for granted in this theory needs, however, to be made explicit. The things done to the criminal, even if they are called cures, will be just as compulsory as they were in the old days when we called them punishments. If a tendency to steal can be cured by psychotherapy, the thief will no doubt be forced to undergo the treatment. Otherwise, society cannot continue.

My contention is that this doctrine, merciful though it appears, really means that each one of us, from the moment he breaks the law, is deprived of the rights of a human being.

The reason is this. The Humanitarian theory removes from Punishment the concept of Desert. But the concept of Desert is the only connecting link between punishment and justice. It is only as deserved or undeserved that a sentence can be just or unjust. I do not here contend that the question 'Is it deserved?' is the only one we can reasonably ask about a punishment. We may very properly ask whether it is likely to deter others and to reform the criminal. But neither of these two last questions is a question about justice. There is no sense in talking about a 'just deterrent' or a 'just cure'. We demand of a deterrent not whether it is just but whether it will deter. We demand of a cure not whether it is just but whether it succeeds. Thus when we cease to consider what the criminal deserves and consider only what will cure him or deter others, we have tacitly removed him from the sphere of justice altogether; instead of a person, a subject of rights, we now have a mere object, a patient, a 'case'.

The distinction will become clearer if we ask who will be qualified to determine sentences when sentences are no longer held to derive their propriety from the criminal's deservings. On the old view the problem of fixing the right sentence was a moral problem. Accordingly, the judge who did it was a person trained in jurisprudence; trained, that is, in a science which deals with rights and duties, and which, in origin at least, was consciously accepting guidance from the Law of Nature, and from Scripture. We must admit that in the actual penal code of most countries at most times these high originals were so much modified by local custom, class interests, and utilitarian concessions, as to be very imperfectly recognizable. But the code was never in principle, and not always in fact, beyond the control of the conscience of the society. And when (say, in eighteenth-century England) actual punishments conflicted too violently with the moral sense of the community, juries refused to convict and reform was finally brought about. This was possible because, so long as we are thinking in terms of Desert, the propriety of the penal code, being a moral question, is a question on which every man has the right to an opinion, not because he follows this or that profession, but because he is simply a man, a rational animal enjoying the Natural Light. But all this is changed when we drop the concept of Desert. The only two questions we may now ask about a punishment are whether it deters and whether it cures. But these are not questions on which anyone is entitled to have an opinion simply because he is a man. He is not entitled to an opinion even if, in addition to being a man, he should happen also to be a jurist, a Christian, and a moral theologian. For they are not questions about principle but about matter of fact; and for such *cuiquam in sua arte credendum*.[1] Only the expert 'penologist' (let barbarous things have barbarous names), in the light of previous experiment, can tell us what is likely to deter: only the psychotherapist can tell us what is likely to cure. It will be in vain for the rest of us, speaking simply as men, to say, 'but this punishment is hideously unjust, hideously disproportionate to the criminal's deserts'. The experts with perfect logic will reply, 'but nobody was talking about deserts. No one was talking about *punishment* in your archaic vindictive sense of the word. Here are the statistics proving that this treatment deters. Here are the statistics proving that this other treatment cures. What is your trouble?'

The Humanitarian theory, then, removes sentences from the hands of jurists whom the public conscience is entitled to criticize and places them in the hands of technical experts whose special sciences do not even employ such categories as rights or justice. It might be argued that since this transference

[1] 'We must believe the expert in his own field.'

results from an abandonment of the old idea of punishment, and, therefore, of all vindictive motives, it will be safe to leave our criminals in such hands. I will not pause to comment on the simple-minded view of fallen human nature which such a belief implies. Let us rather remember that the 'cure' of criminals is to be compulsory; and let us then watch how the theory actually works in the mind of the Humanitarian. The immediate starting point of this article was a letter I read in one of our Leftist weeklies. The author was pleading that a certain sin, now treated by our laws as a crime, should henceforward be treated as a disease. And he complained that under the present system the offender, after a term in gaol, was simply let out to return to his original environment where he would probably relapse. What he complained of was not the shutting up but the letting out. On his remedial view of punishment the offender should, of course, be detained until he was cured. And of course the official straighteners are the only people who can say when that is. The first result of the Humanitarian theory is, therefore, to substitute for a definite sentence (reflecting to some extent the community's moral judgment on the degree of ill-desert involved) an indefinite sentence terminable only by the word of those experts — and they are not experts in moral theology nor even in the Law of Nature — who inflict it. Which of us, if he stood in the dock, would not prefer to be tried by the old system?

It may be said that by the continued use of the word punishment and the use of the verb 'inflict' I am misrepresenting Humanitarians. They are not punishing, not inflicting, only healing. But do not let us be deceived by a name. To be taken without consent from my home and friends; to lose my liberty; to undergo all those assaults on my personality which modern psychotherapy knows how to deliver; to be re-made after some pattern of 'normality' hatched in a Viennese laboratory to which I never professed allegiance; to know that this process will never end until either my captors have succeeded or I grown wise enough to cheat them with apparent success — who cares whether this is called Punishment or not? That it includes most of the elements for which any punishment is feared — shame, exile, bondage, and years eaten by the locust — is obvious. Only enormous ill-desert could justify it; but ill-desert is the very conception which the Humanitarian theory has thrown overboard.

If we turn from the curative to the deterrent justification of punishment we shall find the new theory even more alarming. When you punish a man *in terrorem,*[2] make of him an 'example' to others, you are admittedly using him as a means to an end; someone else's end. This, in itself, would be a very wicked thing to do. On the classical theory of Punishment it was of course justified on the ground that the man deserved it. That was assumed to be established before any question of 'making him an example' arose. You then, as the saying is, killed two birds with one stone; in the process of giving him what he deserved you set an example to others. But take away desert and the whole morality of the punishment disappears. Why, in Heaven's name, am I to be sacrificed to the good of society in this way? — unless, of course, I deserve it.

But that is not the worst. If the justification of exemplary punishment is not to be based on desert but solely on its efficacy as a deterrent, it is not absolutely necessary that the man we punish should even have committed the crime. The deterrent effect demands that the public should draw the moral, 'If we do such an act we shall suffer like that man.' The punishment of a man actually guilty whom the public think innocent will not have the desired effect; the punishment of a man actually innocent will, provided the public think him guilty. But every modern State has powers which make it easy to fake a trial. When a victim is urgently needed for exemplary purposes and a guilty victim cannot be found, all the purposes of deterrence will be equally served by the punishment (call it 'cure' if you prefer) of an innocent victim, provided that the public can be cheated into thinking him guilty. It is no use to ask me why I assume that our rulers will be so wicked. The punishment of an innocent, that is, an undeserving, man is wicked only if we grant the traditional view that righteous punishment means deserved punishment. Once we have abandoned that criterion, all punishments have to be justified, if at all, on other grounds that have nothing to do with desert. Where the punishment of the innocent can be justified on those grounds (and it could in some cases

[2] 'to cause terror'.

be justified as a deterrent) it will be no less moral than any other punishment. Any distaste for it on the part of a Humanitarian will be merely a hang-over from the Retributive theory.

It is, indeed, important to notice that my argument so far supposes no evil intentions on the part of the Humanitarian and considers only what is involved in the logic of his position. My contention is that good men (not bad men) consistently acting upon that position would act as cruelly and unjustly as the greatest tyrants. They might in some respects act even worse. Of all tyrannies a tyranny sincerely exercised for the good of its victims may be the most oppressive. It may be better to live under robber barons than under omnipotent moral busybodies. The robber baron's cruelty may sometimes sleep, his cupidity may at some point be satiated; but those who torment us for our own good will torment us without end for they do so with the approval of their own conscience. They may be more likely to go to Heaven yet at the same time likelier to make a Hell of earth. Their very kindness stings with intolerable insult. To be 'cured' against one's will and cured of states which we may not regard as disease is to be put on a level with those who have not yet reached the age of reason or those who never will; to be classed with infants, imbeciles, and domestic animals. But to be punished, however severely, because we have deserved it, because we 'ought to have known better', is to be treated as a human person made in God's image.

In reality, however, we must face the possibility of bad rulers armed with a Humanitarian theory of punishment. A great many popular blue prints for a Christian society are merely what the Elizabethans called 'eggs in moonshine' because they assume that the whole society is Christian or that the Christians are in control. This is not so in most contemporary States. Even if it were, our rulers would still be fallen men, and, therefore, neither very wise nor very good. As it is, they will usually be unbelievers. And since wisdom and virtue are not the only or the commonest qualifications for a place in the government, they will not often be even the best unbelievers.

The practical problem of Christian politics is not that of drawing up schemes for a Christian society, but that of living as innocently as we can with unbelieving fellow-subjects under unbelieving rulers who will never be perfectly wise and good and who will sometimes be very wicked and very foolish. And when they are wicked the Humanitarian theory of punishment will put in their hands a finer instrument of tyranny than wickedness ever had before. For if crime and disease are to be regarded as the same thing, it follows that any state of mind which our masters choose to call 'disease' can be treated as crime; and compulsorily cured. It will be vain to plead that states of mind which displease government need not always involve moral turpitude and do not therefore always deserve forfeiture of liberty. For our masters will not be using the concepts of Desert and Punishment but those of disease and cure. We know that one school of psychology already regards religion as a neurosis. When this particular neurosis becomes inconvenient to government, what is to hinder government from proceeding to 'cure' it? Such 'cure' will, of course, be compulsory; but under the Humanitarian theory it will not be called by the shocking name of Persecution. No one will blame us for being Christians, no one will hate us, no one will revile us. The new Nero will approach us with the silky manners of a doctor, and though all will be in fact as compulsory as the *tunica molesta* or Smithfield or Tyburn, all will go on within the unemotional therapeutic sphere where words like 'right' and 'wrong' or 'freedom' and 'slavery' are never heard. And thus when the command is given, every prominent Christian in the land may vanish overnight into Institutions for the Treatment of the Ideologically Unsound, and it will rest with the expert gaolers to say when (if ever) they are to re-emerge. But it will not be persecution. Even if the treatment is painful, even if it is life-long, even if it is fatal, that will be only a regrettable accident; the intention was purely therapeutic. In ordinary medicine there were painful operations and fatal operations; so in this. But because they are 'treatment', not punishment, they can be criticized only by fellow-experts and on technical grounds, never by men as men and on grounds of justice.

This is why I think it essential to oppose the Humanitarian theory of punishment, root and branch, wherever we encounter it. It carries on its front a semblance of mercy which is wholly false. That is how it can deceive men of good will. The error

293

began, perhaps, with Shelley's statement that the distinction between mercy and justice was invented in the courts of tyrants. It sounds noble, and was indeed the error of a noble mind. But the distinction is essential. The older view was that mercy 'tempered' justice, or (on the highest level of all) that mercy and justice had met and kissed. The essential act of mercy was to pardon; and pardon in its very essence involves the recognition of guilt and ill-desert in the recipient. If crime is only a disease which needs cure, not sin which deserves punishment, it cannot be pardoned. How can you pardon a man for having a gumboil or a club foot? But the Humanitarian theory wants simply to abolish Justice and substitute Mercy for it. This means that you start being 'kind' to people before you have considered their rights, and then force upon them supposed kindnesses which no one but you will recognize as kindnesses and which the recipient will feel as abominable cruelties. You have overshot the mark. Mercy, detached from Justice, grows unmerciful. That is the important paradox. As there are plants which will flourish only in mountain soil, so it appears that Mercy will flower only when it grows in the crannies of the rock of Justice: transplanted to the marshlands of mere Humanitarianism, it becomes a man-eating weed, all the more dangerous because it is still called by the same name as the mountain variety. But we ought long ago to have learned our lesson. We should be too old now to be deceived by those humane pretensions which have served to usher in every cruelty of the revolutionary period in which we live. These are the 'precious balms' which will 'break our heads'.[3]

There is a fine sentence in Bunyan: 'It came burning hot into my mind, whatever he said, and however he flattered, when he got me home to his House, he would sell me for a Slave.'[4] There is a fine couplet, too, in John Ball:

> Be war or ye be wo;
> Knoweth your frend from your foo.[5]

---

[3] Psalm cxli. 6.

[4] *The Pilgrim's Progress,* ed. James Blanton Wharey, second edition revised by Roger Sharrock, Oxford English Texts (Oxford, 1960), Part I, p. 70.

[5] 'John Ball's Letter to the Peasants of Essex, 1381', lines 11-12, found in *Fourteenth Century Verse and Prose,* ed. Kenneth Sisam (Oxford, 1921), p. 161.

ON PUNISHMENT: A REPLY
TO CRITICISM
by
C. S. Lewis

I HAVE TO THANK THE EDITOR FOR THIS OPPORTUNITY OF replying to two most interesting critiques of my article on the Humanitarian Theory of Punishment, one by Professor J. J. C. Smart[6] and the other by Drs N. Morris and D. Buckle.[7]

Professor Smart makes a distinction between questions of the First and of the Second Order: 'First' are questions like 'Ought I to return this book?'; Second, like 'Is promise-making a good institution?' He claims that these two Orders of question require different methods of treatment. The first can be answered by Intuition (in the sense which moral philosophers sometimes give that word). We 'see' what is 'right' at once, because the proposed action falls under a rule. But second-order questions can be answered only on 'utilitarian' principles. Since 'right' means 'agreeable to the rules' it is senseless to ask if the rules themselves are 'right'; we can only ask if they are useful. A parallel would be this: granted a fixed spelling we may ask whether a word is spelled correctly, but cannot ask whether the spelling system is correct, only if it is consistent or convenient. Or again, a form may be grammatically right, but the grammar of a whole language cannot be right or wrong.

Professor Smart is here, of course, treating in a new way a very ancient distinction. It was realised by all the thinkers of the past that you could consider either (a) Whether an act was 'just' in the sense of conforming to a law or custom, or (b) Whether a law or custom was itself 'just'. To the ancients and medievals, however, the distinction was one between (a) Justice by law or convention, *nomo (i)*, and (b) Justice 'simply' or 'by nature', *haplôs* or *physei,* or between (a) Positive Law, and (b) Natural Law. Both inquiries were about

6 'Comment: The Humanitarian Theory of Punishment', *Res Judicatae,* vol. VI (February 1954), pp. 368-71.

7 'Reply to C. S. Lewis', *Res Judicatae,* vol. VI (June 1953), pp. 231-37.

justice, but the distinction between them was acknowledged. The novelty of Professor Smart's system consists in confining the concept of justice to the First-order questions.

It is claimed that the new system (1) avoids a *petitio* inherent in any appeal to the Law of Nature or the 'simply' just; for 'to say that this is the Law of Nature is only to say that this is the rule we should adopt'; and (2) gets rid of dogmatic subjectivism. For the idea of desert in my article may be only 'Lewis's personal preference'.

I am not convinced, however, that Professor Smart's system does avoid these inconveniences.

Those rules are to be accepted which are useful to the community, utility being (I think) what will make that community 'happier'.* Does this mean that the happiness of the community is to be pursued *at all costs,* or only to be pursued in so far as this pursuit is compatible with certain degrees of mercy, human dignity, and veracity? (I must not add 'of justice' because, in Professor Smart's view, the rules themselves cannot be either just or unjust). If we take the second alternative, if we admit that there are some things, or even any one thing, which a community ought not to do however much it will increase its happiness, then we have really given up the position. We are now judging the useful by some other standard (whether we call it Conscience, or Practical Reason, or Law of Nature or Personal Preference). Suppose then, we take the first alternative: the happiness of the community is to be pursued at all costs. In certain circumstances the costs may be very heavy. In war, in some not improbable future when the world's food runs short, during some threat of revolution, very shocking things may be likely to make the community happier or to preserve its existence. We cannot be sure that frame-ups, witch-hunts, even cannibalism, would never be in this sense 'useful'. Let us suppose (what, I am very sure, is false) that Professor Smart is prepared to go the whole hog. It then remains to ask him why he does so or why he thinks we should agree with him. He of all men cannot reply that *salus populi suprema lex*[8] is the Law of Nature; firstly, because we others know that 'the people should be

---

* See the penultimate paragraph of Professor Smart's article.

[8] Cicero, *De Legibus,* bk. III, pt. iii, sect. 8. 'The safety of the people is the highest law.'

preserved' is not the Law of Nature but only one clause in that Law. What then could a pursuit of the community's happiness at all costs be based on if not on Professor Smart's 'personal preference'? The real difference between him and me would then be simply that we have different desires. Or, rather, that I have one more desire than he. For, like him, I desire the continuance and happiness of my country (and species),* but then I also desire that they should be people of a certain sort, behaving in a certain way. The second desire is the stronger of the two. If I cannot have both, I had rather that the human race, having a certain quality in their lives, should continue for only a few centuries than that, losing freedom, friendship, dignity, and mercy, and learning to be quite content without them, they should continue for millions of millennia. If it is merely a matter of wishes, there is really no further question for discussion. Lots of people feel like me, and lots feel the other way. I believe that it is in our age being decided which kind of man will win.

And that is why, if I may say so without discourtesy, Professor Smart and I both matter so little compared with Drs Morris and Buckle. We are only dons; they are criminologists, a lawyer and a psychiatrist respectively. And the only thing which leads me so far off my own beat as to write about 'Penology' at all is my intense anxiety as to which side in this immensely important conflict will have the Law for its ally. This leads me to the only serious disagreement between my two critics and myself.

Other disagreements there are, but they mainly turn on misunderstandings for which I am probably to blame. Thus:

(1) There was certainly too little, if there was anything, in my article about the protection of the community. I am afraid I took it for granted. But the distinction in my mind would not be, as my critics suppose (Morris and Buckle, p. 232), one between 'subsidiary' and 'vital' elements in punishment. I call the act of taking a packet of cigarettes off a counter and slipping it into one's pocket 'purchase' or 'theft' according as one does or does not pay for it. This does not mean that I consider the taking

---

* I am not sure whether for Professor Smart the 'community' means the nation or the species. If the former, difficulties arise about international morality, in discussing which I think Professor Smart would have to come to the species sooner or later.

away of the goods as 'subsidiary' in an act of purchase. It means that what legitimises it, what makes it purchase at all, is the paying. I call the sexual act chaste or unchaste according as the parties are or are not married to one another. This does not mean that I consider it as 'subsidiary' to marriage, but that what legitimises it, what makes it a specimen of conjugal behaviour at all, is marriage. In the same way, I am ready to make both the protection of society and the 'cure' of the criminal as important as you please in punishment, but only on a certain condition; namely, that the initial act of thus interfering with a man's liberty be justified on grounds of desert. Like payment in purchase, or marriage as regards the sexual act, it is this, and (I believe) this alone, which legitimises our proceeding and makes it an instance of punishment at all, instead of an instance of tyranny — or, perhaps, of war.

(2) I agree about criminal *children* (see Morris and Buckle, p. 234). There has been progress in this matter. Very primitive societies will 'try' and 'punish' an axe or a spear in cases of unintentional homicide. Somewhere (I think, in the Empire) during the later Middle Ages a pig was solemnly tried for murder. Till quite recently, we may (I don't know) have tried children as if they had adult responsibility. These things have rightly been abolished. But the whole question is whether you want the process to be carried further: whether you want us all to be simultaneously deprived of the protection and released from the responsibilities of adult citizenship and reduced to the level of the child, the pig, and the axe. I don't want this because I don't think there are in fact any people who stand to the rest of us as adult to child, man to beast, or animate to inanimate.* I think the laws which laid down a 'desertless' theory of punishment would in reality be made and administered by people just like the rest of us.

But the real disagreement is this. Drs Morris and Buckle, fully alive to dangers of the sort I dread and reprobating them no less than I, believe that we have a safeguard. It lies in the Courts, in their incorruptible judges, their excellent techniques, and 'the controls of natural justice which the law has built up'

---

* This is really the same objection as that which I would make to Aristotle's theory of slavery (*Politics* 1254A *et seq.*). We can all recognize the 'natural' slaves (I am perhaps one myself) but where are the 'natural' masters?

(p. 233). Yes; if the whole tradition of natural justice which the law has for so long incorporated, will survive the completion of that change in our attitude to punishment which we are now discussing. But that for me is precisely the question. Our Courts, I agree, 'have traditionally represented the common man and the common man's view of morality' (p. 233). It is true that we must extend the term 'common man' to cover Locke, Grotius, Hooker, Poynet, Aquinas, Justinian, the Stoics, and Aristotle, but I have no objection to that; in one most important, and to me glorious, sense they were all common men.* But that whole tradition is tied up with ideas of free-will, responsibility, rights, and the law of nature. Can it survive in Courts whose penal practice daily subordinates 'desert' to therapy and the protection of society? Can the Law assume one philosophy in practice and continue to enjoy the safeguards of a different philosophy?

I write as the son of one lawyer and the lifelong friend of another,[9] to two criminologists one of whom is a lawyer. I believe an approximation between their view and mine is not to be despaired of, for we have the same ends at heart. I wish society to be protected and I should be very glad if all punishments were also cures. All I plead for is the *prior* condition of ill desert; loss of liberty justified on retributive grounds *before* we begin considering the other factors. After that, as you please. Till that, there is really no question of 'punishment'. We are not such poltroons that we want to be protected unconditionally, though when a man has deserved punishment we shall very properly look to our protection in devising it. We are not such busybodies that we want to improve all our neighbours by force; but when one of our neighbours has justly forfeited his right not to be interfered with, we shall charitably try to make his punishment improve him. But we will not presume to teach him (who, after all, are we?) till he has merited that we should 'larn him'. Will Dr Morris and Dr Buckle come so far to meet me as that? On their decision and on that of others in similar important offices, depends, I believe, the continued dignity and beneficence of that great discipline the Law, but also much more. For, if I am not de-

---

* See also Lewis: *The Abolition of Man* (London, 1943), especially the Appendix.

[9] Owen Barfield.

ceived, we are all at this moment helping to decide whether humanity shall retain all that has hitherto made humanity worth preserving, or whether we must slide down into the sub-humanity imagined by Mr Aldous Huxley and George Orwell and partially realised in Hitler's Germany. For the extermination of the Jews really would have been 'useful' if the racial theories had been correct; there is no foretelling what may come to seem, or even to be, 'useful', and 'necessity' was always 'the tyrant's plea'.[10]

[10] See Letter 12.

5

XMAS AND CHRISTMAS

A LOST CHAPTER FROM HERODOTUS

AND BEYOND THIS THERE LIES IN THE OCEAN, TURNED towards the west and north, the island of Niatirb which Hecataeus indeed declares to be the same size and shape as Sicily, but it is larger, though in calling it triangular a man would not miss the mark. It is densely inhabited by men who wear clothes not very different from the other barbarians who occupy the north-western parts of Europe though they do not agree with them in language. These islanders, surpassing all the men of whom we know in patience and endurance, use the following customs.

In the middle of winter when fogs and rains most abound they have a great festival which they call Exmas, and for fifty days they prepare for it in the fashion I shall describe. First of all, every citizen is obliged to send to each of his friends and relations a square piece of hard paper stamped with a picture, which in their speech is called an Exmas-card. But the pictures represent birds sitting on branches, or trees with a dark green prickly leaf, or else men in such garments as the Niatirbians believe that their ancestors wore two hundred years ago riding in coaches such as their ancestors used, or houses with snow on their roofs. And the Niatirbians are unwilling to say what these pictures have to do with the festival, guarding (as I suppose) some sacred mystery. And because all men must send these cards the market-place is filled with the crowd of those buying them, so that there is great labour and weariness.

But having bought as many as they suppose to be sufficient, they return to their houses and find there the like cards which others have sent to them. And when they find cards from any to whom they also have sent cards, they throw them away and give thanks to the gods that this labour at least is over for another year. But when they find cards from any to whom they have not sent, then they beat their breasts and wail and utter curses against the sender; and, having sufficiently lamented their misfortune, they put on their boots again and go out into the fog and rain and buy a card for him also. And let this account suffice about Exmas-cards.

They also send gifts to one another, suffering the same things about the gifts as about the cards, or even worse. For every citizen has to guess the value of the gift which every friend will send to him so that he may send one of equal value, whether he can afford it or not. And they buy as gifts for one another such things as no man ever bought for himself. For the sellers, understanding the custom, put forth all kinds of trumpery, and whatever, being useless and ridiculous, they have been unable to sell throughout the year they now sell as an Exmas gift. And though the Niatirbians profess themselves to lack sufficient necessary things, such as metal, leather, wood and paper, yet an incredible quantity of these things is wasted every year, being made into the gifts.

But during these fifty days the oldest, poorest and most miserable of the citizens put on false beards and red robes and walk about the market-place; being disguised (in my opinion) as *Cronos*. And the sellers of gifts no less than the purchasers become pale and weary, because of the crowds and the fog, so that any man who came into a Niatirbian city at this season would think some great public calamity had fallen on Niatirb. This fifty days of preparation is called in their barbarian speech the Exmas *Rush*.

But when the day of the festival comes, then most of the citizens, being exhausted with the *Rush,* lie in bed till noon. But in the evening they eat five times as much supper as on other days and, crowning themselves with crowns of paper, they become intoxicated. And on the day after Exmas they are very grave, being internally disordered by the supper and the drinking and reckoning how much they have spent on gifts and on the wine. For wine is so dear among the Niatirbians that a man must swallow the worth of a talent before he is well intoxicated.

Such, then, are their customs about the Exmas. But the few among the Niatirbians have also a festival, separate and to themselves, called Crissmas, which is on the same day as Exmas. And those who keep Crissmas, doing the opposite to the majority of the Niatirbians, rise early on that day with shining faces and go before sunrise to certain temples where they partake of a sacred feast. And in most of the temples they set out images of a fair woman with a new-born Child on her knees and certain animals and shepherds adoring the Child. (The reason of these images is given in a certain sacred story which I know but do not repeat.)

But I myself conversed with a priest in one of these temples and asked him why they kept Crissmas on the same day as Exmas; for it appeared to me inconvenient. But the priest replied, It is not lawful, O Stranger, for us to change the date of Crissmas, but would that Zeus would put it into the minds of the Niatirbians to keep Exmas at some other time or not to keep it at all. For Exmas and the *Rush* distract the minds even of the few from sacred things. And we indeed are glad that men should make merry at Crissmas; but in Exmas there is no merriment left. And when I asked him why they endured the *Rush,* he replied, It is, O Stranger, a *racket;* using (as I suppose) the words of some oracle and speaking unintelligibly to me (for a *racket* is an instrument which the barbarians use in a game called *tennis*).

But what Hecataeus says, that Exmas and Crissmas are the same, is not credible. For first, the pictures which are stamped on the Exmas-cards have nothing to do with the sacred story which the priests tell about Crissmas. And secondly, the most part of the Niatirbians, not believing the religion of the few, nevertheless send the gifts and cards and participate in the *Rush* and drink, wearing paper caps. But it is not likely that men, even being barbarians, should suffer so many and great things in honour of a god they do not believe in. And now, enough about Niatirb.

6

WHAT CHRISTMAS
MEANS TO ME

THREE THINGS GO BY THE NAME OF CHRISTMAS. ONE IS A religious festival. This is important and obligatory for Christians; but as it can be of no interest to anyone else, I shall naturally say no more about it here. The second (it has complex historical connections with the first, but we needn't go into them) is a popular holiday, an occasion for merry-making and hospitality. If it were my business to have a 'view' on this, I should say that I much approve of merry-making. But what I approve of much more is everybody minding his own business. I see no reason why I should volunteer views as to how other people should spend their own money in their own leisure among their own friends. It is highly probable that they want my advice on such matters as little as I want theirs. But the third thing called Christmas is unfortunately everyone's business.

I mean of course the commercial racket. The interchange of presents was a very small ingredient in the older English festivity. Mr Pickwick took a cod with him to Dingley Dell; the reformed Scrooge ordered a turkey for his clerk; lovers sent love gifts; toys and fruit were given to children. But the idea that not only all friends but even all acquaintances should give one another presents, or at least send one another cards, is quite modern and has been forced upon us by the shopkeepers. Neither of these circumstances is in itself a reason for condemning it. I condemn it on the following grounds.

1. It gives on the whole much more pain than pleasure. You have only to stay over Christmas with a family who seriously try to 'keep' it (in its third, or commercial, aspect) in order to see that the thing is a nightmare. Long before December 25th everyone is worn out — physically worn out by weeks of daily struggle in overcrowded shops, mentally worn out by the effort to remember all the right recipients and to think out suitable gifts for them. They are in no trim for merry-making; much less (if they should want to) to take part in a religious act. They look far more as if there had been a long illness in the house.

2. Most of it is involuntary. The modern rule is that anyone can force you to give him a present by sending you a quite unprovoked present of his own. It is almost a blackmail. Who has not heard the wail of despair, and indeed of resentment, when, at the last moment, just as everyone hoped that the nuisance was over for one more year, the unwanted gift from Mrs Busy (whom we hardly remember) flops unwelcomed through the letter-box, and back to the dreadful shops one of us has to go?

3. Things are given as presents which no mortal ever bought for himself — gaudy and useless gadgets, 'novelties' because no one was ever fool enough to make their like before. Have we really no better use for materials and for human skill and time than to spend them on all this rubbish?

4. The nuisance. For after all, during the racket we still have all our ordinary and necessary shopping to do, and the racket trebles the labour of it.

We are told that the whole dreary business must go on because it is good for trade. It is in fact merely one annual symptom of that lunatic condition of our country, and indeed of the world, in which everyone lives by persuading everyone else to buy things. I don't know the way out. But can it really be my duty to buy and receive masses of junk every winter just to help the shopkeepers? If the worst comes to the worst I'd sooner give them money for nothing and write it off as a charity. For nothing? Why, better for nothing than for a nuisance.

DELINQUENTS IN THE SNOW

Voices 'off', outside the front door, annually remind us (usually at the most inconvenient moment) that the
season of carols has come again. At my front door they are,
once every year, the voices of the local choir; on the forty-
five other annual occasions they are those of boys or children
who have not even tried to learn to sing, or to memorize the
words of the piece they are murdering. The instruments they
play with real conviction are the door-bell and the knocker;
and money is what they are after.

I am pretty sure that some of them are the very same hooligans who trespass in my garden, rob my orchard, hack down
my trees and scream outside my windows, though everyone
in the neighbourhood knows that there is serious illness in
my family. I am afraid I deal with them badly in the capacity
of 'waits'. I neither forgive like a Christian nor turn the dog
on them like an indignant householder. I pay the blackmail.
I give, but give ungraciously, and make the worst of both
worlds.

It would be silly to publish this fact (more proper for a
confessor's ear) if I did not think that this smouldering resentment, against which I win so many battles but never win the
war, was at present very widely shared by law-abiding people.
And Heaven knows, many of them have better cause to feel
it than I. I have not been driven to suicide like Mr Pilgrim.
I am not mourning for a raped and murdered daughter whose
murderer will be kept (partly at my expense) in a mental
hospital till he gets out and catches some other child. My

greatest grievance is trivial in comparison. But, as it raises all the issues, I will tell it.

Not long ago some of my young neighbours broke into a little pavilion or bungalow which stands in my garden and stole several objects — curious weapons and an optical instrument. This time the police discovered who they were. As more than one of them had been convicted of similar crimes before, we had high hopes that some adequately deterrent sentence would be given. But I was warned: 'It'll all be no good if the old woman's on the bench.' I had, of course, to attend the juvenile court and all fell out pat as the warning had said. The — let us call her — Elderly Lady presided. It was abundantly proved that the crime had been planned and that it was done for gain: some of the swag had already been sold. The Elderly Lady inflicted a small fine. That is, she punished not the culprits but their parents. But what alarmed me more was her concluding speech to the prisoners. She told them that they must, they really must, give up these 'stupid pranks'.

Of course I must not accuse the Elderly Lady of injustice. Justice has been so variously defined. If it means, as Thrasymachus thought, 'the interest of the stronger', she was very just; for she enforced her own will and that of the criminals and they together are incomparably stronger than I.

But if her intention was — and I do not doubt that the road on which such justice is leading us all is paved with good ones — to prevent these boys from growing up into confirmed criminals, I question whether her method was well judged. If they listened to her (we may hope they did not) what they carried away was the conviction that planned robbery for gain would be classified as a 'prank' — a childishness which they might be expected to grow out of. A better way of leading them on, without any sense of frontiers crossed, from mere inconsiderate romping and plundering orchards to burglary, arson, rape and murder, would seem hard to imagine.

This little incident seems to me characteristic of our age. Criminal law increasingly protects the criminal and ceases to protect his victim. One might fear that we were moving towards a Dictatorship of the Criminals or (what is perhaps the same thing) mere anarchy. But that is not my fear; my fear is almost the opposite.

According to the classical political theory of this country we surrendered our right of self-protection to the State on condition that the State would protect us. Roughly, you promised not to stab your daughter's murderer on the understanding that the State would catch him and hang him. Of course this was never true as a historical account of the genesis of the State. The power of the group over the individual is by nature unlimited and the individual submits because he has to. The State, under favourable conditions (they have ceased), by defining that power, limits it and gives the individual a little freedom.

But the classical theory morally grounds our obligation to civil obedience; explains why it is right (as well as unavoidable) to pay taxes, why it is wrong (as well as dangerous) to stab your daughter's murderer. At present the very uncomfortable position is this: the State protects us less because it is unwilling to protect us against criminals at home and manifestly grows less and less able to protect us against foreign enemies. At the same time it demands from us more and more. We seldom had fewer rights and liberties nor more burdens: and we get less security in return. While our obligations increase their moral ground is taken away.

And the question that torments me is how long flesh and blood will continue to endure it. There was even, not so long ago, a question whether they ought to. No one, I hope, thinks Dr Johnson a barbarian. Yet he maintained that if, under a peculiarity of Scottish law, the murderer of a man's father escapes, the man might reasonably say, 'I am amongst barbarians, who ... refuse to do justice ... I am therefore in a state of nature ... I will stab the murderer of my father.' (This is recorded in Boswell's *Journal of a Tour of the Hebrides* under 22 August 1773.)

Much more obviously, on these principles, when the State ceases to protect me from hooligans I might reasonably, if I could, catch and trash them myself. When the State cannot or will not protect, 'nature' is come again and the right of self-protection reverts to the individual. But of course if I could and did I should be prosecuted. The Elderly Lady and her kind who are so merciful to theft would have no mercy on me;

and I should be pilloried in the gutter Press as a 'sadist' by journalists who neither know nor care what that word, or any word, means.

What I fear, however, is not, or not chiefly, sporadic outbreaks of individual vengeance. I am more afraid, our conditions being so like that of the South after the American Civil War, that some sort of Ku Klux Klan may appear and that this might eventually develop into something like a Right or Central revolution. For those who suffer are chiefly the provident, the resolute, the men who want to work, who have built up, in the face of implacable discouragement, some sort of life worth preserving and wish to preserve it. That most (by no means all) of them are 'middle class' is not very relevant. They do not get their qualities from a class: they belong to that class because they have those qualities. For in a society like ours no stock which has diligence, forethought or talent, and is prepared to practise self-denial, is likely to remain proletarian for more than a generation. They are, in fact, the bearers of what little moral, intellectual, or economic vitality remains. They are not nonentities. There is a point at which their patience will snap.

The Elderly Lady, if she read this article, would say I was 'threatening' — linguistic nicety not being much in her line. If by a *threat* you mean (but then you don't know much English) the conjectural prediction of a highly undesirable event, then I threaten. But if by the word *threat* you imply that I wish for such a result or would willingly contribute to it, then you are wrong. Revolutions seldom cure the evil against which they are directed; they always beget a hundred others. Often they perpetuate the old evil under a new name. We may be sure that, if a Ku Klux Klan arose, its ranks would soon be chiefly filled by the same sort of hooligans who provoked it. A Right or Central revolution would be as hypocritical, filthy and ferocious as any other. My fear is lest we should be making it more probable.

This may be judged an article unfit for the season of peace and goodwill. Yet there is a connection. Not all kinds of peace are compatible with all kinds of goodwill, nor do all those who say 'Peace, peace' inherit the blessing promised to the peacemakers.[1] The real *pacificus* is he who promotes peace,

[1] Jeremiah vi. 14; viii. 11 and Matthew v. 9.

309

not he who gasses about it. Peace, peace . . . we won't be hard on you . . . it was only a boyish prank . . . you had a neurosis . . . promise not to do it again . . . out of this in the long run I do not think either goodwill or peace will come. Planting new primroses on the primrose path is no long-term benevolence.

There! They're at it again. 'Ark, the errol hygel sings.' They're knocking louder. Well, they come but fifty times a year. Boxing Day[2] is only two and a half weeks ahead; then perhaps we shall have a little quiet in which to remember the birth of Christ.

[2] The first week-day after Christmas.

8

IS PROGRESS POSSIBLE?

WILLING SLAVES OF THE WELFARE STATE

[From the French Revolution to the outbreak of the First World War in 1914, it was generally assumed that progress in human affairs was not only possible but inevitable. Since then two terrible wars and the discovery of the hydrogen bomb have made men question this confident assumption. *The Observer* invited five well-known writers to give their answers to the following questions: 'Is man progressing today?' 'Is progress even possible?' This second article in the series is a reply to the opening article by C. P. Snow, 'Man in Society', *The Observer* (13 July 1958).]

PROGRESS MEANS MOVEMENT IN A DESIRED DIRECTION, AND we do not all desire the same things for our species. In 'Possible Worlds'[1] Professor Haldane pictured a future in which Man, foreseeing that Earth would soon be uninhabitable, adapted himself for migration to Venus by drastically modifying his physiology and abandoning justice, pity and happiness. The desire here is for mere survival. Now I care far more how humanity lives than how long. Progress, for me, means increasing goodness and happiness of individual lives. For the species, as for each man, mere longevity seems to me a contemptible ideal.

I therefore go even further than C. P. Snow in removing the H-bomb from the centre of the picture. Like him, I am not certain whether if it killed one-third of us (the one-third

[1] One essay in J. B. S. Haldane's *Possible Worlds and Other Essays* (London, 1927). See also 'The Last Judgment' in the same book.

I belong to), this would be a bad thing for the remainder; like him, I don't think it will kill us all. But suppose it did? As a Christian I take it for granted that human history will some day end; and I am offering Omniscience no advice as to the best date for that consummation. I am more concerned by what the Bomb is doing already.

One meets young people who make the threat of it a reason for poisoning every pleasure and evading every duty in the present. Didn't they know that, Bomb or no Bomb, all men die (many in horrible ways)? There's no good moping and sulking about it.

Having removed what I think a red herring, I return to the real question. Are people becoming, or likely to become, better or happier? Obviously this allows only the most conjectural answer. Most individual experience (and there is no other kind) never gets into the news, let alone the history books; one has an imperfect grasp even of one's own. We are reduced to generalities. Even among these it is hard to strike a balance. Sir Charles enumerates many real ameliorations. Against these we must set Hiroshima, Black and Tans, Gestapo, Ogpu, brain-washing, the Russian slave camps. Perhaps we grow kinder to children; but then we grow less kind to the old. Any G.P.[2] will tell you that even prosperous people refuse to look after their parents. 'Can't they be got into some sort of Home?' says Goneril.[3]

More useful, I think, than an attempt at balancing, is the reminder that most of these phenomena, good and bad, are made possible by two things. These two will probably determine most of what happens to us for some time.

The first is the advance, and increasing application, of science. As a means to the ends I care for, this is neutral. We shall grow able to cure, and to produce, more diseases — bacterial war, not bombs, might ring down the curtain — to alleviate, and to inflict, more pains, to husband, or to waste, the resources of the planet more extensively. We can become either more beneficent or more mischievous. My guess is we shall do both; mending one thing and marring another, removing old miseries and producing new ones, safeguarding ourselves here and endangering ourselves there.

[2] A general practitioner (doctor).
[3] In Shakespeare's *King Lear*.

The second is the changed relation between Government and subjects. Sir Charles mentions our new attitude to crime. I will mention the trainloads of Jews delivered at the German gas-chambers. It seems shocking to suggest a common element, but I think one exists. On the humanitarian view all crime is pathological; it demands not retributive punishment but cure. This separates the criminal's treatment from the concepts of justice and desert; a 'just cure' is meaningless.

On the old view public opinion might protest against a punishment (it protested against our old penal code) as excessive, more than the man 'deserved'; an ethical question on which anyone might have an opinion. But a remedial treatment can be judged only by the probability of its success; a technical question on which only experts can speak. Thus the criminal ceases to be a person, a subject of rights and duties, and becomes merely an object on which society can work. And this is, in principle, how Hitler treated the Jews. They were objects; killed not for ill desert but because, on his theories, they were a disease in society. If society can mend, remake, and unmake men at its pleasure, its pleasure may, of course, be humane or homicidal. The difference is important. But, either way, rulers have become owners.

Observe how the 'humane' attitude to crime could operate. If crimes are diseases, why should diseases be treated differently from crimes? And who but the experts can define disease? One school of psychology regards my religion as a neurosis. If this neurosis ever becomes inconvenient to Government, what is to prevent my being subjected to a compulsory 'cure'? It may be painful; treatments sometimes are. But it will be no use asking, 'What have I done to deserve this?' The Straightener will reply: 'But, my dear fellow, no one's *blaming* you. We no longer believe in retributive justice. We're healing you.'

This would be no more than an extreme application of the political philosophy implicit in most modern communities. It has stolen on us unawares. Two wars necessitated vast curtailments of liberty, and we have grown, though grumblingly, accustomed to our chains. The increasing complexity and precariousness of our economic life have forced Government to take over many spheres of activity once left to choice or chance. Our intellectuals have surrendered first to the slave-

313

philosophy of Hegel, then to Marx, finally to the linguistic analysts.

As a result, classical political theory, with its Stoical, Christian, and juristic key-conceptions (natural law, the value of the individual, the rights of man), has died. The modern State exists not to protect our rights but to do us good or make us good — anyway, to do something to us or to make us something. Hence the new name 'leaders' for those who were once 'rulers'. We are less their subjects than their wards, pupils, or domestic animals. There is nothing left of which we can say to them, 'Mind your own business.' Our whole lives *are* their business.

I write 'they' because it seems childish not to recognize that actual government is and always must be oligarchical. Our effective masters must be more than one and fewer than all. But the oligarchs begin to regard us in a new way.

Here, I think, lies our real dilemma. Probably we cannot, certainly we shall not, retrace our steps. We are tamed animals (some with kind, some with cruel, masters) and should probably starve if we got out of our cage. That is one horn of the dilemma. But in an increasingly planned society, how much of what I value can survive? That is the other horn.

I believe a man is happier, and happy in a richer way, if he has 'the freeborn mind'. But I doubt whether he can have this without economic independence, which the new society is abolishing. For economic independence allows an education not controlled by Government; and in adult life it is the man who needs, and asks, nothing of Government who can criticise its acts and snap his fingers at its ideology. Read Montaigne; that's the voice of a man with his legs under his own table, eating the mutton and turnips raised on his own land. Who will talk like that when the State is everyone's schoolmaster and employer? Admittedly, when man was untamed, such liberty belonged only to the few. I know. Hence the horrible suspicion that our only choice is between societies with few freemen and societies with none.

Again, the new oligarchy must more and more base its claim to plan us on its claim to knowledge. If we are to be mothered, mother must know best. This means they must increasingly rely on the advice of scientists, till in the end the politicians proper become merely the scientists' puppets.

Technocracy is the form to which a planned society must tend. Now I dread specialists in power because they are specialists speaking outside their special subjects. Let scientists tell us about sciences. But government involves questions about the good for man, and justice, and what things are worth having at what price; and on these a scientific training gives a man's opinion no added value. Let the doctor tell me I shall die unless I do so-and-so; but whether life is worth having on those terms is no more a question for him than for any other man.

Thirdly, I do not like the pretensions of Government — the grounds on which it demands my obedience — to be pitched too high. I don't like the medicine-man's magical pretensions nor the Bourbon's Divine Right. This is not solely because I disbelieve in magic and in Bossuet's *Politique*.[4] I believe in God, but I detest theocracy. For every Government consists of mere men and is, strictly viewed, a makeshift; if it adds to its commands 'Thus saith the Lord', it lies, and lies dangerously.

On just the same ground I dread government in the name of science. That is how tyrannies come in. In every age the men who want us under their thumb, if they have any sense, will put forward the particular pretension which the hopes and fears of that age render most potent. They 'cash in'. It has been magic, it has been Christianity. Now it will certainly be science. Perhaps the real scientists may not think much of the tyrants' 'science' — they didn't think much of Hitler's racial theories or Stalin's biology. But they can be muzzled.

We must give full weight to Sir Charles's reminder that millions in the East are still half starved. To these my fears would seem very unimportant. A hungry man thinks about food, not freedom. We must give full weight to the claim that nothing but science, and science globally applied, and therefore unprecedented Government controls, can produce full bellies and medical care for the whole human race: nothing, in short, but a world Welfare State. It is a full admission of these truths which impresses upon me the extreme peril of humanity at present.

We have on the one hand a desperate need; hunger, sick-

[4] Jacques Bénigne Bossuet, *Politique tirée des propres paroles de l'Écriture-Sainte* (Paris, 1709).

ness, and the dread of war. We have, on the other, the conception of something that might meet it: omnicompetent global technocracy. Are not these the ideal opportunity for enslavement? This is how it has entered before; a desperate need (real or apparent) in the one party, a power (real or apparent) to relieve it, in the other. In the ancient world individuals have sold themselves as slaves, in order to eat. So in society. Here is a witch-doctor who can save us from the sorcerers — a war-lord who can save us from the barbarians — a Church that can save us from Hell. Give them what they ask, give ourselves to them bound and blindfold, if only they will! Perhaps the terrible bargain will be made again. We cannot blame men for making it. We can hardly wish them not to. Yet we can hardly bear that they should.

The question about progress has become the question whether we can discover any way of submitting to the worldwide paternalism of a technocracy without losing all personal privacy and independence. Is there any possibility of getting the super Welfare State's honey and avoiding the sting?

Let us make no mistake about the sting. The Swedish sadness is only a foretaste. To live his life in his own way, to call his house his castle, to enjoy the fruits of his own labour, to educate his children as his conscience directs, to save for their prosperity after his death — these are wishes deeply ingrained in white and civilised man. Their realization is almost as necessary to our virtues as to our happiness. From their total frustration disastrous results both moral and psychological might follow.

All this threatens us even if the form of society which our needs point to should prove an unparalleled success. But is that certain? What assurance have we that our masters will or can keep the promise which induced us to sell ourselves? Let us not be deceived by phrases about 'Man taking charge of his own destiny'. All that can really happen is that some men will take charge of the destiny of the others. They will be simply men; none perfect; some greedy, cruel and dishonest. The more completely we are planned the more powerful they will be. Have we discovered some new reason why, this time, power should not corrupt as it has done before?

9

WE HAVE NO
'RIGHT TO HAPPINESS'

AFTER ALL', SAID CLARE, 'THEY HAD A RIGHT TO HAPPINESS.'
We were discussing something that once happened in our
own neighbourhood. Mr A. had deserted Mrs A. and got
his divorce in order to marry Mrs B., who had likewise got
her divorce in order to marry Mr A. And there was certainly
no doubt that Mr A. and Mrs B. were very much in love
with one another. If they continued to be in love, and if
nothing went wrong with their health or their income, they
might reasonably expect to be very happy.

It was equally clear that they were not happy with their
old partners. Mrs B. had adored her husband at the outset.
But then he got smashed up in the war. It was thought he
had lost his virility, and it was known that he had lost his
job. Life with him was no longer what Mrs B. had bargained
for. Poor Mrs A., too. She had lost her looks — and all her
liveliness. It might be true, as some said, that she consumed
herself by bearing his children and nursing him through the
long illness that overshadowed their earlier married life.

You mustn't, by the way, imagine that A. was the sort of
man who nonchalantly threw a wife away like the peel of
an orange he'd sucked dry. Her suicide was a terrible shock
to him. We all knew this, for he told us so himself. 'But what
could I do?' he said. 'A man has a right to happiness. I had
to take my one chance when it came.'

I went away thinking about the concept of a 'right to happiness'.

At first this sounds to me as odd as a right to good luck. For I believe — whatever one school of moralists may say — that we depend for a very great deal of our happiness or misery on circumstances outside all human control. A right to happiness doesn't, for me, make much more sense than a right to be six feet tall, or to have a millionaire for your father, or to get good weather whenever you want to have a picnic.

I can understand a right as a freedom guaranteed me by the laws of the society I live in. Thus, I have a right to travel along the public roads because society gives me that freedom; that's what we mean by calling the roads 'public'. I can also understand a right as a claim guaranteed me by the laws, and correlative to an obligation on someone else's part. If I have a right to receive £100 from you, this is another way of saying that you have a duty to pay me £100. If the laws allow Mr A. to desert his wife and seduce his neighbour's wife, then, by definition, Mr A. has a legal right to do so, and we need bring in no talk about 'happiness'.

But of course that was not what Clare meant. She meant that he had not only a legal but a moral right to act as he did. In other words, Clare is — or would be if she thought it out — a classical moralist after the style of Thomas Aquinas, Grotius, Hooker and Locke. She believes that behind the laws of the state there is a Natural Law.

I agree with her. I hold this conception to be basic to all civilization. Without it, the actual laws of the state become an absolute, as in Hegel. They cannot be criticized because there is no norm against which they should be judged.

The ancestry of Clare's maxim, 'They have a right to happiness,' is august. In words that are cherished by all civilized men, but especially by Americans, it has been laid down that one of the rights of man is a right to 'the pursuit of happiness'. And now we get to the real point.

What did the writers of that august declaration mean?

It is quite certain what they did not mean. They did not mean that man was entitled to pursue happiness by any and every means — including, say, murder, rape, robbery, treason and fraud. No society could be built on such a basis.

They meant 'to pursue happiness by all lawful means'; that is, by all means which the Law of Nature eternally sanctions and which the laws of the nation shall sanction.

Admittedly this seems at first to reduce their maxim to the tautology that men (in pursuit of happiness) have a right to do whatever they have a right to do. But tautologies, seen against their proper historical context, are not always barren tautologies. The declaration is primarily a denial of the political principles which long governed Europe: a challenge flung down to the Austrian and Russian empires, to England before the Reform Bills, to Bourbon France. It demands that whatever means of pursuing happiness are lawful for any should be lawful for all; that 'man', not men of some particular caste, class, status or religion, should be free to use them. In a century when this is being unsaid by nation after nation and party after party, let us not call it a barren tautology.

But the question as to what means are 'lawful' — what methods of pursuing happiness are either morally permissible by the Law of Nature or should be declared legally permissible by the legislature of a particular nation — remains exactly where it did. And on that question I disagree with Clare. I don't think it is obvious that people have the unlimited 'right to happiness' which she suggests.

For one thing, I believe that Clare, when she says 'happiness', means simply and solely 'sexual happiness'. Partly because women like Clare never use the word 'happiness' in any other sense. But also because I never heard Clare talk about the 'right' to any other kind. She was rather leftist in her politics, and would have been scandalised if anyone had defended the actions of a ruthless man-eating tycoon on the ground that his happiness consisted in making money and he was pursuing his happiness. She was also a rabid teetotaller; I never heard her excuse an alcoholic because he was happy when he was drunk.

A good many of Clare's friends, and especially her female friends, often felt — I've heard them say so — that their own happiness would be perceptibly increased by boxing her ears. I very much doubt if this would have brought her theory of a right to happiness into play.

Clare, in fact, is doing what the whole western world seems to me to have been doing for the last 40-odd years. When I

319

was a youngster, all the progressive people were saying, 'Why all this prudery? Let us treat sex just as we treat all our other impulses.' I was simple-minded enough to believe they meant what they said. I have since discovered that they meant exactly the opposite. They meant that sex was to be treated as no other impulse in our nature has ever been treated by civilized people. All the others, we admit, have to be bridled. Absolute obedience to your instinct for self-preservation is what we call cowardice; to your acquisitive impulse, avarice. Even sleep must be resisted if you're a sentry. But every unkindness and breach of faith seems to be condoned provided that the object aimed at is 'four bare legs in a bed'.

It is like having a morality in which stealing fruit is considered wrong — unless you steal nectarines.

And if you protest against this view you are usually met with chatter about the legitimacy and beauty and sanctity of 'sex' and accused of harbouring some Puritan prejudice against it as something disreputable or shameful. I deny the charge. Foam-born Venus . . . golden Aphrodite . . . Our Lady of Cyprus . . . I never breathed a word against you. If I object to boys who steal my nectarines, must I be supposed to disapprove of nectarines in general? Or even of boys in general? It might, you know, be stealing that I disapproved of.

The real situation is skilfully concealed by saying that the question of Mr A.'s 'right' to desert his wife is one of 'sexual morality'. Robbing an orchard is not an offense against some special morality called 'fruit morality'. It is an offense against honesty. Mr A.'s action is an offense against good faith (to solemn promises), against gratitude (toward one to whom he was deeply indebted) and against common humanity.

Our sexual impulses are thus being put in a position of preposterous privilege. The sexual motive is taken to condone all sorts of behaviour which, if it had any other end in view, would be condemned as merciless, treacherous and unjust.

Now though I see no good reason for giving sex this privilege, I think I see a strong cause. It is this.

It is part of the nature of a strong erotic passion — as distinct from a transient fit of appetite — that it makes more towering promises than any other emotion. No doubt all our desires make promises, but not so impressively. To be in love involves the almost irresistible conviction that one will go on being in love until one dies, and that possession of the beloved will confer, not merely frequent ecstasies, but settled, fruitful, deep-rooted, lifelong happiness. Hence *all* seems to be at stake. If we miss this chance we shall have lived in vain. At the very thought of such a doom we sink into fathomless depths of self-pity.

Unfortunately these promises are found often to be quite untrue. Every experienced adult knows this to be so as regards all erotic passions (except the one he himself is feeling at the moment). We discount the world-without-end pretensions of our friends' amours easily enough. We know that such things sometimes last — and sometimes don't. And when they do last, this is not because they promised at the outset to do so. When two people achieve lasting happiness, this is not solely because they are great lovers but because they are also — I must put it crudely — good people; controlled, loyal, fair-minded, mutually adaptable people.

If we establish a 'right to (sexual) happiness' which supersedes all the ordinary rules of behaviour, we do so not because of what our passion shows itself to be in experience but because of what it professes to be while we are in the grip of it. Hence, while the bad behaviour is real and works miseries and degradations, the happiness which was the object of the behaviour turns out again and again to be illusory. Everyone (except Mr A. and Mrs B.) knows that Mr A. in a year or so may have the same reason for deserting his new wife as for deserting his old. He will feel again that all is at stake. He will see himself again as the great lover, and his pity for himself will exclude all pity for the woman.

Two further points remain.

One is this. A society in which conjugal infidelity is tolerated must always be in the long run a society adverse to women. Women, whatever a few male songs and satires may say to the contrary, are more naturally monogamous than men; it is a biological necessity. Where promiscuity prevails, they will therefore always be more often the victims than the culprits. Also, domestic happiness is more necessary to them than to us. And the quality by which they most easily hold a man, their beauty, decreases every year after they have come to maturity, but this does not happen to those qualities of personality — women don't really care twopence about our *looks* — by which we hold women. Thus in the ruthless war of promiscuity women are at a double disadvantage. They play for higher stakes and are also more likely to lose. I have no sympathy with moralists who frown at the increasing crudity of female provocativeness. These signs of desperate competition fill me with pity.

Secondly, though the 'right to happiness' is chiefly claimed for the sexual impulse, it seems to me impossible that the matter should stay there. The fatal principle, once allowed in that department, must sooner or later seep through our whole lives. We thus advance toward a state of society in which not only each man but every impulse in each man claims *carte blanche*. And then, though our technological skill may help us survive a little longer, our civilization will have died at heart, and will — one dare not even add 'unfortunately' — be swept away.

PART IV

LETTERS

[Though I have reprinted only Lewis's own letters here, I have attempted to place them in their context by citing the sources of the letters from the various correspondents which Lewis was answering, or who were answering him. Thus the sub-divisions (a), (b), (c) and so forth.]

1

THE CONDITIONS FOR A JUST WAR

(a) E. L. Mascall, 'The Christian and the Next War', *Theology*, vol. XXXVIII (January 1939), pp. 53-58.

(b) C. S. Lewis, 'The Conditions for a Just War', *ibid.* (May 1939), pp. 373-74:

Sir, In your January number Mr Mascall mentions six conditions for a just war which have been laid down by 'theologians'. I have one question to ask, and a number of problems to raise, about these rules. The question is merely historical. Who are these theologians, and what kind or degree of authority can they claim over members of the Church of England? The problems are more difficult. Condition 4 lays down that 'it must be morally certain that the losses, to the belligerents, the world, and religion, will not outweigh the advantages of winning'; and 6, that 'there must be a considerable probability of winning'. It is plain that equally sincere people can differ to any extent and argue for ever as to whether a proposed war fulfils these conditions or not. The practical question, therefore, which faces us is one of authority. Who has the duty of deciding when the conditions are fulfilled, and the right of enforcing his decision? Modern discussions tend to assume without argument that the answer is 'The private conscience of the individual,' and that any other answer is immoral and totalitarian. Now it is certain, in some sense, that 'no duty of obedience can justify a sin', as Mr Mascall says. Granted that capital punishment is compatible with Christianity, a Christian may lawfully be a hangman; but he must not hang a man whom he knows to be innocent. But will anyone interpret this to mean that the hangman has the *same* duty of investigating the prisoner's guilt which the judge has? If so, no executive can work and no Christian state is possible; which is absurd. I conclude that the hangman has done his duty if he has done his share of the general duty, resting upon all citizens alike, to ensure, so far as in him lies, that we have an honest judicial system; if, in spite of this, and unknowingly, he hangs an innocent man, then a sin has been committed, but not by him. This analogy suggests to me that it must be absurd to give to the private citizen the *same* right and duty of deciding the justice of a given war which rests on governments; and I submit that the rules for determining what wars are just were originally rules for the guidance of princes, not subjects. This does not mean that private persons must obey governments commanding them to do what they know is sin; but perhaps it does mean (I write it with some reluctance) that the ultimate decision as to what the situation at a given moment is in the highly complex field of international affairs is one which must be delegated. No doubt we must make every effort which the constitution allows to ensure a good government and to influence public opinion; but in the long run, the nation, as a nation, must act, and it can act only through its government. (It must be remembered that there are risks in both directions: if war is ever lawful, then peace is sometimes sinful.) What is the alternative? That individuals ignorant of history and strategy should decide for themselves whether condition 6 ('a considerable probability of winning') is, or is not, fulfilled? — or that every citizen, neglecting his own vocation and not weighing his capacity, is to become an expert on all the relevant, and often technical, problems?

Decisions by the private conscience of each Christian

in the light of Mr Mascall's six rules would divide Christians from each other and result in no clear Christian witness to the pagan world around us. But a clear Christian witness might be attained in a different way. If all Christians consented to bear arms at the command of the magistrate, and if all, after that, refused to obey anti-Christian orders, should we not get a clear issue? A man is much more certain that he ought not to murder prisoners or bomb civilians than he ever can be about the justice of a war. It is perhaps here that 'conscientious objection' ought to begin. I feel certain that one Christion airman shot for refusing to bomb enemy civilians would be a more effective martyr (in the etymological sense of the word) than a hundred Christians in jail for refusing to join the army.

Christendom has made two efforts to deal with the evil of war — chivalry and pacifism. Neither succeeded. But I doubt whether chivalry has such an unbroken record of failure as pacifism.

The question is a very dark one. I should welcome about equally refutation, or development, of what I have said.

2
THE CONFLICT IN ANGLICAN THEOLOGY

(a) Oliver C. Quick, 'The Conflict in Anglican Theology', *Theology,* vol. LXI (October 1940), pp. 234-37.
(b) C. S. Lewis, *ibid.* (November 1940), p. 304:
Sir, In an admirable letter contributed to your October number Canon Quick remarks, ' "Moderns" of every kind have one characteristic in common: they hate Liberalism.' Would it not be equally true to say, more shortly, ' "Moderns" of every kind have one characteristic in common: they *hate?'* The matter deserves, perhaps, more attention than it has received.

3
MIRACLES

(a) Peter May, 'Miracles', *The Guardian* (9 October 1942), p. 323.

(b) C. S. Lewis, *ibid*. (16 October 1942), p. 331:

Sir, — In answer to Mr May's question, I reply that whether the birth of St John Baptist were a miracle or no, it was not the same miracle as the birth of our Lord.[1] What was abnormal about St Elizabeth's pregnancy was that she was an elderly (married) woman, hitherto sterile. That Zacharias was the father of St John is implied in the text ('shall bear *thee* a son', Luke i. 13).

Of the natural conversion of water into wine, what I said was: 'God creates the vine and teaches it to draw up water by its roots and, *with the aid of the sun,* to turn that water into a juice *which will ferment* and take on certain qualities.'[2] For completeness I should, no doubt, have added 'with the aid of the soil', and perhaps other things; but this would not, from my point of view, have materially altered what I was saying. My answer to Mr May's question — where the other raw materials came from — would be the same, whether the list of raw materials be reduced to the mere vegetable and sunlight I mentioned, or extended to bring in all that the skilled botanist might add. I think they came from the same source at Cana whence they come in Nature. I agree with Mr May, of course, that on the hypothesis of the story being fiction, we can attach to it, as our ancestors did to the miracles in Ovid, any number of edifying *moralitates*. What I was doing was to combat that particular argument for its falsity which rests on the idea that, if it occurred, such an event would be arbitrary and meaningless.

4

MR C. S. LEWIS ON CHRISTIANITY

(a) W. R. Childe, 'Mr C. S. Lewis on Christianity', *The Listener,* vol. XXXI (2 March 1944), p. 245.

(b) C. S. Lewis, *ibid*. (9 March 1944), p. 273:

I agree with Mr W. R. Childe that it is no use to say 'Lord, Lord', if we do not do what Christ tells us: that,

---

[1] Mr May was criticizing the essay on 'Miracles' printed in this book. See page 26.

[2] *Ibid.,* p. 29.

indeed, is one of the reasons why I think an aesthetic religion of 'flowers and music' insufficient.[3] My reason for thinking that a mere statement of even the highest ethical principles is not enough is precisely that to know these things is not necessarily to do them, and if Christianity brought no healing to the impotent will, Christ's teaching would not help us. I cannot blame Mr Childe for misunderstanding me, because I am naturally no judge of my own lucidity; but I take it very hard that a total stranger whom I have never knowingly injured or offended, on the first discovery of a difference in theological opinion between us, should publicly accuse me of being a potential torturer, murderer and tyrant — for that is what Mr Childe's reference to faggots means if it means anything. How little I approve of compulsion in religion may be gauged from a recent letter of mine to the *Spectator* protesting against the intolerable tyranny of compulsory church parades for the Home Guard. If Mr Childe can find any passage in my works which favours religious or anti-religious compulsion I will give five pounds to any (not militantly anti-Christian) charity he cares to name. If he cannot, I ask him, for justice and charity's sake, to withdraw his charge.

(c) W. R. Childe, *ibid.* (16 March 1944), p. 301.

5
A VILLAGE EXPERIENCE

C. S. Lewis, 'A Village Experience', *The Guardian* (31 August 1945), p. 335:

Sir, — I think your readers should, and will, be interested in the following extract from a letter I have just received; the writer is an invalid lady in a village:

'This used to be a God-fearing village with a God-fearing parson who visited and ran the Scouts ("Lovely

---

[3] Mr Childe had taken exception to a passage in Lewis's B.B.C. broadcast 'The Map and the Ocean' in which he said, in speaking of a 'vague religion', that 'you will not get eternal life by just feeling the presence of God in flowers or music'. *The Listener*, vol. XXXI (24 February 1944), p. 216. The broadcast was later to become a chapter in Lewis's *Mere Christianity* (London, 1952), Bk. IV, ch. i, p. 122.

troop we 'ad. *And* you should have 'eard our choir of a Sunday," says my bricklayer host). The young were polished up and sent to Sunday school, their parents filled the church to the brim. *Now* they have an octogenarian. No harm in that! My late uncle — at that age was going as strong as most two-year-olds. But this one — I noted for myself, seeing him pass — has been dead for years . . . He does not visit the sick, even if asked. He does nothing. And — listen — he stuck up a notice in the church: *No children admitted without their parents or an adult.* The village . . . went instantly Pagan. I must get away from it. Never before but in the vile pagan West Indies have I been without so much as an *extorted* Holy Sacrament. (*Can* one forbid the church to a Crissom child? — legally, I mean? Pass me a Bishop.)'

6

CORRESPONDENCE WITH AN ANGLICAN WHO DISLIKES HYMNS

(The 'correspondence' consists of two letters from Erik Routley to Lewis (an Anglican), and two letters from Lewis, all of which were published together in *The Presbyter*, vol. VI, No. 2 (1948), pp. 15-20. Lewis's letters appeared over the initials 'A. B.')

(a) Summary of a letter from Erik Routley to Lewis (dated 13 July 1946), p. 15:

'. . . The Hymn Society of Great Britain and Ireland is opening a file of new hymns to which modern hymn-writers are to be asked to contribute. I have been asked to write to you and ask if you will be a member of the panel to whom new hymns may be submitted in order that their merit may be assessed . . .'

(b) C. S. Lewis to Erik Routley (dated 16 July 1946), p. 15:

Dear Mr Routley,

The truth is that I'm not in sufficient sympathy with the project to help you. I know that many of the congregation like singing hymns: but am not yet convinced that their enjoyment is of a spiritual kind. It may be: I don't know. To the minority, of whom I am one, the hymns are mostly the dead wood of the service. Recently in a party of six people I found that all without exception would like *fewer* hymns. Naturally, one holding this view can't help you.

(c) Erik Routley to Lewis (dated 18 September 1946), pp. 15-20.

(d) C. S. Lewis to Erik Routley (dated 21 September 1946), pp. 15-20:

I can't quite remember my own last letter; but I was wrong if I said or implied that (*a*) variables, (*b*) active participation by the people, or (*c*) hymns, were bad in principle. I would agree that anything the congregation *can do* may properly and profitably be offered to God in public worship. If one had a congregation (say, in Africa) who had a high tradition in sacred dancing and could do it really well I would be perfectly in favour of making a dance part of the service. But I wouldn't transfer the practice to a Willesden congregation whose best dance was a ballroom shuffle. In modern England, however, we can't sing — as the Welsh and Germans can. Also (a great pity, but a fact) the art of poetry has developed for two centuries in a private and subjective direction. That is why I find hymns 'dead wood'. But I spoke only for myself and a few others. If an improved hymnody — or even the present hymnody — does edify other people, of course it is an elementary duty of charity and humility for me to submit. I have never spoken in public *against* the use of hymns: on the contrary I have often told 'highbrow' converts that a humble acquiescence in anything that may edify their uneducated brethren (however frightful it seems to the educated 'natural man') is the first lesson they must learn. The door is *low* and one must stoop to enter.

7

THE CHURCH'S LITURGY, INVOCATION, AND INVOCATION OF SAINTS

(a) E. L. Mascall, 'Quadringentesimo Anno', *Church Times,* vol. CXXXII (6 May 1949), p. 282.

(b) C. S. Lewis, 'The Church's Liturgy', *ibid.* (20 May 1949), p. 319:

Sir, — If it is not harking back too far, I would like to make two layman's comments on the liturgical articles in your issue of May 6. Firstly, I would underline the necessity for uniformity, if in nothing else, yet in the time taken by the rite. We laymen may not be busier than the clergy but we usually have much less choice in our hours of business. The celebrant who lengthens the service by ten minutes may, for us, throw the whole day into hurry and confusion. It is difficult to keep this out of our minds: it may even be difficult to avoid some feeling of resentment. Such temptations may be good for us but it is not the celebrant's business to supply them: God's permission and Satan's diligence will see to that part of our education without his assistance.

Secondly, I would ask the clergy to believe that we are more interested in orthodoxy and less interested in liturgiology as such than they can easily imagine. Dr Mascall rightly says that variations are permissible when they do not alter doctrine. But after that he goes on almost casually to mention 'devotions to the Mother of God and to the hosts of heaven' as a possible liturgical variant. That the introduction of such devotions into any parish not accustomed to them would divide the congregation into two camps, Dr Mascall well knows. But if he thinks that the issue between those camps would be a liturgical issue, I submit that he is mistaken. It would be a doctrinal issue. Not one layman would be asking whether these devotions marred or mended the beauty of the rite; everyone would be asking whether they were lawful or damnable. It is no part of my object to discuss that question here, but merely to point out that it is the question.

What we laymen fear is that the deepest doctrinal issues should be tacitly and implicitly settled by what seem to be, or are avowed to be, merely changes in liturgy. A man who is wondering whether the fare set before him is food or poison is not reassured by being told that this course is now restored to its traditional place in the *menu* or that the tureen is of the Sarum pattern. We laymen are ignorant and timid. Our lives are ever in our hands, the avenger of blood is on our heels, and of each of us his soul may this night be required. Can you blame us if the reduction of grave doctrinal issues to merely liturgical issues fills us with something like terror?

(c) W. D. F. Hughes, *ibid*. (24 June 1949), p. 409.

(d) C. S. Lewis, *ibid*. (1 July 1949), p. 427:

Sir, — I agree with Dean Hughes that the connection of belief and liturgy is close, but doubt if it is 'inextricable'. I submit that the relation is healthy when liturgy expresses the belief of the Church, morbid when liturgy creates in the people by suggestion beliefs which the Church has not publicly professed, taught, and defended. If the mind of the Church is, for example, that our fathers erred in abandoning the Romish invocations of saints and angels, by all means let our corporate recantation, together with its grounds in scripture, reason and tradition be published, our solemn act of penitence be performed, the laity reinstructed, and the proper changes in liturgy be introduced.

What horrifies me is the proposal that individual priests should be encouraged to behave as if all this had been done when it has not been done. One correspondent compared such changes to the equally stealthy and (as he holds) irresistible changes in a language. But that is just the parallel that terrifies me, for even the shallowest philologist knows that the unconscious linguistic process is continually degrading good words and blunting useful distinctions. *Absit omen!* Whether an 'enrichment' of liturgy which involves a change of doctrine is allowable, surely depends on whether our doctrine is changing from error to truth or from truth to error. Is the individual priest the judge of that?

(e) Edward Every, 'Doctrine and Liturgy', *ibid*. (8 July 1949), pp. 445-46.

(f) C. S. Lewis, 'Invocation', *ibid*. (15 July 1949), pp. 463-64:

Sir, — Mr Every (quite legitimately) gives the word *in-*

vocation a wider sense than I. The question then becomes how far we can infer propriety of *devotion* from propriety of *invocation?* I accept the authority of the *Benedicite*[4] for the propriety of *invoking* (in Mr Every's sense) saints. But if I thence infer the propriety of *devotions* to saints, will not an argument force me to approve devotions to stars, frosts and whales?

I am also quite ready to admit that I overlooked a distinction. Our fathers might disallow a particular mediaeval doctrine and yet not disallow some other doctrine which we laymen easily confuse with it. But if the issue is so much finer than I thought, this merely redoubles my anxiety that it should be openly and authoritatively decided.

If I feared lest the suggestions of liturgy might beguile us laymen on a simple issue, I am not likely to be comforted by finding the issue a subtle one. If there is one kind of devotion to created beings which is pleasing and another which is displeasing to God, when is the Church, as a Church, going to instruct us in the distinction?

Meanwhile, what better opportunity for the stealthy insinuation of the wrong kind than the unauthorized and sporadic practice of devotions to creatures before uninstructed congregations would our ghostly foe desire? Most of us laymen, I think, have a *parti pris* in the matter. We desire to believe as the Church believes.

(g) Edward Every, 'Invocation of Saints', *ibid.* (22 July 1949), pp. 481-82.

(h) C. S. Lewis, *ibid.* (5 August 1949), p. 513:

Sir, — I hope Mr Every has not misunderstood me. There is, I believe, a *prima facie* case for regarding devotions to saints in the Church of England as a controversial question (see Jewel,[5] *Apologia Ecclesiae Anglicanae*, Pt. II, ch. xxviii, *Homilies*, Bk. II, *Peril of Idolatry*, Pt. III; Laud,[6] *Conference with Fisher*, Sect. XXIII; Taylor,[7]

[4] Found in the Prayer Book service of Morning Prayer, the original source of which is *The Song of the Three Holy Children* (vv. 35-66) in the Old Testament Apocrypha.

[5] John Jewel (1522-71).

[6] William Laud (1573-1645).

[7] Jeremy Taylor (1613-67).

Dissuasive from Popery, Pt. I, ch. ii, sect. 8). I merely claim that the controversy exists. I share Mr Every's wish that it should cease. But there are two ways in which a controversy can cease: by being settled, or by gradual and imperceptible change of custom. I do not want any controversy to cease in the second way.

I implore priests to remember what Aristotle tells us about unconscious revolution (πολλάκις λανθάνει μεγάλη γινομένη μετάβασις τῶν νομίμων *Politics* 1303 a 22).[8] When such unconscious revolution produces a result we like, we are all tempted to welcome it; thus I am tempted to welcome it when it leads to prayers for the dead. But then I see that the very same process can be used, and is used, to introduce modernist dilutions of the faith which, I am sure, Mr Every and I equally abominate. I conclude that a road so dangerous should never be trodden, whether the destination to which it seems to point is in itself good or bad. To write 'No Thoroughfare' over that road is my only purpose.

8
THE HOLY NAME

(a) Leslie E. T. Bradbury, 'The Holy Name', *Church Times*, vol. CXXXIV (3 August 1951), p. 525.

(b) C. S. Lewis, *ibid.* (10 August 1951), p. 541:

Sir, — Having read Mr Bradbury's letter on the Holy Name, I have a few comments to make. I do not think we are entitled to assume that all who use this Name without reverential prefixes are making a 'careless' use of it; otherwise, we should have to say that the Evangelists were often careless. I do not think we are entitled to assume that the use of the word *Blessed* when we speak of the Virgin Mary is 'necessary'; otherwise, we should have to condemn both the Nicene and the Apostles' Creed for omitting it. Should we not rather recognize that the presence or absence of such prefixes constitutes a difference, not in faith or morals, but simply

---

[8] 'The occurrence of an important transition in customs often passes unnoticed.'

in style? I know that as their absence is 'irritating' to some, so their frequent recurrence is irritating to others. Is not each party innocent in its temperamental preference but grossly culpable if it allows anything so subjective, contingent, and (with a little effort) conquerable as a temperamental preference to become a cause of division among brethren? If we cannot lay down our tastes, along with other carnal baggage at the church door, surely we should at least bring them in to be humbled and, if necessary, modified, not to be indulged?

9
MERE CHRISTIANS

(a) R. D. Daunton-Fear, 'Evangelical Churchmanship', *Church Times,* vol. CXXXV (1 February 1952), p. 77.

(b) C. S. Lewis, 'Mere Christians', *ibid.* (8 February 1952), p. 95:

Sir, — I welcome the letter from the Rural Dean of Gravesend, though I am sorry that anyone should have rendered it necessary by describing the Bishop of Birmingham as an Evangelical. To a layman, it seems obvious that what unites the Evangelical and the Anglo-Catholic against the 'Liberal' or 'Modernist' is something very clear and momentous, namely, the fact that both are thoroughgoing supernaturalists, who believe in the Creation, the Fall, the Incarnation, the Resurrection, the Second Coming, and the Four Last Things. This unites them not only with one another, but with the Christian religion as understood *ubique et ab omnibus.*[9]

The point of view from which this agreement seems less important than their divisions, or than the gulf which separates both from any non-miraculous version of Christianity, is to me unintelligible. Perhaps the trouble is that as supernaturalists, whether 'Low' or 'High' Church, thus taken together, they lack a name. May I suggest 'Deep Church'; or, if that fails in humility, Baxter's 'mere Christians'?

[9] 'everywhere and by all'. See St Vincent of Lérins, *Commonitorium,* ii.

10
CANONIZATION

(a) Eric Pitt, 'Canonization', *Church Times,* vol. CXXXV (17 October 1952), p. 743.

(b) C. S. Lewis, *ibid.* (24 October 1952), p. 763:

Sir, — I am, like Mr Eric Pitt, a layman, and would like to be instructed on several points before the proposal to set up a 'system' of Anglican canonization is even discussed. According to the *Catholic Encyclopaedia,* 'saints' are dead people whose virtues have made them 'worthy' of God's 'special' love. Canonization makes *dulia* 'universal and obligatory'; and, whatever else it asserts, it certainly asserts that the person concerned 'is in heaven'.

Unless, then, the word 'canonization' is being used in a sense distinct from the Roman (and, if so, some other word would be much more convenient), the proposal to set us a 'system' of canonization means that someone (say, the Archbishops) shall be appointed

(a) To tell us that certain named people are (i) 'in heaven', and (ii) are 'worthy' of God's 'special' love.

(b) To lay upon us (under pain of excommunication?) the duty of *dulia* towards those they have named.

Now it is very clear that no one ought to tell us what he does not know to be true. Is it, then, held that God has promised (and, if so, when and where?) to the Church universal a knowledge of the state of certain departed souls? If so, is it clear that this knowledge will discern varying degrees of kinds of salvation such as are, I suppose, implicit in the word 'special'? And if it does, will the promulgation of such knowledge help to save souls now *in viâ?* For it might well lead to a consideration of 'rival claims', such as we read of in the *Imitation of Christ* (Bk. III, ch. lviii), where we are warned, 'Ask not which is greater in the kingdom of heaven . . . the search into such things brings no profit, but rather offends the saints themselves.'

Finally, there is the practical issue: by which I do not mean the *Catholic Encyclopaedia's* neat little account of 'the ordinary actual expenses of canonization' (though that too can be read with profit), but the danger of schism. Thousands of members of the Church of England doubt whether *dulia* is lawful. Does anyone maintain that it is necessary to salvation? If not, whence comes our obligation to run such frightful risks?

11
PITTENGER-LEWIS AND VERSION VERNACULAR

(a) W. Norman Pittenger, 'Pittenger-Lewis', *The Christian Century,* vol. LXXV (24 December 1958), pp. 1485-86.
(b) C. S. Lewis, 'Version Vernacular', *ibid.* (31 December 1958), p. 1515.

Sir: Thank you for publishing my 'Rejoinder to Dr Pittenger' (Nov. 26). Now would you, please, complete your kindness by publishing the statement that *'populam'* (p. 1360) is either my typist's or your printer's error for *'populum'*?

An article on 'translation' such as Dr Pittenger suggests in his letter in the Dec. 24 issue certainly needs doing, but I could not usefully do it for Americans. The vernacular into which they would have to translate is not quite the same as that into which I have translated. Small differences, in addressing proletarians, may be all-important.

In both countries an essential part of the ordination exam ought to be a passage from some recognized theological work set for translation into vulgar English — just like doing Latin prose. Failure on this paper should mean failure on the whole exam. It is absolutely disgraceful that we expect missionaries to the Bantus to learn Bantu but never ask whether our missionaries to the Americans or English can speak American or English. Any fool can write *learned* language. The vernacular is the real test. If you can't turn your faith into it, then either you don't understand it or you don't believe it.

12

CAPITAL PUNISHMENT AND
DEATH PENALTY

(a) C. S. Lewis, 'Capital Punishment', *Church Times,* vol. CXLIV (1 December 1961), p. 7:

Sir, — I do not know whether capital punishment should or should not be abolished, for neither the natural light, nor scripture, nor ecclesiastical authority seems to tell me. But I am concerned about the grounds on which its abolition is being sought.

To say that by hanging a man we presumptuously judge him to be irredeemable is, I submit, simply untrue. My Prayer Book includes an exhortation to those under sentence of death which throughout implies the exact opposite. The real question is whether a murderer is more likely to repent and make a good end three weeks hence in the execution shed or, say, thirty years later in the prison infirmary. No mortal can know. But those who have most right to an opinion are those who know most by experience about the effect of prolonged prison life. I wish some prison chaplains, governors and warders would contribute to the discussion.

The suggestion of compensation for the relatives of the murdered man is in itself reasonable, but it ought not to be even remotely connected with the case for or against capital punishment. If it is, we shall be giving countenance to the archaic, and surely erroneous view that murder is primarily an offence not against society but against individuals.

Hanging is not a more irrevocable act than any other. You can't bring an innocent man to life: but neither can you give him back the years which wrongful imprisonment has eaten.

Other correspondents have pointed out that a theory of punishment which is purely exemplary or purely reformatory, or both, is shockingly immoral. Only the concept of desert connects punishment with morality at all. If deterrence is all that matters, the execution of an innocent man, provided the public think him guilty, would be fully justified. If reformation alone is in question, then there is nothing against painful and compulsory reform for all our defects, and a Government which believes Christianity to be a neurosis will have a perfectly good right to hand us all over to their straighteners for 'cure' to-morrow.

(b) Claude Davis, *ibid.* (8 December 1961), p. 14.

(c) C. S. Lewis, 'Death Penalty', *ibid.* (15 December 1961), p. 12:

Sir, — Dr Davis rightly reproves me for using the word *society* as I did. This hypostatised abstraction has already done harm enough. But I only meant 'all of us'. The absurdity of the view which treats murder as an offence against a single family is best illustrated by a case in the private speeches of Demosthenes (I can't turn it up at the moment, but your more scholarly readers no doubt can).

A man, *A,* set free a female slave, *B,* his old nurse. *B* married. Her husband died without issue. Someone then murdered *B.* But under Athenian law no one could prosecute because there was no injured party. *A* could not act because *B,* when murdered, was no longer his property. There was no widower, and there were no orphans.

I am on neither side in the present controversy. But I still think the abolitionists conduct their case very ill. They seem incapable of stating it without imputing vile motives to their opponents. If unbelievers often look at your correspondence column, I am afraid they may carry away a bad impression of our logic, manners and charity.

INDEX

341